"Stories like this often go unheard, but we need to hear them. Aaron Crowley's memoir takes us where few have gone, and along the journey, Aaron destroys the misconceptions many of us have about men in pornography. At times heart-wrenching and at times heartwarming, this book will open your eyes to the lasting trauma inflicted on those in pornography and prostitution and the necessity to end the demand for sexual exploitation."

—DAWN HAWKINS, SR. VICE PRESIDENT OF
National Center on Sexual Exploitation

"This story will bless and shock you. As I read Pastor Aaron's memoir, I laughed, I cried, I felt conviction, and I felt the love of God. When you read this, you will experience the love of God and see firsthand His ability to heal the brokenhearted and set captives free."

—BISHOP RANDY MORGAN, *The Covenant Network*

"A terrific read illustrating the power of God's redeeming grace, which is available to all who are willing to hear God's whisper of life-giving love, hope and strength. I hope Aaron Crowley's book will lead many to find the courage to live in God's peace, provision and freedom."

—JANE CLEMENTI, COFOUNDER AND CEO OF
Tyler Clementi Foundation

"What a great opportunity to learn and see into a world most of us have no real idea about. This memoir is a journey you must read. We must have a strong reaction! Lives depend on it. Maybe yours."

—APOSTLE MIKE WHITED, *New Covenant Ministries of Charlotte*

"*Bought with a Price* is a relevant, bold, and timely memoir. This testament of the presence and power of God to transform lives is truly an evangelistic tool for our generation and specifically to our LGBT+ community."

—APOSTLE MARK LEGEAR, *New Covenant Church of Atlanta*

"This book is a work of art! Aaron Crowley manages to showcase the problems with the porn industry and identify the slippery slop many prostituted people find themselves in; all while remaining true to his new identity in Christ. This is a must-read for those struggling with their salvation and in need of encouragement to leave pornography or any sin, knowing that God is grace, and God is love."

—Pastor Tanzanika Ruffin, Esq., attorney
who has represented those affected by the sex industry since 2000

"Aaron's journey from exploitation to self-actualization turns a floodlight on the realities of the porn industry and on the nature of the fundamental need for intimacy woven into each of our souls. These are the hard lessons I learned through porn addiction, but told from the other side of the camera and all the more compelling for it. This story shines with real empowerment, profound self-worth, and genuine love. It's the most positive view of sex you'll find."

—Paul Creekmore, former porn user

"I met Aaron Crowley early in 2013 while in Los Angeles during a speaking engagement. It was hard to miss the beautiful and joy-filled young man enthusiastically speaking about and worshiping God. When he spoke of his personal faith, it was clear God had touched him to the core. *Bought with a Price* offers a transparent lens through which the reader can follow Aaron on his pilgrimage from the profane to the sacred. Though few of us will have plunged into so dark a world as Aaron did, we have each experienced our own entanglements of seemingly hopeless despair. In Aaron's transparent story, we can celebrate that there is hope for all."

—Kathy Baldock, author of *Walking the Bridgeless Canyon: Repairing the Breach Between the Church and the LGBT Community,* and *Forging a Sacred Weapon: How the Bible Became Anti-Gay,* executive director of *Canyonwalker Connections*

BOUGHT WITH A PRICE

A GAY CHRISTIAN'S MEMOIR FROM PORN SETS TO LOVE

AARON CROWLEY

PUBLISHING

LOS ANGELES

REVIVAL HOUSE PUBLISHING
PO Box 4816
Glendale, CA 91222

Bought with a Price is a nonfiction work. Some names and identifying details have been changed.

Unless otherwise indicated, all Scripture quotations are from The Holy Bible, English Standard Version® (ESV®), copyright © 2001 by Crossway. Used by permission. All rights reserved.

Scripture quotations marked NRSV are from the New Revised Standard Version Bible, copyright © 1989 National Council of the Churches of Christ in the United States of America. Used by permission. All rights reserved worldwide.

Scriptures marked KJV are taken from the King James Version (KJV), public domain.

Cover design by Euan Monaghan
Page design by Aaron Michael Crowley-Guest

Because of the evolving nature of the internet, web addresses referenced in the end-notes section of this book may have changed since publication. However, all online sources were available and accurate when this book was sent to press. This book was fact-checked by Hank Musolf.

Publisher's Cataloging-in-Publication data

Names: Crowley, Aaron, author.
Title: Bought with a price: a gay Christian's memoir from porn sets to love / by Aaron Crowley.
Description: Includes bibliographical references. | Los Angeles, CA: Revival House Publishing, 2021.
Identifiers: LCCN: 2021900307 | ISBN: 978-1-7364626-0-7 (Hardcover) | 978-1-7364626-1-4 (pbk.) | 978-1-7364626-2-1 (ebook)
Subjects: LCSH Crowley, Aaron. | Christian gay men--United States--Biography. | Gay men--Biography. | Male prostitutes--Biography. | Christian biography. | Protestants--Clergy--Biography. | Christian converts--United States--Biography. | Pornography--United States. | BISAC BIOGRAPHY & AUTOBIOGRAPHY / Personal Memoirs | BIOGRAPHY & AUTOBIOGRAPHY / LGBTQ+ | BIOGRAPHY & AUTOBIOGRAPHY / Religious | RELIGION / Christian Living / Personal Memoirs
Classification: LCC HQ75.8 .C76 2021 | DDC 306.7662/092--dc23

10 9 8 7 6 5 4 3 2 1

To those I fell in love with all over again while I wrote this book:
Yeshua, Aaron Michael, and the Covenant Network

CONTENTS

AUTHOR'S NOTE

THIS BOOK might not always read like a traditional memoir. Because the experience of being prostituted is not well understood, I have referenced research to show that what I experienced is not uncommon. Since scripture has played a tremendous role in my transformation, I also reference the Christian Bible throughout this story. Each reference is cited in the endnotes found at the end of this book.

As in any memoir, all descriptions of events, settings, and dialogue come from my memory and have been truthfully recounted to the best of my ability. I referenced old emails, social media, and video recordings to aid my memory. I also had friends who were present at certain events check my retelling. Some event details have been left vague or omitted entirely to serve the narrative better. There may be two sides to every story, but this is the truth of my experience. All names and most personal characteristics have been changed or omitted to protect people's privacy, except for Aaron Michael, Mike, Randy Morgan, and Johnny Layton.

My story contains some scenes that may be uncomfortable to some readers, including scenes involving sexual violence, rape, prostitution, pornography, drug and alcohol use, witchcraft, external and internal homophobia, and suicide attempts. However, it also contains scenes of triumph and redemption.

This is not an easy story to tell, but I am convinced I need to tell it, even if it kills me.

PROLOGUE

FROM THE AUTHOR'S HUSBAND

D RIVING DOWN the 101 Highway in Los Angeles to meet the man who would officiate our wedding, I let out a deep, painful cry. I hit my hands against the steering wheel in an attempt to ground myself, but an overwhelming numbness overtook my body.

Although Aaron and I have the same first name—people call me Aaron Michael to clarify—we come from two completely different backgrounds. Before I knew him, Aaron had lived a life of sexual exploitation in the porn industry while I was waiting for sex until marriage. I thought I was at peace with Aaron's past, but I wasn't prepared for how the world would treat us.

Moments before I headed to meet our wedding officiant, I found out that my friend had intentionally sought out the porn videos of my fiancé. I went into shock. My friend knew Aaron and I were waiting until marriage to have sex, yet he felt comfortable uncovering my fiancé's nakedness.

My mind seemed stuck on one thought, *I haven't even seen Aaron naked.*

I was awestruck that my friend felt emboldened to exploit Aaron's trauma, knowing how Aaron was exploited in the porn industry. Even now, he didn't seem bothered or affected by my despair. I could no longer breathe, realizing that this might not be the last time someone would do this. Worse, it likely wouldn't be the last time someone would act so unconcerned talking about it. People saw porn as glamorous. How could we tell the truth about Aaron's trauma without leaving ourselves open to more hurt? I was alone, unsure anyone could understand the grief I was going through, or if they would even care.

Aaron never shied away from his past. Right after we met, he shared his testimony with me. I was amazed at how God could take Aaron's pain from the porn industry and use it to give him power and purpose.

Since I was struggling with porn addiction when I met him, Aaron's story resonated with me personally. With him in my life, I was able to see the humanity behind the videos I used to binge. I saw how it hurt me. My brain was rewired by porn to see sex as shameful and dirty, instead of something special and intimate. I had attached this shame to my orientation as a gay man. I knew I needed to make a change. I asked God for help, and He showed me how to let go of my guilt and love myself as a gay Christian.

The more I got to know Aaron and the passionate man of God he is, the more quickly I began to fall in love with him. Only a year after we had met, we were planning our wedding. Coming from a background that didn't believe someone could be gay and Christian, it was beautiful to think that I would be in a gay-affirming marriage with someone who also loved God intensely. It no longer mattered where we came from or what our lives had been like before; Aaron and I would now have a future together with God at the forefront.

I couldn't wait to explore the power of love and intimacy with this incredible man who had been through so much. Blinded by my excitement, I wasn't prepared for the storm that was still to come.

Not long after we were married, several more people came up to me and let me know that they had pulled up Aaron's past. Each time, I grew more and more devastated. I questioned why they would do such a thing, but they always shrugged it off as a harmless curiosity. It was clear they believed they had every right to my husband's body, anytime and anywhere they wanted. They wouldn't let themselves see his trauma or mine. They saw only what they wanted to see, orchestrated by the people behind the scenes to make the exploitation of his vulnerability seem sexy. Nevertheless, Aaron seemed determined to press on and share the truth God gave him. I was quickly wearing down. The feeling that people—*even friends*—could carelessly steal graphic moments of my husband at any time was hard to shake. It was as if anyone could have an affair with my husband's trauma, and I had to be okay with it.

I told Aaron I couldn't handle him telling people about his past anymore. I believed that if people didn't know his story, they couldn't use it to hurt me. Resentment grew. I put up walls. I stopped making friends. The guilt and shame that followed were overwhelming. I had panic attacks. I fell into a spiraling depression that made me suicidal. I let the shame and fear of other people's actions take over my life.

It was in my darkest moment when Jesus met me and reminded me of where I came from. I wasn't blameless. I used to watch porn too. Once again, Jesus saved me. God showed me a way to love people and give grace despite what they may or may not do, while still giving me the space to feel and express my deep pain and anger. The Lord reminded me of the real fight; "For we do not wrestle against flesh and blood, but against the rulers, against the authorities, against the cosmic powers over this present darkness, against the spiritual forces of evil in the heavenly places."[1]

Aaron's testimony has power. My testimony has power. And I believe that God will use our story to bring freedom and love. No matter what the enemy may throw at us, Jesus will take it and turn it for good.[2] I take this promise from God and hold fast to it. I use it as a shield against the enemy's schemes and the pain people may inadvertently cause us.

That's why I know that this book isn't just my husband's testimony or mine; it's a chance for love to win and for more lives to find freedom. I pray that you take the words of this book to heart. No matter where you come from or what you think of pornography or the "sex" industry, I challenge you to dwell on this book without getting defensive. Ask God where He wants you to go from here, and never forget that you are fearfully and wonderfully made.[3]

No matter what, no matter who you are, I love you.

—AARON MICHAEL CROWLEY-GUEST

ONE

JESUS LOVES GAY PORN STARS

"DO YOU KNOW who I am?" I drunkenly shouted at the bouncer, who refused to let my friends and me into the club.

"You just look like some skinny white boy to me," the bouncer said. "You can wait in line like everyone else."

"This is some bullsh—!" In my drunken arrogance, I hoped that some level of recognition from being in gay porn or even just pretending to be famous would give my friends and me immediate VIP access into the club.

Eventually, the bouncer relented and lifted up his puke-stained velvet rope to let us in. As I walked through, the bouncer closed the barrier behind me. When I looked back, I noticed he had left out a couple of guys from my group.

"Wait, wait!" I shouted towards the bouncer, "They're part of my group." Then I yelled towards the rest of my friends who had already gone inside, "Wait! This a—hole isn't letting them in!" My voice was drowned out by the bass of the electronic dance music shaking the entire building.

The bouncer raised his voice, "They have to wait. We're at capacity."

"No, that's straight-up f—ing bullsh—. They're part of my group. We stick together."

He lifted his sorry-looking velvet rope, which separated the club entrance from the street in front of us. As I tried to wave the rest of my friends into the club, the bouncer stopped them and looked straight at me. "You can leave."

"Fine!" I yelled at his face as I stomped in protest through the rope opening he made to the street. "F— this!" I headed down the street in search of another club.

Although the lights of West Hollywood shined around me, the night seemed darker than normal. There were life and busyness. People were running across the street to get in line for the clubs, but everything seemed dead. Empty. Meaningless. It was pitch black except for the dim glow of a few scattered streetlights along the road in front of me. On my path, a spotlight shined on a small crowd of people who looked neither drunk nor homeless. As I passed them, I heard someone mention the name "Jesus."

Maybe it was the alcohol in my system. Maybe it was the adrenaline leftover from my excitement with the bouncer. But something caused me to jump into the middle of their group and obnoxiously shout, "I *love* Jesus!"

I was mostly mocking them, but in a way, I did love the *idea* of Jesus even though I was definitely not one of His followers. I knew a bit about Him, but I didn't *know* Him. Although my mother took me to church a handful of times when I was growing up, by the time I was old enough to understand that I'm gay, I had no interest in any organized, religious version of God. I believed that all anyone needed was to be a good person. I believed if we sought a connection with the universe or God, or *whoever* through *whatever* path we'd like, then we'd be fine.

After drunkenly interrupting the group, I realized they were a Christian outreach group. Most of them looked at me like they were thinking, "Who is this super annoying drunk guy interrupting our prayer?" One of the young women nearest to me watched with wide eyes as if she was afraid of me. They began to whisper among themselves, possibly anxious about what else I might do. But one man smiled at me. He glowed as the streetlamp above us cast a halo around him. His bright eyes pierced my heart and held my focus captive. He was the only one from that group to speak to me.

"You love Jesus, man?"

Something about him sobered me for a moment. His look was gentle. It made me feel like he actually, authentically cared. I looked down and thought about everything I had heard about Jesus. From what I knew about Him, Jesus seemed great, but everyone said He was anti-gay. After all, He is supposedly the son of a god who destroyed two cities because there were gay people living there.

"I guess," I finally answered the man. "But I don't think He loves me."

Their entire group grew silent.

"No, man," the guy corrected me. "Jesus *loves* you!"

The words hit my heart like a seed falling on hard, rocky earth.

I don't believe that, I thought. *This guy wouldn't say that if he knew I'm gay and in porn.*

I was too incoherent to remember what happened the rest of that night. Still, somehow, this moment remained vividly etched in my memory. A seed somehow fell upon my solid stone heart and found a crack where it landed into soft, wet soil to plant itself. No amount of alcohol could drown it out, but it would still be a while before that seed would grow.

THE SET LIGHTS erupted in my irises until all I could see was the dark eye of the camera and the shadowy silhouettes who watched behind it. The camera lens pushed in and out to better focus on its subject—me, completely exposed, except for my tight boxer-briefs.

As I watched the camera, I thought about the thousands of eyes who would end up watching me through that one lens. They would all see me in my underwear, and they would all see more of me in the scene we had just finished shooting. As soon as the camera slid into focus and its aperture opened to the right setting, the producer began to ask me a series of salacious questions.

"What's a sexual fantasy of yours?"

"Where's the kinkiest place you've had sex?"

"Are you a top or a bottom?"

I knew what was expected of me, so I answered him in a way that would keep the viewers turned on. But when he got to the last question, it was like a crack broke through the façade, and the answer I knew he wanted just wouldn't come out.

In the darkness, on the other side of the camera, my producer's voice asked, "Is there anything else you want your fans to know about you?"

As soon as he said it, the words echoed within me, "Jesus *loves* you."

Through the glare of the studio lights, I looked at his silhouette, and without thinking, the words fell out of my mouth.

"I want people to know that there is more to me than all of this."

My eyes widened at the realization of what I had just said. It didn't matter that I couldn't see his face; my producer's displeasure was palpable. I had just broken one of the most important but unspoken rules of the "sex" industry: do not be real.[a] We're in the business of peddling fantasies. We need to look cute. Be enticing. But never show a deeper side. We must betray our humanity for the camera.

"What do you mean?" the producer pressed in a tone that implied he wanted me to stick to my pornified persona. I looked down, trying to think of something that would keep the fans watching. It was a simple question, but I didn't have any other answer.

"I don't know," I responded.

When my porn videos were released to the public and when people I knew found them—because everyone has a "friend" who watches gay porn—I owned it proudly. I hid behind boastfulness and acted like my life was glamorous. It was all a lie. I not only lied to other people about what the "sex" industry is like, but I also lied to myself. And I lied to myself so much that it became difficult for me to distinguish between myself and the persona I played in porn, a person who enjoyed being used for sex.

My excessive lifestyle was the only way I could get myself to play the part I was expected to play in front of the cameras. Alcohol, drugs, parties, all of it numbed me enough so that what happened to me in front of the cameras would look fun to a porn viewer. It had to look fun so that those who watched it could get off. Acting like it is pleasurable is a part

---

[a] I'll explain in a later chapter, but I hate the phrase "sex industry." Because I used this term when I was in porn, I will use it in this section, but I will put "sex" in quotation marks to emphasize that there is no real sex in the "sex" industry.

of commercialized "sex." In any business, you must cater to the consumers' needs.

As I tried to think of a response to my producer's final question, the consumers' desires were overshadowed by the Christian's words resonating within my heart, "Jesus *loves* you!" The night I ran into the outreach group was such a small moment, but I couldn't escape it. The thought was too astounding to someone like me. That man did not know me, yet he confidently claimed that his God loves me. Hearing that Jesus loves me captivated me, and the thought made it difficult for me to keep my mind focused on the character I was supposed to play in front of the camera. It caused me to wonder if I was worth more and made for more than all of this. It caused something within me to become uncomfortable with what I was doing.

Why would Jesus love me? What about me is lovable? Does Jesus love gay porn stars?

My producer grew irritated with my lack of an answer to his question. He used his hand to gesture silently and urged me to give him something he could use. I didn't usually have to think this much in my shoots. Normally, I just had to let people do things to me, but now I had to think of an answer that the producer wanted. But the answer he wanted would betray what was stirring in my heart.

"I mean, like," my mind stumbled around, looking for the right response. "There are deeper things to who I am beyond what the camera can capture."

My producer let out an audible sigh. Next to him, my co-performer, Scott, cocked his head to the side as if he was thinking about what I was saying. It seemed like I was making everyone uncomfortable. Even I was uncomfortable, but I couldn't think of a sexy answer to that question.

If I had any fans, all they knew about me was from porn. They knew what the most intimate parts of my body looked like, but they didn't know *me*. They didn't even know my real name. They didn't know I worked my butt off in high school to go to a good university with the hopes that I could one day provide a better life for myself. They didn't know that to pay for that education, I needed to sell myself. They didn't know that I was starting to wonder if there was more value to me than the couple hundred dollars I was given for letting men use and abuse me.

It echoed within me, "Jesus *loves* you!"

If Jesus loves me, then how does He feel about what I am doing?

If Jesus loves me, then by doing what I'm doing, am I being degraded?

My producer's question shook that thought awake in me.

Who am I really?

Deep inside of me, I knew that I had lost myself in the "sex" industry, and I had ignored this feeling out of necessity. I kept doing porn shoots, escorting, and go-go dancing because I needed the money. I kept partying, drinking, and abusing prescription drugs because I needed to cope with the fact that I felt empty and powerless inside. My deeper self, my spirit—who I truly am—had been killed by who the world wanted me to be: nothing more than a human sex toy. I didn't realize it at the time, but I was dead.

Thankfully, God is in the business of raising the dead!

TWO

PIMPED OUT

ONTHS BEFORE I ran into the Christian outreach group, I began my "career" in porn. I was a senior in college when I met the man who would spend the next year pimping me out to the highest bidder: clubs who needed go-go dancers, porn producers who needed bodies, and personal clients who wanted escorts.

I was easy to recruit into the "sex" industry. I lived off scholarships, grants, financial aid, a part-time, minimum-wage job, and student loans throughout my time in college. Still, after tuition, books, and supplies, I barely could afford to eat. Ramen noodles and peanut butter and jelly sandwiches left me desperately malnourished.

When it was time to pay my tuition, I didn't have enough money. My student loans wouldn't come in for a couple more weeks. I could get a short-term loan to help pay for tuition until my student loans came in, but even after that, I wouldn't have enough for food and rent.

Financial aid was the main reason I wasn't homeless. Before college, during my senior year of high school, I didn't feel safe at home anymore, so I left. There was a lot going on with my family at the time, but a part of why I left is that I was terrified about how some in my family would react to the fact that I am gay. So I ran away. I slept on my friends' couches until I could move to college. When I got to my university, financial aid helped me to afford dorm rent. As I entered into my senior year, I knew that I would soon need a new income source for rent, and I would have to start repaying my student loans shortly after graduation.

While staring at my bank account online and trying to figure out how to pay my tuition with over-drafted funds, my phone buzzed. I had several notifications that someone had messaged me on a hookup app I was using. I opened it to see a mirror selfie of a heavy set, forty-something year old guy trying to make the early 2000's teenage-duckface-kissy-lips. According to his profile, his name was Sean.

SEAN

> Hey, cutie. I'm a talent scout for a couple of gay porn studios. I'm looking for cute twinks to cast in shoots that we have going on. I saw your profile, and I thought you might be interested.

In gay slang, "twinks" refer to young, naive, skinny, gay men, and in the gay community, I was a twink. I was twenty-one, but I looked way younger. I could even pass as underage, fifteen or sixteen, which was the most attractive asset that the porn industry wanted from me. Porn that depicts underage teens—*children*—has been a consistently popular search on porn websites.[1]

I thought Sean was probably some sleazy, older man trying to hook up with me, but because I needed the money, I hoped he was telling the truth.

ME

Really? I might be interested. How would we do that?

SEAN

You'll just need to come over so that I can take pictures of you to submit to the studios.

ME

How do I know you're for real?

SEAN

Go to my Facebook profile and ask any of my friends. Most of them work with me. I think you can be big in the industry, but you need someone like me to protect you.

Since I was a kid, I had been watching porn, and just from watching it, the people seemed to be having fun and making a lot of easy money. Sean's offer seemed like a rescue to catch up on bills. I wanted to be sure, though, so I reached out to some of his Facebook friends to see if he was really a porn talent scout. All of them verified it, and some of them even sent me some of their own videos. Since everything checked out, I decided to meet up with Sean.

At his house, Sean asked me to take off my clothes and model against a bare wall while he took pictures. It was nothing new for me. In my freshman year of college, a friend had taken pictures of me while I was blackout drunk and someone else had "sex" with me. That friend shared the pictures online before I even knew about it, so Sean's photoshoot wasn't my first time having graphic pictures taken of me to be shared with others. I was numb to the experience.

While Sean took the pictures, he kept his eyes on me like a hungry carnivore, salivating over a piece of meat. Then after several poses, Sean's face changed as he sat down in a chair. He became stoic and straight-faced. He didn't look up at me as he unzipped his pants.

With his eyes on the floor, Sean said, "I need to see what you can do. If you want to be in this industry, this is a part of it."

I stood there, staring at his genitals. Sean was not someone I wanted to have sex with. His age, his appearance, his size, his stoic expression reminded me too much of another older man who had sexually assaulted me earlier in college. I didn't want to hook up with Sean, but I didn't want to hook up with that older man either. That man forced himself on me. If I refused Sean, I was afraid that he would force himself on me as well.

"Do you want to make money or not?" Sean asked after a glance up to see my not-too-excited face.

I did. I needed the money, and he knew that. I did what he asked.

There's so much to why I gave in to him. My desperation for money was only a part of it. Another big reason I gave in to him is that I wasn't sure if I had a choice. I was at Sean's house. He could easily take advantage of me, and no one else would ever know. When I was assaulted before, I didn't want to have sex with those people, but they had "sex" with me anyway. If people were going to have "sex" with me regardless of my choice, it seemed much less traumatic if I would just let men do what they wanted to do. Giving in was my self-defense.

By convincing myself that I chose to let men do to me what they otherwise would have done through assault, I thought I had regained some control over myself. By giving in and always complying with what men wanted to do to me, I gave myself an illusion that I had power over the situation. The idea of empowerment removed me from the reality of my trauma.

I let Sean do whatever he wanted to my body. I comforted myself with the thought that this would open up the opportunity to feed myself, pay my bills, and finish school.

What Sean did to me was a grooming technique to make sure I could handle the porn industry where the same stuff would happen. I didn't want to have sex with Sean, but in porn, there would be countless times that I would be having unwanted sex. I didn't decide what happened to my body anymore. I was now at the direction and command of others. Sean needed to make sure I knew that.

Although Sean was my "agent," from the moment I gave in to him, Sean became my pimp. Today, I choose the word "pimp" when referring to Sean because there is a difference between the dynamic of what an agent is and what Sean was to me. An agent helps writers, singers, actors, models, and other artists find clients who need their talents. Actors have a talent to portray a character on stage or screen, and models have a photogenic talent to market a product. But I wasn't an actor or a model. Sean didn't find people who needed my talents. He found people who wanted to rent and use *me* as a sex toy so that he could get a cut of the pay. And like any pimp, Sean used his merchandise—me, and other men in porn—as he pleased. Sean was no agent. He was my pimp.

. . .

THERE WERE four guys, including myself, waiting in the holding room for hair and makeup. It was my first industry-produced porn scene. One of the guys was a little bit chubbier than the rest of us, and he was suffering from a bad acne breakout. The shallow person who I was did not want to perform with him. Fortunately, for shallow me, the producers pulled that guy aside and escorted him out of the studio. Part of me was relieved I wouldn't have to perform with him, while another part of me felt sorry for him. However, that was overshadowed by anxiety that made it hard to breathe.

What if the producers don't find me attractive either? What if they escort me out?

I still wonder today if the producers removed that guy in front of us on purpose to cause anxiety in me and the other first-timer. I wonder if that guy was an example to indirectly tell us, "If you don't keep up your appearance, we will remove and shame you too." We had to maintain a sexy image to sell our product—ourselves. Being unattractive would mean poverty.

The third guy waiting with us wasn't new to porn, so he helped prepare us for what to expect. He had first done porn years prior, but he admitted that he quit when he was dating his boyfriend because his boyfriend took care of all of his financial needs. But when his boyfriend broke up with him, he returned to porn to make a living. I ignored this thought at the time, but I realize now that he didn't really want to be there having sex with us. He felt he had to be there to survive. Just like I did.

Actually, everyone I ever knew from porn and prostitution was in it because of poverty. We all needed the money.

As I prepared to do my first porn scene, panic overcame me. It helped that the production crew had some vodka on the set. The alcohol helped me to dissociate, but I also sensed Sean's voice in my head telling me, "Don't worry. You'll do great. You're cute."

Sean was skilled at grooming me for the "sex" industry. Pimps and traffickers groom the people they prostitute by building a relationship with them before manipulating and exploiting them. Sean built a relationship with me by taking me to exclusive clubs, movie premieres, and theme parks. He made me feel that because I knew him, I had social status. He did this to build my trust, so he could tear down any ounce of self-worth I had outside of my sex life. When you're in the middle of it, it's hard to tell what's happening, but looking back, I can see exactly how he manipulated me and made me feel like I needed him.

For example, Sean and his friends, all of whom were twice my age, would talk about something going on in the news or pop culture. I'd ask a question or try to get involved in the conversation. After a moment, he and his friends would all stop, laugh, and say, "Good thing that he's cute."

Moments like this reminded me that I was a ditzy, dumb twink. This subtle way of making me feel inept broke down any self-worth I had built around my intelligence or any other accomplishments and reminded me that I was only good for sex.

For the same reason, Sean would make sure to build me up when it came to my sexuality. The night before I was to perform my first scene, I confessed to him I was anxious the producers wouldn't find me attractive. He replied, "Don't worry. You'll do great. I think you're cuter than you realize."

As I went to porn sets, I kept hearing the same thing, "Wow! You're cuter in person than Sean's pictures of you." It was almost scripted like Sean had asked them all to say it, and it worked. My appearance and sexuality became the only things that I had any confidence in. With a rush of encouragement from the on-set alcohol and Sean's voice in my head, I was able to get through three of my first porn scenes that week.

When it was pay time, the producers called me into their office. "Don't mention how much you're getting paid to the other guys. Sean worked out a deal for you, but we are paying the other guys less."

It was five-hundred dollars per scene. One scene was a few hundred dollars short of a month's rent. I had to do several scenes each month to catch up on my bills.

My FIRST meeting with Sean wasn't the only time he used me. Whenever he wanted, Sean would text me to come over to his house because he wanted to use my body. At first, there were many times where I told him that I didn't want to have sex with him. He would always reply, "I guess you just don't need any money right now."

But we both knew that I needed the money. When financial aid from school ran out, porn kept me fed and housed. That's what kept me bound to Sean. Hunger. Poverty. Vulnerability.

Today, I hate hearing the phrase "pimped out" when referring to something cool or when something has had a lot of money spent on it. It implies that being pimped out is fun, or that the object or person being pimped out is glamorous. As someone who has actually been pimped out, I know it is not fun and glamorous. The use of the phrase "pimped out" as cool is evidence of just how deeply our society has normalized and grown desensitized towards prostitution.

After I encountered the Christian outreach group, as I'd lie there while Sean used me, I continued to hear it. "Jesus *loves* you!" It was impossible to escape the reverberation of those words within me because when I had to dissociate—which I did every time Sean called me to his house—my mind seemed to keep going to that moment when I ran into those Christians. While Sean would use my body, I would be trying to understand what it meant that Jesus loves me.

Because of the time that Sean invested in mentally and emotionally grooming me, I became accustomed to thinking that I was only worth being used for sex. I believed it was my value. But when I heard the man say, "Jesus *loves* you," everything began to change.

THREE

ASKING FOR IT

I WAS CALLED into a shoot as a stand-in because the previous model had suffered a seizure. What I didn't realize—or what I didn't *want* to realize—is that the scene I was about to perform was so rough that it incited painful convulsions in the original model to the point where he needed to be rushed to the hospital. At the time, I refused to recognize that I was getting myself into something dangerous because Sean had always promised to protect me.

When I got to the studio, the production team sat me down to sign the consent forms. While I rarely read every single word of a consent form before I signed it, that day especially, I knew that I needed to hurry because they were already behind schedule. Being naive and pressured by the circumstances, I signed the papers as soon as the producer handed them to me. Then I was rushed to set, where I was eventually bound, gagged, and found myself in a brutal rape scene.

I had been raped so many times by this point in my life that as soon as it began happening, I had already dissociated. I was completely detached from my body and took all the aggression as if it were nothing. Every now and then, I might have winced in pain, but there was no empathy for the trauma. Instead, the other performer and the viewers were supposed to derive pleasure from the violence acted against me.

Today, when I describe the type of porn scenes I appeared in, it may sound like hardcore, fringe porn, especially to older generations who are not familiar with the widespread, graphic porn of today's internet. But all of the porn videos I appeared in are considered mainstream. My generation has grown up with this material, and we are desensitized to it. It's normal porn to us.

I was first exposed to porn when I was nine years old. The first video I ever saw had a group of men acting out sexual aggression on a woman. From that, I learned that sex is violent, so everything that happened to me on porn sets seemed normal.

Rape and sexual violence are viral porn categories and searches.[1] Because of its increasing popularity, producers continue to make more and more violent content to appease the demand of porn fans. Today's violent porn normalizes sexual violence for viewers and portrays it as pleasurable. It suggests that people enjoy rape and sexual aggression. It portrays the idea that nonconsensual sex is arousing. It tells viewers that violence is a part of sex. It tells society that rape victims were asking for it.[2]

I had done scenes like this rape scene before, but this was the first scene I did after the drunken night when I met the Christian outreach group. On the porn set, as my mind drifted elsewhere while sexual aggression was poured out upon my body, the voice of the Christian man continued to echo within me. "Jesus *loves* you!"

. . .

A FEW YEARS EARLIER—

The rays of sunlight through the window pierced through my eyelids. As I rolled over to avoid the light, my head began spinning. The bitter taste of vomit rose to the back of my throat. I needed to find a toilet fast.

Blinking, my eyes squinted open. I was not in my dorm. My bare leg knocked into someone else's as I moved to get off the bed.

An upperclassman I met the night before, Brandon, was lying next to me. Another guy, José, was sleeping on the floor below, his digital camera lying next to him. I looked around the room for my clothes. They were scattered around except for my boxers, which were pulled down around my thighs. As I crept out of bed, I didn't have time to put on more than my underwear before my stomach reminded me that I needed to find the toilet.

As I hurried and stumbled out of the room, I opened the first door I found, and thankfully it was the bathroom. Another guy, Zach, was passed out with his arms wrapped around the toilet seat. I tried to use my foot to push him off, but he was too heavy. I gave him a quick kick. He gave out a grunt and rolled over onto the floor.

Zach's stale vomit filled the toilet. I'm not sure whether seeing it or smelling it was the final straw, but in seconds, I was retching up all of my stomach's contents. When there was nothing left to throw up, I flushed the toilet and stumbled back to the bedroom. José was now up, gathering his things.

"We probably should go," he said.

On the car ride back home, neither José, Brandon, Zach, or I said anything. We were all too hungover. I tried to remember the night before, but each time I tried to make sense of the blurred images, my skull felt like it would burst open. All I could remember was that this was the first week of my freshman year in college. I wanted to make new friends, and I had met José online. He invited me to a small party at Brandon's house. We took some shots, and then I woke up.

When we pulled up to my dormitory, I mumbled, "Bye," before slamming the car door behind me. Somehow, I managed to make it to my room, chug several water bottles, and fall onto my bed as I passed out to sleep off the rest of my hangover.

I woke up several hours later to a text message.

JOSÈ

> That was really hot last night.

ME

> What do you mean?

JOSÈ

> You and Brandon.

The image broke through like I had locked it away in some dark corner of my mind. Brandon forced himself on me while I was completely blacked out. Brandon *raped* me.

Back then, I didn't want to use that word—*rape*—to describe what Brandon did. I couldn't bring myself to speak that word. Now, though, I know the importance of calling it exactly what it was. I was *raped*. Had I been sober and more aware, I wouldn't have consented to have sex with Brandon since I had just met him.

I especially would not have consented to what I found out next.

JOSÈ

The pictures came out really hot too.

ME

What the f— are you talking about?!

While Brandon raped me, José had been standing at the foot of the bed, taking pictures of the whole thing. By the time any of this was revealed to me, José had already shared these photos online. This was the first time I was pornographed. My first porn was my rape.

I ran to José's dorm. "You better f—ing delete those!"

"Why?" He laughed like I was joking. "Guys think these are hot."

José thought that I would be flattered. He found me attractive, so to him, there was nothing wrong with what he did. Our culture told him "boys will be boys" and "men always want sex," so he thought what happened last night was normal.[3] It's hard to see what's wrong with something you think is normal.

Pushing through the lump in my throat that only comes when I'm about to cry, but trying with everything in me not to, I whispered, "I don't want everyone to see me naked." José had already shared the pictures, so I was powerless. "Please delete them."

"Okay, okay. Fine."

I watched as José went through his camera and computer to delete every nude photo of me, and I left his dorm that evening, believing that every photo was gone.

A couple of weeks later, I ran into Zach on my way to class; he was the bigger guy who was passed out with his arms hugging the toilet. He wasn't like José and Brandon, though. Before we all started drinking, Zach had told us that he was a Christian and that he was waiting until marriage to have sex. Neither Brandon, José, or I took it seriously. I laughed out loud when he said it.

A gay man waiting to have sex? A gay Christian?

When I ran into Zach on campus, he told me that José didn't delete the pictures and was still sharing them. I confronted José about it again, but he insisted that he no longer had them. I wanted to believe him, but everywhere I went, if there was another gay man from my university, I couldn't shake the feeling that he had already seen me naked.

I didn't go to the police. What could they have done? The photos were already on the internet. They could be downloaded and shared a million times. There was no way to delete them for good, so I thought there was nothing I or anyone else could do.

Also, I blamed myself. Today, I know that nothing anyone does is deserving of rape, but back then, like many people who experience rape, I believed that it was somehow my fault. I chose to go to Brandon's house. I chose to get drunk. That's why it was so hard for me to realize it was rape.

Even when I did start to wonder if it was rape, I didn't tell anyone what happened to me. Who would have believed me? A man who didn't want to have sex? Our culture doesn't even think that exists. I wouldn't have gotten sympathy. Our society laughs at male-on-male rape. *"Don't drop the soap!"* I would have been ridiculed. If someone actually believed me, the fact that I was raped would make me less of a man in their eyes. I would be even less of a man than I already am to some people because I'm not just a man; I'm a gay man.

Since gay men are men, and since people think all men want sex constantly, society seemed to paint gay men as exceptionally lustful. Through porn and other media, I had always seen gay men portrayed as having wild, insatiable sex regardless of consent. Even Christians seemed to describe gay men like this, and especially after being raped, I had a lot of reason to believe it was true.

Imagery of Sodom and Gomorrah flooded my mind as I thought, *Maybe this happened because I'm gay.*

It became difficult for me to mentally separate gay sex from what I realize now is rape. They became the same thing in my mind. And being raped as a gay man made me hate myself.

BY THE TIME I was learning to cope with what had happened at Brandon's house, I was raped again. I was raped several times in my early years of college. Each time, it was like more and more of my humanity was chiseled away.

During either my sophomore or junior year, I was out at the clubs with some friends from my university's student TV program. It was a straight club, so when I got drunk, I ditched my friends to go to the gay bars. As I was ordering a drink, I noticed an older man staring at me. He wasn't my type, and he gave me the creeps. So I avoided him as I made my way to the dance floor.

The rest of the night is a hazy blur. All I remember is noticing the older man watching me for what seemed like the entire night. Even when I made every effort to avoid him, he seemed to be lurking somewhere.

When the club began to close, and people around me started to leave the dance floor, I realized that the only thing keeping me from falling on my face was the crowd. As the mass of people dissipated, I fought just to stay conscious. When I noticed the older man start to approach me, I realized that I might be *more* than just drunk.

It took everything in me, but I made it out of the club and found some guys who looked like they were my age. Through what I'm sure was a slurred and incoherent speech, I tried to communicate to them that I needed to get to the bus stop back to campus. They were going in that direction, so they let me follow them.

I have no idea what happened, but the next thing I knew, the same guys who let me follow them to the bus stop were putting me into a car. I looked beside me and saw that the driver was the older man from the club—the man I was trying to escape from.

As he strapped the seatbelt around me, one of the young men whispered in my ear, "This guy says he can take you home. Have fun. He looks like he'll be good in bed."

Before I could say anything, the young man slammed the car door in my face.

The next thing I remember, the older man was on top of me, raping me.

I remembered back to a moment at my freshman orientation when a volunteer upperclassman lectured us, "If you say, 'No,' they must stop, or it becomes sexual assault."

As the older man abused my body, I couldn't feel my lips or tongue. It was slurred, and I was mumbling. But I was saying it.

"No." It didn't matter. "No." I had no choice. "No." He was raping me.

I could barely say a monosyllabic word, let alone defend myself or escape. I accepted my fate and lay there, waiting for him to finish and for everything to be over.

Even though I said "No," I still blamed myself. Shame kicked in and reminded me that I chose to get drunk. I chose to ditch my friends. I chose to go to a gay club alone. It seemed that something about my presence at that club that night screamed that I wanted this. Something about me told this man that I was asking for it, and a part of me wondered if I really did want it because I had made decisions that led to it.

My mind drifted, desperate to be anywhere but there. I hovered above the entire scene with my back turned to avoid seeing what was happening to my body below. I continued to drift further into the nightly heavens that lay beyond the cage I was trapped in. The stars became my friends as I floated along the black ocean sky.

I had completely dissociated from the object I used to call my body. It was the first time I can remember my mind completely detaching itself from the physical form to cope with the trauma I was experiencing, and it wouldn't be the last. There would be many more times when I had to dissociate from sexual trauma before I found myself doing the same thing on set for violent rape scenes.

FOUR

UNWANTED

WHEN I GOT HOME from the rape scene that had hospitalized the guy before me, the rest of the cast and the crew were still all over me. Their sweat, their grease, their fingerprints covered every inch of my body. I got into the shower, wishing that the water would wash away what had just been done to me, but nothing could undo it. My body had been used and abused, and it would continue to be used and abused every time someone watched that video. No matter how hard I scrubbed, no matter how much water washed over me, there was no undoing what had just been done to my body.

I got out of the shower and furiously dried off, desperate to find a way to escape my dirty, ugly, powerless, used body.

Maybe I can get away if I die.

I dug through my medicine cabinet. I had prescription drugs that were given to me to help with anxiety attacks. The doctors thought I had anxiety because of demanding schoolwork, but I didn't tell them that I had been raped. I took one of those pills. Then I took another. And then I took a handful. I had some sleeping pills. I took a handful of them as well.

For the next day and a half, I was in and out of sleep. I'm not sure what exactly was happening in my body. I would suddenly jolt awake as I convulsed and twitched while my heart beat like it was trying to burst out of my chest. Then I'd pass out again.

Two days later, when the pills' effects began to wear off, I wasn't immediately able to get out of bed. I lay there in paralysis.

How am I not dead right now?

"No, man. Jesus *loves* you!"

If Jesus is real and loves me, why is He so horrible to allow my life to be like this?

THE SAME PRODUCERS who produced the rape scene continued to bring me in to do more of their scenes, which always involved me being humiliated and raped. It seemed I was the type of person people wanted to rape. As I went to these porn shoots, I thought I was simply portraying sexual violence. Still, something about hearing the Christian man tell me that Jesus loves me caused something within me to begin to awaken. I wondered if maybe I was actually being sexually traumatized.

I had never heard the term "grooming." I had no idea what it meant to become desensitized to sexual trauma and violence through teachings, social norms, and experiences. Today, I know that I was groomed for sexual trauma because I grew up in a culture that told me that my sexual orientation was lustful and violent. I know that being exposed to violent porn from a young age desensitized me to think that violent sex is normal. On top of that, being repeatedly raped in college, I now know that rape was one of the biggest factors contributing to me feeling comfortable with eventually surrendering to unwanted sex by selling myself.

No little boy or girl grows up wanting to sell their bodies. It is no one's "dream come true." In reality, many factors contribute to grooming an individual for the "sex" industry. The most powerful grooming technique is rape.

Rape was used to groom me because, like most people who were raped, I took a lot of the blame for being raped. Because it happened to me more than once, I thought something about me led these men to rape me. There seemed to be this constant, inescapable sense of shame and guilt, which nagged me that it was my fault. I survived being raped by dissociating. While being traumatized, my mind left my body, and I would just lie there. At the time, just lying there seemed to mean to me that I consented to the sex. That made me feel out of control of my own body, which led me to search for some outlet to regain control.

I became hypersexual. Many rape survivors try to cope with being raped by having an excess amount of sex to regain control and empowerment over their bodies.[1] When porn presented itself as an opportunity, it seemed to be a viable option to conquer the lingering feeling that I had no authority over myself.

When I entered the porn industry, I thought it would be fun and glamorous. I grew up watching porn. It looked exciting. On the outside, I kept up that enticing, sexy image, but on the inside, deep down, being on set and having things done to me that I otherwise wouldn't have consented to was just as unwanted as rape. And, as with the times I was raped, I survived it by dissociating. Through dissociation, I was able to ignore how I really felt. When dissociation was too difficult, I drank heavily to keep my mind numb and mentally checked out, so I could be used, abused, smacked around, and then discarded. And when it was too hard to dissociate with alcohol, suicide often seemed the best opportunity for escape. I attempted suicide often after I was raped and while in porn.

The part of me that blamed myself for being raped was the same part of me that was convinced that being in porn was empowering. Convincing myself that porn was fun seemed to medicate the part of me that blamed myself for being raped. Still, I was paid to have otherwise unwanted sex, with people watching who I otherwise wouldn't want to have watching, all so that I could afford to live. I would have never done any of it without the money, but that kind of stuff was already happening to me anyway. I thought I might as well get paid for it.

The only difference between the times I was raped and these filmed rape scenes is that I was paid to participate in the scenes. I convinced myself that getting paid gave me control over these experiences. At least through porn, I exploited for my own gain that which others had already exploited—myself. I thought it was empowering. It was much less traumatizing to give in to what the rapists had already assumed—that I wanted what was happening to me. That I wanted all of this. That I was asking for it.

After hearing that Jesus loves me, it became too difficult to ignore how little control I actually had in porn. Hearing "Jesus *loves* you" seemed to sober me. It triggered my mind to return to my body, and it became too difficult to ignore that I was still being traumatized in much the same way as when I was raped. After all, I wasn't the one calling the shots; the producers were. And they were acting based on the demands of porn consumers. I didn't decide what happened to me. The consumers did, and to do what the consumers wanted,

I had to keep myself in a state of constant dissociation.

Unwanted sex is traumatizing. It tells a person that they have no autonomy over their own body. Unwanted sex for money is *still* just as traumatizing. Money doesn't have some miraculous power to erase the trauma of unwanted sex. The fact that cameras were there does nothing to take away the trauma, either; in fact, the money and the cameras strengthened that sense of shame and guilt that festered within me due to the trauma. The money and the cameras are often seen as evidence that I wanted everything that happened to me. They are often used as evidence that I was to blame for any trauma I experienced on set. Interlocking trauma with self-blame tells us that we deserve the trauma we experience, so I owned it. I gave in to it. Everyone seemed to say that I was asking for it, so I complied. I convinced myself that porn was empowering me. I told myself that I enjoyed it. I told everyone that I enjoyed it. I convinced everyone that it was fun. All while I had to let my mind dissociate while I acquiesced to unwanted sex.

I did porn because I thought it was what I deserved, and we, all of us as humans, are deeply flawed. We do not, by nature, accept what we are truly worth. Instead, we accept only that which we believe we deserve. And it *kills* us.

Yet, even in the midst of some of the most degrading porn scenes, I continued to hear the words echo in my heart. "No, man. Jesus *loves* you!"

FIVE

THE END OF MYSELF

A s I WAS LEAVING my apartment to go to a porn shoot, one of my roommates asked me, "What if porn ends up becoming your career? Like, even after graduation?"

"It won't," I said. "I'll get a real job eventually."

"But what if you don't?"

"Then I'll have a career in porn," I laughed. I shrugged it off and headed out the door.

Before graduating, I applied to every job I was qualified for, but I wasn't getting hired. I wasn't even getting interviewed. My inability to find work only seemed to prove the point that Sean had always hinted at: I was only good for sex. Selling myself was the only thing that kept food in my stomach and rent paid.

I graduated from college in 2011 as the economy was weakly recovering from the Great Recession. There weren't many new entry-level positions, but I continued to apply to every job I could. Still, I didn't have any luck even getting interviews. Because I now had to pay all my bills without financial aid, I depended more on doing porn shoots. I didn't know of any other way to make the money I needed to continue to pay my living expenses. I survived by selling my body.

After a prolonged month of no porn shoots, I had to tell my roommate I was afraid that I wouldn't make rent.

"Can you do a porn video to get the money?" she asked.

"There aren't many productions going on right now," I said. "But my agent did mention some opportunities to be an escort. I don't really want to, but I can do that. I still might be a few days late, though."

She sighed and sat down next to me. "I thought about doing sex work once. But when I moved out here, my dad told me that if I'm ever in a bind, and sex work was my last resort, that I should call him. He said he would help me out, so I wouldn't have to do it."

Why are you telling me this? I thought to myself. *I don't have that luxury.*

I was raised by a single mother who worked her butt off to take care of my siblings and me. I was the only one in my immediate family to graduate from high school, let alone college, so my mom wasn't financially well-off enough to pay for my living expenses during and after school.

When I needed money quickly, and porn studios didn't have many productions for me, Sean booked me escorting gigs. These were always the hardest part of the "sex" industry for me. In other parts of the "sex" industry, I was able to leave my body through dissociation, but when escorting, the men who bought me wanted to talk and have intimate company. With them, I had to stay mentally present.

People who buy sex are often called johns, tricks, or punters. I used to call them my "clients." Today, I see these terms as too much of a mask to hide the reality of what these men do. They buy humans for sex. They are sex-buyers. Today, I can't call them anything less than that.

My sex-buyers tended to want me to sit on their lap while we talked. It was as if they liked to treat me like a child. Often, it seemed, they spoke about things that they thought would impress me. They'd talk about how nice their house or the hotel room was, as if it was such a privilege for me to be there with them. Or they'd talk about their nice careers or their money as if I should appreciate that they were going to share some with me. It seemed that my sex-buyers liked to brag and have me grovel in recognition that they had what I needed.

It was too difficult for me to stay completely present during these conversations. As he'd drone on and on, my mind would often wander to a blank spot on the wall where I'd stare. I'd drift deep into the paint and swim through it.

Then my sex-buyer would notice that I'm not paying attention. "Is everything okay?"

I'd force myself to snap back to reality by shaking myself awake, smiling, and looking him in the eyes. "Yeah, I'm fine. I was just noticing…" and I'd talk about something on his wall where I was staring. Sometimes family pictures. A calendar. His diploma. And then I'd try to carry on with the small talk.

I had to smile, nod, refrain from dissociating, and respond to him as he seemed to rub it in my face that he had what I needed. To get it, I needed to do exactly what he wanted: act like I enjoyed being with him. Then, finally, he'd use me, and I was allowed to dissociate. Then he'd be done. He'd pay me, and I'd get into my car to head to either my next sex-buyer or home.

As I'd drive away, ignoring the trauma raging inside of me, I'd always hear it. "Jesus *loves* you!"

As I CONTINUED to look for a job, one of my friends gave me some hope. She was a Wiccan spiritualist. I would often pay her to read my astrological star charts and consult tarot cards. When I told her that I was struggling to find work, she suggested a prosperity potion. Every morning and night, I would wash my hands in this potion that my friend helped me concoct. Then I would breathe out a little chant. This practice was supposed to summon the power of the universe, or something, to help me find work, but I still wasn't even getting interviewed.

After repeatedly hearing, "Jesus *loves* you" echoing within me, I decided to say a little prayer one night. "Jesus, if You're real, please help me find a job, so I can quit selling myself."

The next day, I applied for a position as a post-production assistant at a television production company. That week, the hiring manager called me to come in for an interview. After a series of questions and answers, he hired me on the spot. It happened so quickly that I could hardly believe it.

As I drove down the highway back home, my foot trembled on the gas pedal. I thought back to hearing the Christian man say, "Jesus *loves* you."

Did I get this job because I prayed to Jesus?

I was so caught up trying to figure out what happened that I forgot that I was driving home. I ended up accidentally driving several miles into the desert north of Los Angeles county. As I caught myself and did a U-turn off the highway to head back home, I decided that it was a pure coincidence that I prayed to

Jesus and then got a job. I had also been washing my hands in my friend's prosperity potion, so it could have been the potion finally kicking in. Whatever it was, "the stars" seemed to align in my favor finally.

Sean was one of the first people I texted to tell the good news. Except to him, this was bad news.

SEAN

> Does this mean that my favorite rent-boy won't want to work with me anymore? :(

It was my original plan to get a job and then stop doing porn. Yet, after that new job was a reality, there was something too terrifying about the thought of quitting porn. The sense of blame for my rapes conditioned me to tolerate unwanted sex. To too many people, that tolerance and the exchange of money are received as evidence that we enjoy everything that happens to us in porn. Today, I see this thinking as evidence that we, as a society, have all been groomed to normalize sexual trauma. When I was in porn, I agreed with society; I agreed that the money meant that I had complete power over what was happening to me. So when Sean asked me if I was leaving porn, shame and guilt cornered me.

If I quit porn, it would have been a confession that I was *not* really being empowered by porn. To me, leaving porn because I found a job would be admitting that I *didn't* really want to be in porn but only did it because I needed the money. At the time, I thought if I left porn, it would have been like diving right back into the shame and guilt that porn seemed to save me from. If porn was so empowering, why would I ever want to leave it?

I was unwilling to admit that in prostitution, I was still being abused and victimized like I had been when I was raped. It was still unwanted sex, but I had acquiesced and tolerated the unwanted sex because I needed the money. And the exchange of money gave me a false sense of pride because it made me believe that I was finally in control.

Pride was my protection from the shame and guilt that haunted me every day since I had been raped. Pride hid the truth of the trauma in my heart. I thought it was a good thing, a normal thing, for a gay man to be hypersexual, so I turned my shame into pride. To me, it seemed much stronger to own it and take pride in being a "porn star" than it was in admitting that I was a victim of sexual trauma. I couldn't admit to myself that porn wasn't as fun as I had portrayed it to be. I couldn't bring myself to admit I was wrong, that I needed help. I was too prideful to admit I still had no control.

As I continued to think through Sean's text, I thought about my new job's salary. I would make in a week what I was used to making from one porn scene. After my new job took out the taxes, I would need to work two weeks to barely make rent, which was already the cheapest I could find in the San Fernando Valley at that time. Then I would have to wait another week to afford groceries, and I wouldn't be able to pay all of my bills with my new job alone.

I also didn't think I was good enough to keep this new job for too long. Sean and my experiences had so conditioned me that I doubted that I had any other value beyond being used for sex. I expected that my new employer would realize this and eventually fire me.

I finally replied to Sean.

ME

LOL. No. I can still do shoots. I'll still be available nights and weekends. ;)

I thought I had to keep doing porn. It seemed like the best backup for when I would inevitably fail at my new job. So I became a post-production assistant during the day and continued to do porn during my time off.

But the words "Jesus *loves* you" nagged at me. It got to the point that, in my on-camera interview where my producer asked me, "Is there anything else you want your fans to know about you," it was too difficult to keep up the lie.

"I want people to know that there is more to me than all of this."

That question shook my heart awake. If it was true, if I was worthy of love, if Jesus really loves me, then there was actually more to me than all of this. There were deeper, more intimate parts of me that no one would ever know if they only knew me from porn. All anyone knew of me was the fake version of me. By this point, all *I* knew of me was the fake version of me, but hearing that Jesus loves me made me wonder, *Who am I that Jesus would love me?*

I didn't realize it, but the seed that was sown in me the night of my encounter with that Christian outreach group was starting to sprout. A sapling stretched out from the stoniness of my heart. That little sprout was evidence that I had subconsciously hidden something softer deep under the hardness that I was groomed to portray. There was more to me hidden under the surface.

. . .

A FEW MONTHS BEFORE I started my new job, before one porn shoot, the producer called me and said, "Please get tested before you come in. I just heard that someone you performed with tested positive for syphilis."

If there was a chance that a performer had caught a sexually transmitted infection (STI), the producers required everyone who had recently performed with them to get tested. If we tested positive for anything, we couldn't do porn again until we were healthy. Although performers can wear condoms, they aren't one-hundred-percent effective. Since porn viewers want more and more scenes without condoms, the industry feels more and more pressure to produce bare scenes, leaving us all exposed.

I never did a scene without a condom, but not all of my peers were so lucky. If I performed with one of those not-so-lucky performers, that put me at risk. Also, porn wasn't the only place where I had sex. Sean and my sex-buyers often wanted to have unprotected sex with me.

Thankfully, I tested negative for syphilis, but this was only my first scare with an STI. While in the "sex" industry, I caught several infections. I had never caught an STI until I was in porn, and I did not expect the burden of taking care of them without health insurance. Neither porn nor my TV production job offered health insurance. To pay for my medical expenses, I had to keep selling my body. Then I would catch another STI. I'd get treatment because I couldn't do porn if I was infected. Then immediately, I would have to go back to selling myself to pay for my medical bills. Then I'd catch another STI. It was a vicious cycle of no escape.

Sometime after I started working for the TV production company, I caught chlamydia, so I couldn't have sex or perform in porn until I was healed. During that time, I relied more on go-go dancing to keep up with my bills. After the doctor told me not to drink any alcohol because it could prevent the medicine from killing all of the bacteria, I was forced to dance completely sober for the first time.

I stood on the stage and tried to pretend like I was enjoying the party, but I couldn't escape the full, sober awareness that I was naked. Just as in that nightmare where you're out in public and realize you forgot to put your pants on, I was wearing nothing but a revealing, tight pair of underwear. Only, unlike that nightmare, this was reality.

While trying to dance sober, one drunk man grabbed my underwear and attempted to pull them down in the front. The bouncers didn't come to protect me like they were supposed to. I had to wrestle the man's hands off me, and because of my role, I had to laugh it off and continue to act like I was having fun. I continued to dance as a knot developed in the back of my throat, but I couldn't cry. I had to maintain the image. I had to perform my job. I had to be sexy.

I was finally saved when the club manager motioned for me to take my break. I went to the dressing room and looked in the mirror.

Who are you?

As I sat on the bench in front of my locker, I stared at the ground and took a moment to try to dissociate without alcohol. As I breathed in and breathed out, trying to calm myself, I heard it again.

"Jesus *loves* you!"

Around that same time, I caught a medically incurable STI, human papillomavirus (HPV). I told Sean about it, and he said that if I had it, he wouldn't be able to book me any more porn shoots. I didn't know what to do. I needed the money, especially because I had an infection, so I denied it. I panicked and said it was a false alarm, just another common ailment that went away. Sean took my word for it and never had me get tested to confirm. He continued to pimp me out. HPV was easy to hide as long as the breakout wasn't too bad, and I would continue only to do scenes with condoms. I thought everything would be fine.

Then, in 2012, several months after hearing the Christian man say, "Jesus *loves* you," I got a text message from someone I had recently had sex with.

HIM

> I just tested positive for HIV.

My heart stopped. I had unprotected sex with this guy.

ME

> Please tell me you're kidding.

HIM

> Dude, I wouldn't joke about something like that. You need to get tested.

"F—! I could have HIV…"

I couldn't breathe. I opened my mouth and tried to expand my diaphragm, but I was paralyzed. My heart pounded like it was going to break through my ribs and beat out of my chest. White noise buzzed in my ears. When I finally was able to take a gasp of air, my breaths came in short, quick bursts as if there wasn't enough oxygen in the room. I panicked as my mind plunged into anxiety. *I can't work anymore. I can't afford treatment. This is it. I'm going to die. Why wouldn't God just let me die when I wanted to? Why is He going to kill me like this? HIV. HPV. Medical bills. No money. Death. God. Porn. HIV. Bills. No money. Death. God. Porn. HIV. HPV. Sex. Death. God. Sex. HIV. God. Porn. God.*

I shouted through angry tears that poured down my face, "God, why do You hate me?!"

In the midst of my panic, something suddenly snapped. Everything around me seemed to shut off. My mind stopped. Peace descended upon me like a cloud of hushed silence. I fell to my knees in the middle of my room. Time froze at the moment. My body stilled. His Presence alone brought me to the end of myself, the end of my *old* self.

A deep, soft, yet powerful voice roared, *"No, Aaron. I love you!"*

SIX

THE OPPOSITE OF LOVE

M Y HEART STILLED when I heard His voice. The words touched me, embraced me, clothed me in the most tranquilizing hug I have ever known. My angry, fearful tears erupted into tears of relief, tears of surrender. The words hit me even more forcefully than those of the man who told me, "Jesus *loves* you!" The moment I heard the voice of God, the sprout of the words that were seeded into my heart broke through the hard concrete and finally reached the life-giving sunlight. I knew that the voice I heard was Jesus, the real Jesus.

His voice was soothing. *"You are not meant for this life you're living. I am Who you have been searching for all along. Only I can satisfy you. Turn to Me. I will make you new."*

The words melted into me. His words softened every rocky crevasse of my bruised and broken heart. I gave up. I stopped pretending. I knew that I needed help. God's help.

I realized what a part of me had known all along: it was a sense of worthlessness and lovelessness that had coerced me to live the life I had been living. I had craved love, real love, but I thought sex was love. I thought being wanted, even to the point of being abused, was love. I thought being in porn would make me into someone people would love, but all it did was make me into someone people wanted to rape. To hurt. To humiliate. I had confused love with lust, but hearing God's voice confirm that I was not only worthy of love, but loved already, made me question everything I once thought.

When the Christian man told me that Jesus loves me, that man didn't know me. Still, he knew it didn't matter who I was or what I did. Jesus loves me, unconditionally. Even though He probably would prefer that I not sell myself, a part of me knew Jesus would still love me, even if I did. Before I could even question why Jesus had waited so long to reveal His love to me, I realized that God had been trying to reach me for years.

After I graduated from high school, one of my teachers, a gay Christian, reached out to me and offered to take me to lunch to introduce me to her wife. Afterward, they took me to their church for a Bible study. It was my first experience with an LGBT+ affirming church.[b]

Back in university, I was looking in the library for a movie and stumbled upon a documentary about gay Christians and how they reconcile their faith with their orientation. I checked it out, not so much to see if I could be a Christian but to

---

[b] I use "LGBT+" to refer to the entire community of lesbian, gay, bisexual, and transgender people. This also includes people questioning their sexual orientation and identity, intersex people, asexual people, and anyone else who falls under the sexual or gender minority category. I use the word "affirming" when referring to Christian churches and movements that believe that LGBT+ people should be fully included in the Church and are allowed to marry according to their sexual orientation.

strengthen my argument for the legalization of gay marriage in my speech class. That documentary told me that even if I am gay, Jesus is for me.

Then there was that drunken night outside the club when a stranger looked me in the eyes and told me that Jesus loves me. The more I went through my memories, the more I noticed time after time, Jesus had tried to show His love for me. He had never stopped trying, even though I kept refusing to listen.

The weight of His words brought me to my knees in the middle of my room. Tears rolled down my cheeks as I cried, "Jesus, if this is You, please, I know You can heal me. If it's really You, please, make me clean like I've never done porn or sold myself or anything. I'll do whatever You ask. I'll follow You. I'll give You my life."

THE NEXT DAY, I went to the clinic to get tested. The cold, dim, gray waiting room was a familiar acquaintance, but I trembled more than usual.

The nurse called me into her office to read my rapid HIV test results. Negative. I didn't have HIV. An overwhelming sense of peace came over me.

The voice whispered, *"I have protected you. Are you ready to follow Me?"*

The calm was interrupted by the nurse. "You will need to get tested again in three months, just to be sure."

"Three months?"

"Yes, if you've been with someone who tested positive for HIV, you need to get retested in three months. Sometimes it takes the virus a couple of months to be detectable."

The clinic couldn't guarantee a negative test result. My heart tried to escape my body. My blood pressure was eager to rise. But the moment anxiety attempted to take over me, a gentle hand calmed my nerves and steadied my heart.

"I have protected you."

I agreed to come back in three months, but a conviction sat upon my heart that God healed me. I couldn't even find the physical symptoms of HPV anymore, and I saw the negative rapid HIV test results as a full sign that Jesus had a new life for me. All I had to do was follow Him.

I was done living in constant fear that I was going to catch another STI. I was done letting Sean do whatever he wanted to do to my body. I was done giving my body to anyone to use me for their own pleasure. I was ready for a new life. I was ready to live my *own* life.

When I got home from the clinic, I went to my room and kneeled on the floor with the test results out in front of me.

I cried, "Jesus, thank You for loving me. Thank You for forgiving me. Thank You for healing me. If You want my life, You can have it. I give it to You."

I gave my life to Jesus, or Yeshua, as I will refer to Him throughout the rest of this book. Yeshua is Jesus' Hebrew name, and I enjoy identifying the Messiah by His Hebrew heritage. I call Him Yeshua because I know Him now as an intimate friend. His closest friends back in the first-century would have called Him Yeshua, a name in their native tongue, which means "salvation from God."

That week, I had a go-go dancing gig, but I didn't show up for it. And the next time Sean contacted me, it was a little awkward.

SEAN

> I have a shoot for you. Come over so that we can talk about it. I've been missing my favorite rent-boy.

ME

> I can't do this anymore.

SEAN

> :(I guess you don't need the money right now.

I wasn't sure yet what I was going to do about money. My post-production assistant work by itself was still not enough to take care of me, but something within me wouldn't let me get anxious about it. It was a huge step of faith, but I knew that I needed to get out of the "sex" industry.

ME

> Yeah. I'm not for sale anymore.

I had found Yeshua, and He loved me out of porn.

I DIDN'T LEAVE porn merely because I knew selling your body is looked down upon in Christianity. I left porn because when I encountered God, His love caused me to repent, change my mind, and turn away from everything that held me back from a full relationship with Him. I changed my mind because Yeshua's

Light revealed to me the darkness of what porn really is. Abuse. Trauma. Exploitation. It is the opposite of love.

When it comes to discussions about the "sex" industry, many people insist that consent is all that matters. Consent is often understood as the person desired the sex, but the mere presence of a "Yes" is too low of a bar. We should also consider what's behind the "Yes." The question shouldn't just be, "Did the person agree to it?" but also, "Did the person really want to have sex, or did they feel like they *had* to have sex for whatever reason?"

If they felt like they had to have sex, they didn't really *want* to have sex. There's a difference between enthusiastic consent in which someone ecstatically enters into erotic intimacy and the "consent" in which someone has "sex" out of necessity or pressure. When money is exchanged for sex, it is a hint that the prostituted person may not really want to have sex with the person renting them. They're having sex because they *need* the money. True consent can't be bought. The sex is unwanted.

In reality, surveys show that the *overwhelming* majority of prostituted people—nine out of ten—want to leave the "sex" industry, but they aren't sure how else to survive.[1] Most people who enter the "sex" industry do so because their need for survival coerces them to submit to being prostituted.

The reality is that sex in exchange for money is produced through economic and social inequality. The most marginalized communities have the most desperate need for money, and prostituted people are most likely to come from these more vulnerable communities.[2]

The LGBT+ community is immensely affected by prostitution. Transgender people are often less likely to get hired by employers because of discrimination against their gender identities.[3] LGBT+ youth are often rejected by their families and experience homelessness at much higher rates than their heterosexual, cisgender peers. LGBT+ people in these situations often resort to prostitution to survive.[4] It isn't because prostitution is an inherent part of being LGBT+ or that LGBT+ people desire to be prostituted. This happens because LGBT+ people are often marginalized and left vulnerable.

In the "sex" industry, people's vulnerabilities and desperation to survive are used against them for the pleasure of the more privileged in society. The porn industry even acknowledges that it exploits low-income people. It's no secret. Many videos have titles with words like "broke," "desperate," and "needs money." This eroticizes poverty, which for the porn viewer, normalizes the sexual exploitation of the most vulnerable economic classes.

Another common reason someone might enter the "sex" industry is that they are victims of sexual abuse.[5] Sex abuse survivors often try to cope through hypersexuality, and sex abusers and society groom victims of sex crimes to tolerate unwanted sex. Like me, many enter the "sex" industry because they sense that it "empowers" them over their sexual assault. If we're going to get raped anyway, it might as well happen for our own benefit. Eventually, exploitation becomes normal to us. It's hard for anyone to see what's wrong with what they think is normal. By submitting to the world's exploitation of us, we refuse to realize that we are still being violated in the "sex" industry. We believe we have gained control and power, but the truth is that we are enslaved by the power of our sexualized culture and its money. We are exploited.

I didn't see myself as exploited until the moment I encountered God. Many prostituted people do not see themselves as exploited because we've been groomed to normalize what happens to us. The reason that some prostituted people claim to enjoy being in the "sex" industry will vary from person to person. Still, I do know that dissociation and self-betrayal are inherent to the prostitution experience. I know many prostituted people paint their experiences in more positive terms for the sake of their buyers or their pimps, or to convince themselves that what is happening to them is acceptable or enjoyable. Except in cases with intentionally abusive sex-buyers, which are common, it's usually easier to be bought for sex if your buyer thinks you enjoy it. And it's easier to cope if you convince yourself that you are having fun.

While we're in it, we often don't want to admit that prostitution is destroying us. Dissociation and grooming help to hide that reality from us. But for those who claim they enjoy the "sex" industry, if we were able to dive into the depths of their hearts, I wouldn't be surprised if we would find their hearts broken, just like mine was, and like everyone else I ever knew, and know, in porn. I wouldn't be surprised if, like me, they preferred to deny their heartache by convincing themselves that they are being empowered. Even if that is not the case, and these prostituted people truly enjoy what happens to them, an overwhelming majority of prostituted people still admit that they would prefer to leave the "sex" industry. The presence of the minority who claim they like prostitution tells society that being bought for sex is fun and glamorous for *all* of us. It increases the demand for exploiting the most vulnerable who want to leave but have few other options to survive. It tells society that we are all asking for it.

When it comes to consent and choice within prostitution, we have to consider the context in which a prostituted person made that "choice." A lot of assumptions surround the word "choice." It often implies that someone had at least one desirable option available. "Choice" tends to imply something wanted. It implies the person was happy to make that choice. In the "sex" industry, "choice" implies that the "sex" is fun, desired, and enjoyed.

Years since leaving porn, I hear it over and over, "Well, you wanted to do that. It was your choice." This is often said to downplay the trauma I testify to have experienced in the "sex" industry. It's as if people think my trauma is not real because I signed consent forms and received money for it. This has been said to me to justify that people are entitled to view the pornographic images of me. But to me, this concept rings with the same tone that society often tells rape victims: "Well, maybe you shouldn't have dressed like that." "You knew better than to go to that party." "Maybe you shouldn't have been drunk." "Maybe you shouldn't have *chosen* to do porn."

This thinking puts *all* of the blame on the person experiencing trauma and *none* on the trauma-causer. In the case of porn and prostitution, the trauma-causer is a society that normalizes the idea that prostituted people are okay with sexual trauma as long as they get paid for it. This clothes the traumatized person in shame.

I was traumatized by my experiences in porn. *Everyone* I know from porn was traumatized. It leaves lasting scars on those who survive it. Studies show that more than two-thirds of prostituted people meet the criteria for being diagnosed with post-traumatic stress disorder (PTSD). This rate is comparable to combat veterans, abused women, rape survivors, and torture survivors.[6] Many prostituted people experience depression, suicidal tendencies, dissociation, substance abuse, and eating disorders.

When navigating through a pornified culture that justifies our trauma by saying, "Well, that was your choice," these scars can reopen. This thinking causes shame, and shame shackles a person to their trauma.

Over and over, society has told me, "You sold your body. You got your money. That's what you wanted. It's your fault." This is the worst thing that can be said to a person who has experienced sexual trauma. And the worst thing that a traumatized person can do in response is to own it and convince themselves that the trauma empowers them because they made that "choice." When I encountered God, I decided that I would no longer submit to the world's view of my trauma. I will no longer own the idea that I enjoyed being in porn when I know that the whole time my soul was screaming for help.

When it comes to "choice," there is not always a desirable option for everyone in any given situation. If we consider a prostituted person's role as absolutely consensual, then we must also assume that literally, every decision everyone has ever made has been a choice they were happy to make. But if a decision is made based on fear, desperation, hopelessness, and/or trauma, is that a real choice?

I'll admit that in prostitution, we acquiesce. We acquiesce to our trauma. We comply with our grooming. We abdicate autonomy in our own bodies because our autonomy has already been taken. But I hate the low-bar concept of "choice" and "consent" when it refers to prostitution. It is too shallow, too cheap to explain the experience of being prostituted.

That is why, throughout this book, I will not use the phrase "sex workers" when referring to porn performers, escorts, exotic dancers, prostituted people, or anyone in the "sex" industry. The phrase "sex worker" comes directly from the "sex" industry as a way to normalize what the "sex" industry does to people. And I will no longer comply with the "sex" industry. Instead, I will refer to people in these situations as *prostituted people*. Prostituted people are prostituted by a society that allows humans to be treated as products. I cannot, in good conscience, call what used to be done to me, and what is still done to many others, "work."

I cannot even bring myself to call it the "sex industry" anymore. That phrase implies that it sells sex, but it doesn't sell *real* sex, any more than rape is real sex. Today, I know that sex has a deeper, more powerful meaning than the "sex" I sold in porn and prostitution. Sex is natural, but porn is produced. Sex is inherently intimate, but there is no real intimacy involved when sex is exchanged for money. What the "sex industry" does sell is the exploitation and traumatization of the desperate and vulnerable. Buying sex with mere human currency cheapens humanity into mere products. It commodifies people into sex objects. This is inherently exploitative. Instead of the "sex industry," throughout the rest of this book, I must call it exactly what it is: *sexual exploitation*. Or, as it's more commonly known: *prostitution*.

Yeshua's love opened my eyes to see how vastly different prostitution is from real love. Yeshua's love showed me that I was exploited when people rented me in exchange for worthless, human-made, paper money. That is why I had to leave porn.

But porn is different from all other forms of prostitution. It allows people to continue to watch some of the most horrific things that have ever happened to me. As I left porn, I didn't realize that it would try to follow me into my new life.

SEVEN

WORTH DYING FOR

T HE ENCOUNTER I had the night when God spoke to me in my room left me hungry to hear His voice again, and that hunger led me to the Bible. Because I didn't own a physical Bible, I used the internet. As I read the words, I recognized God's voice in them—the same voice I heard in my room—and I became obsessed with the Bible. I couldn't stop thinking about Yeshua, reading about Him, and talking about Him to anyone and everyone I could.

"You know that's all a bunch of crap, right?" my friend, David, said before passing the bong to Sarah. Some of my friends had come over to watch TV and smoke weed. We sat in a semicircle on the floor of my room. Since rumors about my new faith had been spreading, they all wanted to know what was going on with me.

"No, you don't understand," I argued. "God came right here in this room and touched me."

"He *touched* you?" Sarah laughed. "Sounds like God should be reported."

"I mean, I don't know. The Bible talks about Him like He can come and, like, hang out with you. Like, He's here with us right now."

"I don't feel anything," Molly argued as Sarah passed the bong to her.

"Dude, the Bible's riddled with errors," David continued. "You believe in fairy tales."

After Molly exhaled the bong's smoke, she continued, "Yeah, I'm pretty sure that book has been changed and translated and retranslated so many times throughout 2,000 years that it isn't even reliable anymore. Just seek God, or *goddess*, or the universe or whatever on your own, man. You don't need some messed up book."

Are they right? Do I believe in a fake fairy tale just to feel better about my life?

When I looked it up online, I found that the Bible is actually the *most* reliable historical document from the first-century. The New Testament has over 24,000 early copies of the original manuscripts. The earliest copies date back to within a few decades of the original writings. That is unheard of, considering that the next most reliable historical documents from the time period have only a handful to no more than 2,000 copies. They date between 200 and over 1,000 years from the original.[1] Yet no one doubts the reliability of these other historical documents. Because of the Dead Sea Scrolls, the Old Testament now has 42,000 copies that date back to around the time of Yeshua.[2] It's almost as if a great Power has protected the scriptures throughout millennia!

After I found all this out, I prayed, "God, if You really did come and say all those things to me, if You really healed me, if You really are the God of the Bible, would You please send me a Bible?"

A week later, I came home from work to find a package waiting for me. Within it was a Bible sent by a Christian woman who had also been prostituted in porn. When she heard that I left the porn industry, she felt compelled in her spirit to send it to me. It was the proof I needed to know that I heard and still hear the voice of God. That is why I also call the Bible "the Word of God." I hear Him speaking His words through the written words on the Bible's pages.

When I got my Bible, the first thing I did was open it to one of the so-called "clobber passages." These are the verses traditionally used by non-affirming Christians to say that LGBT+ people cannot be Christian, essentially clobbering our faith in God.

From the documentary I found in college, I heard the word "homosexual" wasn't used in any Bible translation until 1946, and it is an inaccurate translation of what the original writers intended. I wanted to know if my new Bible was one of those translations, so I turned to 1 Corinthians 6:9 and read from my English Standard Version (ESV) Bible.

"Or do you not know that the unrighteous will not inherit the kingdom of God? Do not be deceived: neither the sexually immoral, nor idolaters, nor adulterers, nor men who practice *homosexuality…*"

There it was. Although the documentary I had seen years before told me that this was a mistranslation, it still shook some fear in me. The words gripped my heart and squeezed like a constrictor on its prey.

Is that right? That would mean that my high school teacher was not a Christian. But she loves Jesus and her wife.

I kept reading, and then the Word jumped out at me as I read from 1 Corinthians 6:11-20,

> And such were some of you. But you were washed, you were sanctified, you were justified in the name of the Lord Jesus Christ and by the Spirit of our God.
>
> "All things are lawful for me," but not all things are helpful. "All things are lawful for me," but I will not be enslaved by anything… The body is not meant for sexual immorality, but for the Lord, and the Lord for the body. And God raised the Lord and will raise us up by His power. Do you not know that your bodies are members of Christ? Shall I then take the members of Christ and make them members of a prostitute? Never! Or do you not know that he who is joined to a prostitute becomes one body with her? For, as it is written, "The two will become one flesh." But he who is joined to the Lord becomes one spirit with Him. Flee from sexual immorality. Every other sin a person commits is outside the body, but the sexually immoral person sins against his own body. Or do you not know that your body is a temple of the Holy Spirit within you, whom you have from God? You are not your own, for you were bought with a price. So glorify God in your body.

The words hugged me in the same soothing embrace in which God had hugged me when He first said, *"I love you."* I wasn't sure about what the clobber passages meant for me yet, but I was sure about this one. This was about me.

I am bought with a price.

According to this passage, my behavior before I knew the Lord was evidence that I was not a part of the Kingdom of God. The Word calls out prostitution as an institution that should *never* be among Christians. But the Word also says, "Such *were* some of you." Now, I am *bought with a price.*

As a prostituted man, I submitted my body to whoever had the money that I needed to pay rent, buy groceries, and finish school. That's the value I gave my body: mere human currency.

But the God of the Bible bought me with a much higher price. From what I knew about the Gospel, God came to the earth as Yeshua, lived a completely loving life, and then He was murdered. He took a disfiguring whipping. His torturers placed a crown of thorns upon His head. They spit upon Him and mocked Him. Despite the pain from His fresh flesh wounds, they forced Him to carry the weight of His cross throughout the city of Jerusalem. When He arrived at the execution site, they drove nails into His wrists and feet to pin Him to a wooden cross, which was lifted for all to see Him, mourn for Him, mock Him, criticize Him until He bled and asphyxiated to death. And Yeshua did it willingly.

The price He paid for me was His own life. He died for me. He laid His life down for me. As the revelation washed over me, His words echoed in my heart, *"I love you."*

I reread the passage. *"You were bought with a price."*

The price was Yeshua's life. He sees me as worth dying for.

BOUGHT WITH A PRICE

I read it over and over and found it interesting that the Bible would mention prostitution so close to one of the clobber passages. While looking it up online, I found another translation, the New Revised Standard Version (NRSV), of 1 Corinthians 6:9, which specified "male prostitutes"[3] and not "men who practice homosexuality." Prostitution is so different from sexual orientation. This other translation made so much more sense to me.

Through prostitution, I was giving myself away too cheaply compared to the worth God gave me. Porn was a cheap, exploitative exchange of my body for money, but God paid for me with my true value. As the Word of God says elsewhere, I was ransomed, "not with perishable things such as silver or gold, but with the precious blood of Christ."[4]

I am worth dying for.

AT MY JOB as a post-production assistant, I struggled with my low wage. One month of pay was barely enough to cover my rent and other basic living expenses. After I quit porn, once most of my bills were paid, all of my money was gone, and I found myself in a place of poverty once again. I took out payday loans to get groceries. Then I had to use the next month's rent to pay back my payday loans. Then I'd have to get another payday loan to pay my rent. And it became a cycle of living off payday loans.

A part of me was tempted to go back to porn to pay my bills, but every time that thought crossed my mind, I remembered the impact of the Presence of God. I couldn't go back to selling myself. Yeshua was so much better. My financial situation may have been harder, but I decided that I would rather starve than go back to porn. God said I was worth so much more.

Although I had only been at my new job for a few months, I had been doing more work than expected. I was a post-production assistant (post-PA), which basically meant that I did the typical office paperwork, made coffee, and did some deliveries. When my boss found out that I knew how to use the professional video editing software, he had me start doing a lot more assistant editing work. An assistant editor (AE) is a nice step up from a PA. But I wasn't given any raise, and my position title did not change. When an editor found out that I was a PA doing AE work, she insisted that I talk to the producers to get paid for the extra work that I was doing.

I stepped into my boss' office with a bit of hesitation. "Jack," I said when I was able to grab his attention. "I've been doing a lot of assistant editor type of work, and—"

"You have," he interrupted with a sly smile. "When we hired you, we didn't think you knew as much as you know. I'm glad we can give you this experience. It will really help you going forward in your career."

"Well, that's what I wanted to talk to you about. I'm doing AE work, but I'm still credited and paid as a PA."

Jack's smile faded. He took his attention off me and began typing at his computer.

I continued, "I'm struggling quite a bit with my bills, and I thought that maybe just a slight raise would help out a lot."

Jack continued to work on his computer. I stood awkwardly in the sound of his typing, wondering if I should walk away. After a long moment, he finally looked back up at me.

"Look," he said, "I'm glad we're able to give you the experience as an AE. That's actually worth a whole lot in itself. And I'd be glad to give you the assistant editor credit, but right now, the budget is pretty tight. Maybe we can help you out a bit in a few more months."

Months later, I worked more than ten hours a day for them, and I was still paid the same starvation wage. I had my AE credit, but I was still barely able to pay to live. I was working overtime, but I was still in poverty. I knew leaving porn would be a drastic cut to my income, but I also learned how to be content in all things and trust in God.

At home, as I read my Bible, I came across Yeshua's teaching where He says, "The laborer deserves his wages."⁵ When someone works, they should earn enough to take care of their basic needs; otherwise, they are being exploited.

I took this Scripture, and I prayed, "Lord, please help me. I left porn because I know You have better for me. Please, help me to make a living. If the laborer deserves his wages, please show me what I need to do to make the wages I need to live. Whether that be getting a raise where I work now, or something else."

That week, I got a phone call from another production company. The same editor who suggested that I ask for a raise referred me to one of her friends. That friend called me and offered me a position as an assistant editor. The pay was slightly higher. After I paid the bills, I had a little left to spend however I wanted. I still wasn't making what I made in porn, but I knew the Lord was providing for me.

AFTER THREE MONTHS since my last STI test, I walked into the clinic with such an easy calm that the cold, dim waiting room couldn't have recognized me if it tried. I sat in the office a completely different person than the last time I visited. Last time,

I was anxious and on the verge of a panic attack. This time, I knew that Yeshua had healed me.

As I filled out the clinic's form, I checked off every test on the list of which tests I needed. The guy sitting across from me watched covertly as I ticked off the entire sheet, and I chuckled to myself, wondering if he thought that I had just had a promiscuously busy weekend. I actually hadn't had sex since my last tests.

After the procedures were all done, the rapid HIV test came back negative again! I knew God had saved me in more ways than one, and I only had to wait two more weeks for the other tests' results.

EIGHT

BORN AGAIN

As my friends continued to argue against the Bible with me, I pointed out the facts that I had found, but they thought I was now a crazy Christian. I realized that I needed to find Christian friends who would understand and support my new faith. I needed a church.

I found my first church online. As I drove into its parking lot, the atmosphere reminded me of what my bedroom felt like when God spoke to me. When I entered the building, the air smelled so fresh, so pure, like a bookstore full of new books.

At this church, families greeted other families with big smiles and hugs. There were all types of people. There were Black families, white families, Latino families, and mixed-race families with their children running around playing, unconcerned about each other's skin color. It broke the stereotype of white churches and Black churches; this was clearly an "everybody" church. They seemed joyful and loving, like one big family, and I longed to be a part of their family. I wondered if they also broke the stereotype of straight churches and gay churches. I looked around for any gay families like my high school teacher, her wife, and their kids.

When the service started, a Black man with dreadlocks welcomed the congregation. His name was Pastor Andrew, an associate pastor. He bounced and moved on the stage with exuberance, and something about him made my gaydar go off.

I thought, *Surely, he is gay.*

As I continued to look around, I thought Heaven must look a lot like this. Everyone from every race, nationality, gender, and sexual orientation worshiping God together as one tribe.

When the worship band started, a few people gathered in front of the stage. They lifted their hands into the air as if reaching up to grasp the intangible. Others clapped along to the music and swayed where they stood.

Then the sermon started. Pastor Pete, an older, slender, white man with glasses, was the lead pastor. He read from Luke 15:11-32, one of Yeshua's parables about a son who took his inheritance from his father to spend the money on prostituted people and other reckless things. Then the son found himself broke and needed to feed pigs to make a living.

As Pastor Pete read aloud, I followed along in my Bible: "When he came to himself, he said, 'How many of my father's servants have more than enough bread, but I perish here with hunger!'" Pastor Pete stepped away from his podium and addressed the room as if he spoke to each of us one-on-one. He repeated, "'*When he came to himself.*' Sometimes, we find ourselves in situations where we realize that we made some bad decisions. But if we would just come to our senses and turn to God, our Father, there is an opportunity for a new start, a new life."

I leaned forward in my seat. It was as if he knew I was in his congregation, and he was speaking directly to me. The idea of coming to myself grounded me to reality. In prostitution, I lived by dissociation. I left myself so that I could survive. I allowed myself to drift elsewhere so that others could use my body. But now, God was bringing me back to myself. For the first time in a long time, I was present.

Pastor Pete continued to tell the story about how the son returned to his father expecting that he would need to become one of his father's hired servants, but from "a long way off, his father saw him and felt compassion, and ran and embraced him and kissed him."

The father welcomed his son home, not as a hired servant, but as a son. Even though he did not deserve it, the son was restored to his true position.

The father cried, "My son was dead, and is alive again; he was lost, and is found."

I was dead and am alive again. I was lost, but now, I'm found.

But the older brother did not like that his father allowed the prodigal son to return home after living the life he lived.

"Sometimes, religious people can't handle the grace of God," Pastor Pete continued. "They think that God needs to give people what they deserve for their actions, or that the sinner needs to somehow make up for their sin. But that mindset never saved anyone. That has actually pushed people further from God and further into sin. In reality, regardless of what they've done, God welcomes them home with open arms." He took a moment to let it sink in. "No matter who you are, I want you to know that you are welcomed in the Kingdom of God. You are welcomed here."

This church must be the right church for me. They welcome everyone.

Like the prodigal son, I once lived my life, spending it in the way I wanted, or rather, the way others wanted me to live. Then I came to my senses, and now, I wanted to come home to my Father. I wondered how my older brothers and sisters would handle someone like me, a former porn prostitute. At least at this church, it seemed Pastor Pete promised me that I would be welcomed no matter what.

At the end of his message, Pastor Pete reminded the church, "We have our beach baptisms coming up. If you'd like to be baptized at the Santa Monica Pier, please make sure you sign up today."

Before I left church that day, I made sure my name was on that list.

ON THE MORNING of the beach baptism, I headed to the Santa Monica Pier. The church had set up a huge area just for us. The August sun glistened off the Pacific Ocean waves that stretched beyond the horizon. The pier had just come to life. The rollercoaster and Ferris wheel were running. Seagulls flew from their nests in search of trash that tourists had dropped. The ocean waves roared over the soft murmur of voices laughing and sharing in the beauty of the day.

I signed in at my church's booth, where most of the baptism candidates were gathered together, discussing why they chose to get baptized. Many of them were getting re-baptized out of a desire to rededicate their lives to God.

"I've never been baptized," I said when they finally asked me. "I just want to start a new life with Jesus, and I thought this would be the best way to show that."

"Wow! Good for you," one woman said with a smile.

Pastor Andrew, the associate pastor who welcomed everyone to the church on my first visit, pulled all the baptism candidates away from the rest of the crowd to give us a private message. He read from Romans 6:1-4.

"The Word says, 'What shall we say then? Are we to continue in sin that grace may abound? By no means! How can we who died to sin still live in it? Do you not know that all of us who have been baptized into Christ Jesus were baptized into His death? We were buried therefore with Him by baptism into death, in order that, just as Christ was raised from the dead by the glory of the Father, we too might walk in newness of life.'

"Your baptism is *not* just a religious ritual," Pastor Andrew preached. "If you are doing this for the right reasons, it is because you want to outwardly express something that is already happening inside of your heart. You want to die to your old life and resurrect into a new life with Jesus. As you go into the water, that is your old self dying, and as you come out, that is your resurrection into your new Jesus-bought life."

I was ready. I wanted to be clean. I wanted porn to be washed from me. I wanted the hands that had touched me, groped me, molested me to be cleansed off. I wanted the eyes that had devoured me to be wiped away. I was ready for my new life.

My baptism would be an outward expression of what I experienced the night I decided to follow Yeshua. I had read in my Bible that that experience is called being born again.[1] Inside every human being is a spirit, the part of us connected to God. Our spirit goes deeper than our flesh and far beyond our mental capacity. It is the part of us that causes us to be *us*. But without God, our spirits are dead.[2] That's why our spiritual selves need to be born again.

My life in prostitution was proof that my spirit was dead. I had been living in sin, and sin utterly separates us from God.[3] Just as the Word says, "*All* have sinned and fall short of the glory of God."[4] Nothing, including sin, will separate us from God's love towards us,[5] but sin does separate us from His Presence.

We *all* have sinned. From the human perspective, we vastly underestimate our sin, its power over us, and its effects on the world around us. If we opened our eyes to see sin the way God sees it, we would be utterly devastated, but on the other side of that revelation is freedom.

Maybe we haven't murdered anyone, but Yeshua taught us that to hate someone is to murder them in our hearts.[6] Maybe we haven't committed adultery, but Yeshua taught us that to look at someone with lust—*including pornography*—is to commit sexual sin with them in our hearts.[7] From Yeshua's point of view, all sin is birthed in the heart.[8]

When it comes to pornography, many people get defensive about using it, but they don't see that when they engage in porn, they have the same thing in their heart as sex traffickers and rapists. Because today's porn consistently depicts violence, it desensitizes and grooms its viewers' hearts towards sexual aggression.[9] In the same way, pornography fuels the demand for sex trafficking. Traffickers and sex-buyers often show porn to trafficking victims to desensitize them to the types of acts that will be performed on them, and porn is often used for advertising sex trafficking. Although not every person who watches porn will act on it by purchasing a trafficked person, porn is a catalyst for sex-buyers who do use trafficked people.[10]

Porn also increases the demand for sex trafficking simply by normalizing the idea that people can buy other people for sex.

4

In fact, in societies where buying sex is normalized through legalization, sex trafficking rates rise because traffickers can more easily masquerade trafficking as a legal form of prostitution.[11] So porn not only raises the demand for sex trafficking, but sometimes, porn *is* sex trafficking.

According to the United States' Trafficking Victims Protection Act of 2000, sex trafficking is a form of modern slavery that occurs when "a commercial sex act is induced by force, fraud, or coercion, or in which the person induced to perform such act has not attained 18 years of age."[12] And according to the National Human Trafficking Hotline, pornography is one of the top industries in which sex trafficking occurs.[13] This means that when someone watches porn, they very well may also be watching and participating in sex trafficking without even knowing it. And sex trafficking is not hidden in the darkest crevasses of porn. It is mainstream porn!

Many gay porn fans do not even realize that one of the gay porn industry's most famous porn stars was underage when he first appeared in porn, which means he was *sex trafficked!*[14] This gay porn "star" is a sex trafficking victim, and we have glamorized his abuse.

Recently, there was a fourteen-year-old girl who survived being kidnapped and raped. A couple of months later, she found out that her classmates were sharing porn videos of her trauma with descriptions like "teen getting destroyed." The girl pleaded with the porn website—one of today's *largest* porn websites—to remove the videos, but the website ignored her. It wasn't until she reached out posing as a lawyer that they paid attention and removed the videos.[15]

Her story is not the only one like it. The industry even acknowledges that porn is violent and may even depict sex trafficking because they promote videos that contain words like "abused," "brutal," "forced," "raped," "punished," and "destroyed."

While not every porn scene may be a direct result of sex trafficking, what should concern everyone is that there's no way to know. *That is the problem!*

Even in my situation, I may not have been trafficked, but I was clearly exploited. I may have been the epitome of what pro-prostitution activists envision for their support of prostitution. I was trying to pay my way through college. I claimed to enjoy what I was doing. I even claimed that I was being empowered. Everything I did was technically legal, yet I was in porn because of poverty and vulnerability from sexual trauma. I experienced exploitation and abuse, but no one would ever know that just by watching the porn I was in.

Even though it should worry everyone, in the eyes of God, whether the porn is sex trafficking or not, it's all sin. To God, it all starts from the same seed inside the heart of porn viewers: *lust.* Lust is something that separates us from God's glory because God is love,[16] but lust is *not* love. Porn is *not* love. Prostitution is *not* love.

As much as we may want justice for crimes like sex trafficking, God wants justice too. He tells us, "The wages of sin is death,"[17] and "The soul who sins shall die."[18] If we all have sinned, then we all deserve death!

But God is also merciful. To enact His justice and His mercy at the same time, God came in the flesh as Yeshua,[19] and He died the death that all of us deserve for our sins. God displayed His eternal love by laying His life down for us so that we could have an intimate relationship with Him.[20]

If love is to lay one's life down for others, then sin is to live at the *expense* of others. We have all, in one way or another, lived at the expense of others. But through Yeshua's resurrection, all the dead in spirit—all humans—can resurrect. We can be born again, and we must be born again because otherwise, our spirits remain dead and separated from God.

As I stood on the beach watching the ocean waves and listening to Pastor Andrew's message, I thought about how my participation in porn was not just the acquiescence to my own exploitation. My sin also fed the demand for the exploitation of others. That's what I was most eager to have washed away from me—the harm I had indirectly done to humanity.

It was time to get baptized, to die to the old and resurrect into the new. I was ready to die to the sin that once enslaved me. To rise to a new life. To be set free.

I stepped forward into the surf towards Pastor Andrew. Each molecule of the freezing Pacific water stabbed my skin as I waded through the waves until the water rose just above my waist. Pastor Andrew held me for a moment.

"Have you accepted Jesus into your life as your Lord and Savior?"

"Yes-s-s!" I said through a slight shiver.

"Then I baptize you in the name of the Father, the Son, and the Holy Spirit." As he dunked me, Pastor Andrew said, "Die with Jesus." As a wave crashed against us, my body was immersed in the chilly Pacific water. The baptism washed away the grease, the grime, the fingerprints, the stains, the sweat, the spit, everything from prostitution. As I rose from the water, he said, "Rise with Jesus." I arose pure, fresh, and clean.

I am new!

As I walked back onto the beach, a little girl behind me cried out, "Mommy, look!"

I turned around, and not far from where I was baptized, a pod of dolphins leaped from the water like they were dancing and rejoicing with us.

"What a great way to get baptized," the girl's mother said. "It's a sign from God."

THAT EVENING, as I headed home, something inside me sensed an urgency to pick up my STI test results. They should have been ready. I turned the car from the route to my apartment and headed towards the clinic.

At the medical office, I stared in almost disbelief at my results. They were *all* negative. Even HPV! I hadn't had any symptoms in months, and the tests were not able to detect it. Although HPV is not medically curable, the body sometimes sheds the virus. But the speed that my body shed it seemed to be miraculous. At that moment, I knew it was because Yeshua had healed me!

I took the test results home, rejoicing. "Thank You, God! Thank You. Thank You, Jesus."

When I entered my room, my eyes caught a paper bag that sat under my bed. It was my sex bag. I used it to store my condoms for when I had a hookup or needed extra condoms on porn sets or escorting. I also had all of my old STI test results in it to show anyone that I was negative. As I looked at it, the words I read from my Bible echoed in my heart.

"You are not your own, for you were bought with a price. So glorify God in your body."

I felt so new from baptism, so washed. I looked from my test results to the bag under my bed. The same passage also mentioned that to have sex is to become one with another person. I use to have sex the way the world had groomed me to have sex, but that way had left me depressed and broken-hearted. Now, I wanted to try it God's way.

I got on the floor and pulled out my sex bag. It would have been simple to throw the bag away, but I wanted to keep it as a reminder of what God had done for me and where I believed He was leading my new life. I folded my new test results and put them inside, then I grabbed a piece of paper and wrote a note to myself:

> Before opening this bag, please consider if you are in love with the person with whom you will commit your entire life and that you have made a promise to love him from this moment on. Otherwise, close this bag and walk away. To unite the bodies is to create a covenant before God, and God shall forever unite them. To unite the bodies and then disunite them is not an act of love because you will be breaking a promise to yourself, whom you must love. You will be breaking a promise to this other person, whom you must love. And you will be breaking a promise to God, Whom you love.

I grabbed my stapler and sealed the bag shut with my test results inside and the note I had written to myself on the outside. I decided that I was going to glorify God in my body. I was going to wait until marriage before having sex again.

NINE

SEEK, AND YOU WILL FIND

O NE SUNDAY, our lead pastor, Pete, preached on the importance of serving in the church. He mentioned that we are all called to "the work of ministry" and that we need to serve in the church to grow in spiritual maturity.[1]

"You are not called to sit in a chair. We're supposed to be a team. If you feel like you are not connecting with people in this church as much as you'd like to, then one of the best ways to build godly relationships is to join a group and serve together."

I bounced in my seat! I had been going to church every Sunday and sometimes several times a week. Still, I felt like I struggled to connect with other believers. I decided to take Pastor Pete's advice by signing up to serve in the youth ministry.

After I signed up, they gathered us for an orientation. They went through all kinds of paperwork, including a contract-like form called the "Standards of Ministry," which listed what was expected of people who served in the church. It included things like, "I attend this church regularly," "I only use over-the-counter or doctor-prescribed drugs," and "I do not drink in excess." But also, "I will live by God's standard of a heterosexual, monogamous marriage."

I reread it to make sure I got it right. My heart was like a piece of glass with a small crack that slowly spread and grew until the whole thing shattered. I understood that many churches where I grew up in the conservative South didn't allow gay people, but I didn't expect it from this church in liberal Los Angeles. Crushed by the weight of those words, I admitted to the administrator that I couldn't sign the "Standards of Ministry," and I left the orientation. At first, I kept the reason to myself.

For as long as I can remember, I have been attracted to the same sex. As a kid, my first crushes were the red Power Ranger and Zack from *Saved by the Bell*. I thought they were cute, and just seeing them on TV gave me those excited, butterfly feelings in the pit of my stomach.

As I got older, I learned to suppress my sexual orientation out of fear of what would happen if people found out. I even tried dating girls to prove that I could be straight, but every time it seemed like I was dating a sister. There wasn't that romantic attraction that inspires people to marry each other, so those relationships were always more awkward than romantic. In high school, I had a secret gay relationship. Even though we wouldn't admit it, we both had real feelings for each other, but neither of us wanted to be openly gay.

Things were different when I went to college and moved to Los Angeles. People were more accepting, so I came out. I couldn't have imagined that my church in LA would have this non-affirming view. Someone else might have tried to find another church, but since I was new to Christianity, I wanted to understand why they didn't allow gay people to serve. If they were right, I needed to know because I wanted to follow the Lord no matter the cost.

DURING A BIBLE STUDY group at my church, one of the women leaders mentioned something that encouraged me to come out to her.

She said, "I was raised Baptist, and in the Baptist church, women aren't allowed to preach, teach, or serve in any way other than maybe the children's ministry or to sing during worship. That left a bad taste in my mouth for God. It wasn't until I was older and discovered God for myself that I realized that He isn't like that. He doesn't see women as a second thought. We are co-heirs with men in the Kingdom."[2]

She was right. Some Christian churches believe that women can't be leaders. They would use scriptures that say women should remain quiet.[3] I didn't even think anything of it because, at my church, several women were invited to preach. Clearly, my church didn't hold these scriptures at face value. If someone had pulled out those scriptures to rebuke women for preaching, they'd say that the passages needed to be understood in their context.

Also, there are many examples of women in leadership roles throughout the Bible. Deborah was a woman judge and prophetess.[4] Jesus told the women who saw Him risen from the grave to "go and tell."[5] Priscilla was a woman preacher who even corrected a man on his doctrine.[6] Philip's daughters prophesied.[7] Paul mentioned a woman apostle named Junia,[8] and he mentioned wives praying and prophesying.[9] If the Bible meant that women could never speak or preach in the Church, then the Bible would contradict these other scriptures with clear examples of women leaders. My church understood all of this, so I couldn't understand why they were using a handful of passages to prevent someone like me from serving.

After the Bible study, I pulled the woman leader to the side. "I liked what you said about women in the church, but why don't we handle gay people in the same way? Like, why can't I marry another guy and serve in this church?"

As if she had the answer scripted, she replied, "Because God made marriage between one man and one woman." I gave her a dissatisfied look, and she continued, "But maybe we could call a same-sex relationship a 'domestic partnership.'" She was clearly hoping that would be a more satisfying answer. This happened the year before the 2013 Supreme Court ruling that declared California's Prop 8 ban on same-sex marriage unconstitutional.

I hope I came off as patient, but I was annoyed. I tried to smile and remain kind as I said, "But that's the same thing as separate but equal. We've tried that before, and we now see that as wrong."

She looked at me for a moment. "I don't know," she admitted, "But let me get you in contact with Pastor Andrew. He may be able to answer your question better than I can."

I MET with Pastor Andrew the following week. He was the man with dreadlocks who baptized me. I assumed that he was gay, but I later learned that Pastor Andrew was married to a woman and had kids. Much later, after I no longer attended this church, I found out that he identified as ex-gay. He never once mentioned that to me in any of the times that he and I spoke.

We met in the children's ministry room. The walls around us displayed a cartoony scene of Noah's ark. As he greeted me and pulled up a chair, he had almost a plastic smile, like he was a Ken doll with dreadlocks.

After we shared some small introductions, I said, "I wanted to talk to you because I'm gay. I want to serve in the youth ministry, but I saw on the 'Standards of Ministry' that I have to," I said it using air quotes, "'*live by God's standard of a heterosexual marriage.*' But I'm gay, so I'm wondering if I can have a place in this church and still be me."

He nodded his head as if he understood, and he said with a smile, "We want nothing more than for you to be you." Then he slightly relaxed his smile. "We have the 'Standards of Ministry' in place, especially with the kid's and youth ministries, because we want parents to know that their kids are in good hands. Some of them might not be comfortable with a homosexual man watching their kids."

I gave out a deep sigh. I knew some Christian groups compared gay people to pedophiles. I wondered if that's what he meant.

Pastor Andrew continued, "I wouldn't mind if you watched my kids, though. You seem like a decent guy, but not all of our parents are to that point yet."

I tried to see if there was some room for a compromise. "What if two men are in love, live together, share a bed, adopt kids, but don't have sex? Is that okay?"

Pastor Andrew shrugged. "I would think not because if those men struggle with same-sex attraction, then they would be opening themselves up to temptation. And the Bible says to stay away from even the *appearance* of evil."[10]

I tried not to cringe at him calling being gay "evil," but my face distorted with discomfort as I readjusted in my seat.

"Let me put it this way," Pastor Andrew went on. "I don't live with women other than my wife and other female family members because I don't want to be tempted by another woman."

"Then how can I get more involved in this church? I recognize the Presence of God here, and I want to be more involved if I can."

Pastor Andrew listed some options like volunteering on the community service team. "Also," he said, "I would recommend that you join me in our recovery groups. We have all kinds of groups from codependency recovery, substance addiction, sex addiction, and same-sex attraction. You're welcome to join any of the groups you feel you need, but you will probably feel most comfortable in the same-sex attraction recovery group."

I looked at him in silence. He wanted me to join a group of guys trying to recover from being gay. I didn't know what to say. I wasn't angry, but I was confused about what to do in that situation. In college, I learned that some churches tried to "pray the gay away" in reparative or conversion therapy. I also knew that all major mental health associations deemed ex-gay therapies dangerous for causing mental health issues, including thoughts of suicide.[11] I wasn't sure if I should subject myself to something like that, especially after the trauma of prostitution, but Pastor Andrew suggested it.

I had heard a phrase mentioned before in the church. It seemed to be the best go-to phrase Christians used when they didn't know how else to respond. I looked at Pastor Andrew and said, "Let me pray about that."

While driving home, I did pray. "Lord, I believe I encountered You, and You told me that You love me. But I don't know what to think if You don't like gay people. This is a part of me. I left porn, but I don't know if I can give up being gay."

86

His response was startling. *"Anyone who does not renounce all that he has cannot be My disciple."*[12]

It hit me hard. I wanted nothing more than to follow the one Who said He loved me and saved me from prostitution. I cried, "Then is my church right? Do I need to somehow not be gay?"

As I sat in Los Angeles traffic praying, a stillness descended upon me in a warm embrace. He said, *"I love you."* Every time He said it, it calmed my heart and filled me with a peace that surpassed my understanding. *"Seek, and you will find, knock; and the door will be opened..."*[13] *You will recognize them by their fruit."*[14]

"Lord, I will seek Your will with this. Please, help me to understand."

TEN

THIRSTY

—————

// I 'M SO GLAD to see you here, Aaron," Pastor Andrew greeted me with a huge smile and a hug as I walked into the church.

"I thought I would go ahead and check out the recovery group that you told me about," I said as he released me.

Pastor Andrew's body bounced in excitement as he clapped his hands together. "Yes! Go ahead and find a seat in the auditorium. We're about to get started."

The church organized the recovery services like a regular church service. All of the recovery groups gathered together in the auditorium for worship and to share testimonies about how they overcame their struggles with sin through the power of God. Afterward, everyone split up to go to the small group that catered to their specific struggle.

After worship, one woman who I knew from the church pulled me to the side. "I have someone I'd like for you to meet," she said as she led me towards another young man. "This is Ryder."

As soon as I saw Ryder, I thought he looked familiar, but I wasn't sure from where. He was maybe a few years older than me. He wore a purple fedora, and he looked like he had on some makeup. I thought that maybe I had seen him around at church, but that didn't seem right. I knew I had seen him before from somewhere else.

"Ryder is one of the leaders of the same-sex attraction group," the woman explained.

After some quick introductions, Ryder led me to the group. We met outside of the church's main building in a room they rented next door. With only five or six men, including myself, this group was the smallest of all the recovery groups.

When the meeting started, Ryder and another leader, Preston, explained the rules. Everyone got a few minutes to talk about what they were going through with their struggle against same-sex attraction (SSA). They started by saying, "I'm *so-and-so*, a grateful believer in Jesus Christ, and I struggle with same-sex attraction" and any other struggles that they were trying to overcome.

It was odd to me that they called it "same-sex attraction." Being gay means that you're attracted to the same sex, so it was like they were claiming the definition, but not the word itself. For them, by calling it "same-sex attraction," their sexual orientation became something that was an ailment to be cured, not something that was inherently a part of themselves.

But I had learned in a cultural anthropology class back in college that someone's sexual orientation *is* a part of them, as much a part of them as whether they are right or left-hand dominant. It didn't occur to me that all of that would be challenged by finding God and going to church. Although I didn't necessarily agree with it, I wanted to make sure I understood where the Lord was calling me to go with my sexual orientation.

I listened to everyone speak, but I couldn't bring myself to speak. I decided that on that first night, I would only view the group as an anthropologist. I studied them. They had a culture that I wanted to understand.

As everyone went around describing their situations, a part of me wondered if maybe they were right. Many of their stories revolved around similar situations to what I did before I knew the Lord. Many of them had watched gay porn. Some had rented prostituted men. Most had promiscuous sex. They equated all of that to homosexuality. And because I had been down similar roads, I wondered if my time in prostitution had flowed out from me identifying as gay.

After the meeting, an older man with short white hair and bushy white eyebrows, who had introduced himself as Mike in the session, followed me out.

"I get the sense that you don't necessarily agree with everything in this group," he said.

"I don't," I confessed. "But I'd like to think I'm open-minded."

"Well, I believe you can be gay and Christian. I've been in and out of these groups for years. I even used to be a pastor, and I've never seen a gay person turn straight."

"Why do you come to this group then? Why did you say you struggle with same-sex attraction?"

"Because I have other things I'm working on, but because I'm gay, if I went to any of the other groups, they'd just recommend that I come back to the SSA group."

Mike's situation interested me. He was another example of a gay Christian who God brought into my life. But Mike wasn't out to everyone at church, and it made me wonder if I should not be out at church either. The other guys in the SSA group had developed strong friendships because of this idea that they struggled with same-sex attraction. I wondered if I needed to keep my sexual orientation to myself if I wanted to make Christian friends.

What had started as a tiny seed of faith in the inhospitable environment of my heart had found its way from a crack in the cement with just enough soil to sprout. Eventually, the sapling found itself planted in a pot, but as I grew in faith and my roots continued to stretch through the soil, the pot became too restraining. I couldn't help but wonder if it was the pot's fault that I didn't fit in it. Or was it my fault?

AFTER MY FIRST SSA group, I went home and prayed about what the Lord thought about me being gay. He kept saying, *"You will recognize them by their fruits… every healthy tree bears good fruit, but the diseased tree bears bad fruit. A healthy tree cannot bear bad fruit, nor can a diseased tree bear good fruit."* [1]

Fruit is often used in the Bible to symbolize the consequences that come from spiritual teachings. Specifically, fruit has to do with whether or not the teaching causes someone to repent and turn to God. [2] We are the plants of God, and when we turn our lives to Him, He causes us to bear the fruit of repentance. The fruit of a life transformed by the Spirit of God is "love, joy, peace, patience, kindness, goodness, faithfulness, gentleness, self-control; against such things there is no law" because these are the fulfillment of the Word of God. [3] The fruit of the Spirit is God's love flowing freely from a once-sinful heart. We can discern whether a teaching is of God or not by whether or not it helps believers bear the fruit of the Spirit.

As I prayed and considered the fruit analogy, I remembered where I recognized Ryder from. I got on my phone and opened the gay hookup app that I had previously used to find sex-buyers and casual hookups. I had still been using it, hoping that I could find a boyfriend at some point. When I opened the app, his face was on a little thumbnail, complete with his purple fedora. He was on the app at that exact moment. I messaged him.

ME

Ryder? Is that you?

After just a couple of seconds, I refreshed the app. His profile was gone. No response. Just gone. Either he blocked me, or he deleted his profile.

The next week when I went back to the SSA group, Ryder was there, but he was definitely avoiding me. After the meeting, while everyone exchanged goodbyes, I approached him.

"How's it going, Ryder?" I smiled. I wanted to tell him that his secret was safe with me, and I wanted to know if he was okay.

"Hey, Aaron," he replied through a smile that seemed to be an attempt to hide embarrassment. "Excuse me, but I have to run to a meeting with my accountability partner."

"Oh, okay." I shouted as he rushed off, "Well, good to see you."

After just a short time in the group, I noticed that because the guys in SSA recovery were taught that being gay is sinful, they hated the part of themselves that was attracted to other men. Still, that hatred towards their orientation did nothing to take it away.

Long before I came out as gay, I found other guys attractive and beat myself up about it because I feared the public ridicule of being gay. I would have crushes on boys, and I wanted to act on those crushes by simply saying "Hi" and smiling at them in the school hallways. But that would be complying with the feelings that I didn't want to have. Eventually, though, I grew exhausted from trying to be and act straight. It isn't who I am, and it's tiring trying to be someone you're not.

I wondered if that's how the guys in SSA felt, exhausted from the constant war with a part of themselves that no matter how much they tried to change, avoid, or pretend wasn't there, it was still there. And for the first time since I came out in college, I wondered if I should have that same battle again so that I could be a part of my church.

Seeing Ryder and the rest of the guys in the SSA group struggle made me look inward at myself and my own struggles. After all, I found Ryder on a hookup app, the same app that I had used in prostitution. After being saved by Yeshua, I used the hookup app to share the Gospel with other gay men, and I used the Gospel as an excuse to keep using the app. But the app also became a huge door that would lead me right back to my old way of life because I also used the app to meet other men to "fool around" with. Even after meeting Yeshua and planning to wait until marriage, there was still something within me that clung to my unhealthy ways of finding intimacy.

AT THE AGE OF NINE, I walked in on my older brother and his friend watching porn. My brother's friend jumped up and tried to hide the screen.

"Hold on. It's cool," my brother said. "He needs to see this." He looked at me. "All men watch this, and I think it's time for you to become a real man."

I was nine. My brother was only fourteen. We were both children. He had me sit down on the floor in front of the couch to watch porn with him and his friend. That porn video was my first sexual experience.

As we watched, I heard my brother whisper to his friend, "I told you he isn't gay."

It seemed that my brother thought that if I liked porn, that would mean I'm not gay. To many men, viewing porn seems to make them feel more masculine, and from the moment my brother said those words, I bought into that lie.

His friend replied, "I don't know. He could be watching the guys."

I had no idea what I was watching. It was the first time I had seen *everything*. I do not remember if I had ever seen an adult man or woman naked before that moment, and I wasn't just watching a man and a woman make love. I was watching a group of men and one woman doing things that my nine-year-old brain could not understand.

Watching what that group of men did to that woman created a perverse connection in my mind between sexual arousal and trauma. Because this was my first experience with sex, I grew to think trauma was a part of sex. A part of me was nauseated and knew that something wasn't right, but the porn attracted another part of me. I was too young to realize that a cocktail of chemicals released by my brain was coursing through my bloodstream and bonding me to porn.

Through watching that first porn video, I learned how to masturbate. I didn't know that when I orgasmed for the first time to porn, my brain was programmed to understand this new experience was sex. In that instant, my body created a neurological connection between me and pornography.

When the human body orgasms, the brain releases a neurochemical combination of dopamine, norepinephrine, oxytocin, serotonin, and endorphins, some of the same chemicals released in the brain during narcotic drug use. In a healthy sexual relationship, these bonding chemicals strengthen our connection with our partner. The Lord purposefully designed this so that married couples would be drawn together for mutual satisfaction and bonding, but when we engage in unhealthy sex, like porn, this process gets hacked. These same chemicals can cause a person to become dependent on pornography, promiscuity, the internet, or anything else that the brain associates as rewarding.[4]

Today, most children have their first sexual experience when they first encounter pornography between the ages of eight[5] and eleven.[6] When these children watch porn, these bonding chemicals are released in their brains, causing them to bond to the images they see on the screen. A young, developing brain cannot tell the difference between real sex and the "sex" shown in porn, so the child develops a persistent sexual dependency on porn.

Children cannot consent to sex. Their brains are not yet developed enough to understand the lifelong consequences that can come with sex, so when exposed to porn, it is exploiting their vulnerable youth. When children are exposed to porn, it is *sexual assault*. Porn has essentially raped generations of children, and just like many people who enter prostitution, these children grow up trying to reclaim their power by accepting sexual exploitation as the norm.

Something porn viewers don't often think about is its impact on them. Porn causes the viewers' brains to bond to a screen and not another person. This bond can be so strong that the person needs porn to function sexually. For example, many young men develop erectile dysfunction (ED) due to dependency on pornographic videos.[7] It is not typical for young men to experience ED. Yet because internet porn is so normal to today's young generations, younger men experience it at much higher rates than previous generations. Porn doesn't just affect the ability to perform sex. Studies also show that porn can cause overall dissatisfaction with real-life relationships and contributes to higher infidelity rates.[8] In the end, porn stunts our ability to intimately connect with another human being through sex.

After my first encounter with porn, I began to seek it as often as I could. I knew where my brother hid his videotapes, DVDs, and magazines, and I would frequently watch them when no one else was home. When my family finally got the internet, I looked up porn as soon as I had the chance. Throughout my teenage years, all that stood between me and every sexual experience I ever wanted was a computer. Like most people in my generation, porn was a normal part of my life growing up.

When I had my first physical, sexual experience with another guy as a teenager, I finally felt a romantic connection with another human being. Even though we told each other that we were just "experimenting," we both knew that having sex created a deeper connection than we expected. Our relationship eventually ended because we didn't want people to find out that we were gay, so I experienced my first heartbreak.

The pain was visceral. It was like my heart was being squeezed in someone's fist and about to burst. My heartache was so intense because my body was physically trying to cope with the loss of the bond created through sex. The breakup made it seem like all the intimacy we shared was nothing. Like it was meaningless and worthless; like *I* was meaningless and worthless. As the Bible says, in sex, two people become one.[9] I gave him a part of myself, and when that relationship ended, it was like I was being thrown away.

That relationship was the first time I came out to someone as gay. Having someone to share that realization with made it easier than it had ever been, but when we broke up, I was once again alone. Because I wasn't out as gay, I couldn't openly work through my pain and healthily express my grief. After suicide attempts failed, I self-medicated with alcohol and porn.

Gay male porn is exceptionally homophobic. It consistently portrays gay sex as violent and aggressive. It was common to hear prostituted men in gay porn use homophobic, transphobic, and misogynistic slurs towards one another. What gay porn taught me about gay sex is that gay men do not make love to each other. They make hate.

Then during my first week in college, Brandon raped me. It seemed to prove porn to be true. Gay men only wanted violent, meaningless sex. It seemed to prove what I felt after my "experiment" relationship was over, that I was worthless. Then I was raped again and again, and my sexuality spiraled out of control. It snowballed into hypersexuality as a way to cope with being raped. I was hooking up with men regularly to the point that I sold myself in a desperate attempt to find a sense of worth, value, and control.

When I became a believer in Yeshua, my sexuality wasn't immediately set free from what porn taught me about sex. I thought I had to "fool around" with guys I met on hookup apps, or else I would never find a real, meaningful relationship. After being born again, I wanted to wait until marriage, but I still tried to see how far we could go without officially breaking the line into "actual sex." What I didn't realize is that I had a deep-seated void within my heart, and I wanted a boyfriend to come along to fill that void. I had pain, and I wanted someone to heal it.

I was *thirsty*, and I wanted someone to satisfy my thirst.

As I THOUGHT about the same-sex attraction group and why I still used that hookup app, the Lord seemed to move me to read a certain story in the Bible from John 4:7-29. It was about a Samaritan woman at a water well. She was thirsty.

When Yeshua met her, He said, "Give Me a drink."

She must have been surprised because Yeshua was a Jewish man, and the Jewish people had nothing to do with the Samaritans, especially women. It was first-century racism and sexism.

The woman asked, "How is it that You, a Jew, ask for a drink from me?"

Yeshua responded, "If you knew the gift of God, and Who it is that is saying to you, 'Give Me a drink,' you would have asked Him, and He would have given you living water... whoever drinks of the water that I will give him will never be thirsty again. The water that I will give him will become in him a spring of water welling up to eternal life."

The woman said, "Sir, give me this water, so that I will not be thirsty or have to come here to draw water."

"Go, call your husband, and come here," He said.

"I have no husband."

As I read it, I saw Yeshua lean forward, lock eyes with the woman, and give her a gentle smile. "You are right in saying, 'I have no husband'; for you have had five husbands, and the one you now have is not your husband. What you have said is true."

I imagined the woman's jaw dropped and her eyes widened. She said, "Sir, I perceive that You are a prophet."

She did not know Yeshua, but He somehow knew her and her secrets. If by "five husbands," Yeshua referred to men she had sexually become one with, He somehow knew that she had had five sexual partners at this point in her lifetime. He somehow knew that she was again having marital relations with a man to whom she was not married. This would have needed to be kept a secret because if someone had found out, the woman's sexual partner would have been required to marry her.[10] But Yeshua knew her secret. He knew she was *thirsty*. And He knew she wasn't just thirsty for water or sex. There was something within her that craved deeper satisfaction. It seemed that she tried to satisfy herself through relationships and sex, but after five sexual partners, she was still unsatisfied. She didn't realize that she longed for something more. But Yeshua knew she needed Him.

After Yeshua revealed Himself to her as the Messiah, the woman excitedly ran around proclaiming, "Come, see a man who told me all that I ever did. Can this be the Christ?"

Yeshua was the only one Who could ever truly satisfy her, not through sex, but through true spiritual intimacy between a human and her Creator. This is why Yeshua said He could make a river of living water spring up from within her, referring to His own Spirit.[11] God sought to satisfy this woman through true godly intimacy by putting His own Spirit in her heart.

When I encountered Yeshua for the first time, I encountered love, real love. The satisfaction His love brought caused me to leave prostitution and decide to wait until marriage because I wanted to know real, romantic love in my next relationship. But even after meeting the Lord, there was still something lacking, something that hadn't been fully satisfied yet. And that thirst left me unable to walk fully in my conviction to wait until marriage. I wanted to, but I pushed the limits.

I was thirsty, but Yeshua is the only one who could satisfy that thirst. There is nothing wrong with sexual desire, but sex will never fulfill my life the way Yeshua can. I didn't need hookups. I didn't need to "fool around." I needed Him.

Through the SSA group, I was able to take the first step necessary to recover from my struggle. The first step to overcoming sin is to confess it as a sin. The Word of God says, "Confess your sins to one another and pray for one another, that you may be healed."[12]

I caught everyone's attention in the SSA group when I admitted, "I'm Aaron, a grateful believer in Jesus Christ, and I struggle with sex addiction." It may not have been a confession to same-sex attraction, but it was a start to healing from my past.

ELEVEN

HEART TRANSFORMATION

D URING THE FIRST months of attending my church, I was still trying to figure out how to worship in a public setting. I followed most of the people around me, who worshiped in front of their seats and read along to the lyrics. I stood with my hands in my pockets or my arms crossed. If it was a moving song, I might tap to the beat with my fingers on the chair in front of me.

During one service, God's Spirit pointed out a young man who worshiped at the front altar. There were a few other people at the front, but he definitely seemed the most into it. He had both of his hands lifted high in the air and sang with passion as he moved his body in a swaying dance before the Lord like he was at a concert all by himself.

As I watched, the Lord spoke to me. *"This man worships Me in the way you feel on the inside. Why don't you let it out?"*

My immediate thought was, *No, that's weird.*

Still, I sensed the Lord insisting. At first, I remained at my seat and hesitantly lifted my right hand to about shoulder height.

When I did, it was like a tiny drop of watery fire trickled upon my right hand and rushed down my arm, straight into my heart. The sensation caused a short, soft laugh to burst from my lips. I lifted my left hand to the same height. The warm, watery fire sensation trickled down my left arm and, again, straight into my heart.

I sensed an urgency to step forward to the altar like the young man I had been watching, but I resisted. I wouldn't let my feet move.

As the worship team transitioned into another song, I heard the Lord say, *"This is the last song. Please, don't miss your chance to step out and worship Me."*

Finally, I stepped out of my seat and waded through a pool of that warm, liquid fire to the front altar. When I arrived in front of the stage, I raised my hands high above my head. As soon as they both arrived at the pinnacle of their reach, the warm, watery, fiery trickle of God's Spirit rushed upon me like I was standing under a waterfall. The force of His Presence nudged tears from my eyes. It was similar to my first encounter with the Lord, but so much more powerful.

God wanted intimacy with me, but He isn't a rapist. He wasn't going to force Himself upon me. He is a gentleman. He wanted to see if I would allow Him to pour into me. He wasn't going to overstep my boundaries, so I had to take my boundaries down. Raising hands in worship to the Lord may seem weird to some people, but it is a sign of surrender in the Bible.[1] It is the outward expression of a heart that longs to be yielded to God.

As I worshiped with hands lifted high, the waterfall became a river that rushed from deep within me and out my mouth causing words to bubble up inside my throat. They tingled upon my tongue. Without thinking much about it, I began to murmur a series of syllables and phrases that made no sense. As I did, I sensed the fiery waterfall melt away weights and break off chains that I didn't even know were in my heart.

WHEN I GOT HOME after church, the Spirit led me in my Bible to where Yeshua said, "You heard from Me; for John [the Baptist] baptized with water, but you will be baptized with the Holy Spirit not many days from now... you will receive power when the Holy Spirit has come upon you."[2]

I had to look up what this meant online. I found that before Yeshua came, God promised His people, "I will put My Spirit within you, and cause you to walk in My statutes and be careful to obey My rules."[3] God promised that He would be so intimate with His people that He Himself would be inside of us and enable us to overcome sin.

When I was born again, the Word says that the Holy Spirit was sealed upon my heart,[4] but there's a separate experience called the baptism in the Holy Spirit. The Bible shows several examples where people were born again and *then* filled with the Spirit.[5]

As I read the Word, I got goosebumps. I realized that I had experienced the Spirit baptism. It happened because I yielded to the Spirit of God inside of me. The power I received was beyond anything I could imagine. I once believed that porn had empowered me, but it did nothing but degrade me. When God poured His Spirit into me, that was true empowerment.

The revelation excited me, so I made a post on Facebook.

Aaron Crowley   Just Now · Public

God's power is so tangible. He is so accessible today if we would just reach out for Him.

Like · Comment · Share

After a moment, an old acquaintance from high school—actually, more of a bully—commented on that post.

> **Him**
> Honestly, you're the worst kind of Christian. Jesus doesn't have gay sex on camera!
>
> Like · Reply

As I read the comment, I stopped breathing. My past was public knowledge to people who knew me from high school and college, and I was aware that some people shared my porn with others as a way to cyberbully me. This was one reason I insisted that I was empowered by porn; it made their torment have less impact on causing me shame. But since leaving porn, I hadn't spoken about it to those who knew me as a Christian. While staring at this bully's public comment, I wondered how many people had seen it before I did. I started to hyperventilate.

At that moment, I became aware of what I can only describe as three shadowy presences: guilt, shame, and fear. They weren't new. They had been there for a long time. Only, I was finally consciously aware of them.

Guilt, shame, and fear seemed to choke the air from my lungs. Guilt wanted me to doubt everything I had experienced from God because how could someone who did what I did ever experience God to that degree? Shame wanted me to believe that there was no help for me because I made my bed; I should lie in it. Fear wanted me to be afraid that I could not have a relationship with God because I'm gay. Together, they seemed to taunt me that porn and prostitution would never be in my past. They seemed to argue that my sexual orientation and porn go hand in hand, and Jesus would never save me from porn without first having me repent for being gay.

But I knew enough of the Word of God by this point to understand that these were lies. I got on my knees, closed my eyes, lifted my hands high above my head, drew in one deep gulp of air, and prayed, "Father, I need You more than anything else. Please, fill me with Your Presence."

From within my heart, a light bursted as bright as an atomic bomb, filling the room around me. The guilt, shame, and fear that had gripped me only moments ago wailed in agony and fled from God's power. Shadows cannot exist in the Light!

The Light of Yeshua revealed that those demonic presences were what held sin so strongly to my life. Guilt, shame, and fear held me to mindsets that kept me enslaved to sin.

When those shadows fled, it was as if they left me empty. Then God filled me with a rushing torrent of that watery, fiery *love* that pulsed through every cell in my body and every thought in my mind. Love flowed into me and out of me like a mighty, raging, rushing river! The room around me quivered.

There is a consistent pattern in the Bible that when someone experiences the baptism in the Holy Spirit, they begin to pray in tongues.[6] I prayed in tongues. The torrent of love rushed to my lips and tongue, causing them to quiver. My mouth cried sounds of praise that were in a poetic, musical language. I was not possessed; I was able to control myself. God doesn't force Himself on people through possession. Instead, He gave me utterances as I let my mouth speak.

As I looked back at the comment that my high school acquaintance left, I smirked. It meant nothing to me anymore. I sent him a private message.

ME

That's not who I am anymore. God has changed my life. If you want, He can change yours too.

The bully unfollowed me, but I couldn't care less. God's love was all that mattered.

The baptism in the Holy Spirit was a turning point for my faith. I was set on fire for God. Since that moment, every time I worship and pray, I worship and pray in tongues. I also worship and pray in English, but there is something deeper when I let my mind get out of the way to allow the Spirit within me to pray. It is my way of yielding to God as He builds me up and cleanses me from the inside out.[7]

The baptism in the Holy Spirit isn't just about praying in tongues, though; it is also about holiness. As the prophet said, God puts His Spirit inside of us to cause us to walk in His ways. He puts His Spirit inside of us to transform our hearts.

SOMETIME AFTER I experienced the Holy Spirit baptism, I met up with a guy from the hookup app. He invited me to his apartment to play video games. One thing led to another, and my body craved sex. So we "fooled around."

At the moment that my hands drifted where they should not have gone, God's Spirit called out, *"Wait! You're worth more than this! He's worth more than this!"*

When a believer is filled with the Spirit, it doesn't mean they won't have the ability to sin anymore. They still have to make the constant decision that they will continue to yield to

God. In that moment, I did not yield to God; I yielded to my body's desire instead.

When I stopped yielding to the Spirit, I immediately realized the true source of my spiritual thirst. Because I did not yield to Him, God was not in what I was doing because sin separates us from God's Presence. When I was separated from Him during my sin, I became painfully aware of His absence. Like the Samaritan woman who met Yeshua at the well, my thirst wasn't really for sex. It was a deep, spiritual thirst for Him.

I could not enjoy anything that I did with the guy that night because while we "fooled around," everything inside me desperately cried out for the Spirit of God. I knew that Yeshua wasn't in what I was doing, and I wanted Him. I longed for Him. I missed Him.

As the guy from the hookup app and I went further and further, within me, I felt drier and drier. My heart became dehydrated. I needed the Spirit of God. Not "fooling around." Not sex.

After the baptism in the Holy Spirit, the things that once satisfied me were now horribly dissatisfying compared to Yeshua. He was the only one Who had been able to satisfy me truly. While I was with that guy, I realized how unsatisfied I was without the Lord.

As I left that guy's apartment, I tried to justify what we did.

We didn't go all the way. We just fooled around. There's nothing wrong with that.

As I got in my car, it was as if Yeshua had been waiting for me in the passenger seat. He didn't leave me because He never leaves us nor forsakes us,[8] but when I sensed that the Spirit was in the car waiting, I realized that I had left Him.

When I shut the car door, Yeshua and I sat silently for a moment. The time lingered as I waited to see if He would say something to condemn me for what I had just done. He didn't have to say a word. Within my heart, I could sense He was grieved. He was heartbroken, and His pain broke my heart.

All of my sin put Him on the cross. My shame was the crown of thorns upon His head and the nails driven through His hands and feet. My twisted heart caused Him to asphyxiate to death. Yeshua's torture and torment at the hands of humanity reveal how sin pains God, how *my* sin anguishes Him.

"Okay!" I threw my face into my arms and fell into the steering wheel, wailing as tears splashed beneath me in godly sorrow. "Please, forgive me!"

It wasn't shame or guilt. I was grieved that I broke the heart of God. After being baptized in His Spirit, I was more sensitive to His disappointment.

As gently as He appeared in my room during that first encounter, yet as powerfully as He appeared within me when He filled me with His Spirit, His warm, tangible Presence fluttered all around me and within me. He embraced me and comforted me.

"I do not condemn you. Go, and sin no more.[9] *My grace is sufficient for you."*[10]

The cross displays the grief God goes through because of humanity's sins, but it also displays His grace. His forgiveness. His love. He bore the cross because He loves us.

I drove home that night, praying in tongues as tears streamed down my face. As I prayed, I sensed layers of darkness were being ripped away to leave a purer core of myself, the true me. His grace and mercy were so sweet, like honey on my lips. His Presence was a fresh, cool breath of air. Yeshua is so much more satisfying than anything else. He is all I ever wanted.

The Lord said that He didn't condemn me. I knew Yeshua was speaking because I had read in the Bible that He had said those same words to a woman caught in adultery.

The religious people caught her cheating on her husband. They grabbed her and dragged her to Yeshua, saying that she deserved to die for her sin.

But Yeshua responded, "Let him who is without sin among you be the first to throw a stone at her."

After a moment, one by one, the religious people walked away because they all knew that none of them were innocent of sin. Then Yeshua looked at the woman.

"Woman, where are they? Has no one condemned you?"

She cried, "No one, Lord."

"Neither do I condemn you; go, and from now on sin no more."[11]

This is the grace of God displayed over sexual sin. He says that He does not condemn us, and therefore, we *can* go and sin no more.

I knew it was Yeshua Who said His grace was sufficient for me because I had read that He said that to Apostle Paul.

Paul confessed that he struggled with sin. He said,

> A thorn was given me in the flesh, a messenger of Satan to harass me, to keep me from becoming conceited. Three times I pleaded with the Lord about this, that it should leave me. But He said to me, "My grace is sufficient for you, for My power is made perfect in weakness."

Because God's grace caused him to become strong over his weakness to sin, Paul then declared, "When I am weak, then I am strong."[12]

The power to overcome sin comes from God's grace. Just as Paul also wrote, "the grace of God appeared… training us to renounce ungodliness and worldly passions, and to live self-controlled, upright, and godly lives in the present age."[13]

After being baptized in the Holy Spirit, my desire for God became much stronger than any desire for sin. God's grace was so much more satisfying, and I found myself more in love with the Lord. If it broke Yeshua's heart, then I couldn't find enjoyment in it.

One of my favorite Bible stories is when a religious man invited Yeshua to his house. As the two were hanging out, a sinful woman rushed in, "and standing behind Him at His feet, weeping, she began to wet His feet with her tears and wiped them with the hair of her head and kissed His feet and anointed them with ointment."

When the religious man saw this, he judged Yeshua, thinking that if He really were a prophet, He wouldn't let a sinner touch Him.

But Yeshua said, "Her sins, which are many, are forgiven—for she loved much. But he who is forgiven little, loves little."[14]

It was Yeshua's forgiving grace that moved the woman to love Him. Because of the Lord's mercy over sin, the sinful woman fell in love with Him, and her display of worship at His feet was an outward expression of that love.

Yeshua also promised, "If you love Me, you will keep My commandments."[15]

This is often read as a command that we have to prove our love for God by trying really hard to live a sinless life, but I see these words as a promise. If we love Yeshua, we *will* keep His commandments. It's going to happen supernaturally from within the heart, where the Holy Spirit dwells. After all, Yeshua taught that if we love Him, then we fulfill the Word of God.[16]

HEART TRANSFORMATION

If the sinful woman loved Yeshua, then she kept the Lord's commandments. How was she able to do that? Because Yeshua's grace forgave her, and His forgiveness empowered her to love much. Love empowered her over her sin. This is also how the woman caught in adultery was empowered to "go and sin no more." Yeshua's grace caused her to fall in love with Him, so she went away keeping His commandments and sinning no more. Love is also how God's grace empowered Paul to overcome his weakness to sin.

That was how God empowered me. Because of Yeshua's loving grace, I fell in love with Him, and that love encouraged me to leave prostitution. As I grew in relationship with Him, my heart was transformed by the overflow of love through the baptism in His Spirit. Then I realized that no matter how small we think it is, all sin breaks Yeshua's heart, and because I love Him, I didn't want to break His heart anymore. Instead, I wanted to live a life devoted to Him.

Because I know that I have been forgiven of so much, I love so much. Loving Yeshua makes me sensitive to what hurts Him, and that compels me to keep His commandments. My love for Him causes me to yield to His Spirit, and while yielding to Him, I do not sin. I only fall into sin when I forget to yield to Him. But when I forget to yield to Him, His grace empowers me back out of sin, and then I find myself even more in love with Him. Now, I cling to Yeshua because I know that He is the only one with the power to set me free from sin.

After being filled with the Holy Spirit, the idea of casual sex repulsed me. Yeshua made it to where I no longer desired sex unless it was with someone willing to love me in the way that Yeshua loves me. If I'm worth dying for, then I'm worth waiting for. In fact, after that moment, when I knew that I had grieved God's Spirit, I did not even see another person naked until the night of my wedding. It was because God's Spirit transformed my heart and empowered me to walk in His love.

But if God could transform my desire for promiscuity into a desire for marriage and intimacy, could He also transform my sexual orientation?

TWELVE

THE FRUIT

"AM I STILL attracted to other men?" the guest speaker asked rhetorically.

Mitch was an ex-gay man whom my church invited to share his testimony. While telling his story, he explained, "I was arrested for prostitution. I went from being a prostitute to a pastor." But the church introduced Mitch as someone who was delivered from *being gay*. In his story, there seemed to be no distinction between prostitution and homosexuality.

Mitch's most striking statement was his response to his own question.

"Yes," he admitted. "I still find myself attracted to other men. There are still things about men that compel me to want to know them more than what I believe is okay. It's definitely going to be something that I will wrestle with for the rest of my life. But that doesn't mean I'm gay."

I was shocked. To me, that meant he was gay.

By Mitch's own confession, same-sex attraction, or being gay, is an immutable trait, so to me, there was something that seemed off about his description of his deliverance. I experienced God's power to transform my heart, so it didn't make sense that if being gay actually is a sin, it wouldn't be something God would transform. Of course, the Word says that we are "*being* transformed into the same image [of Yeshua] from one degree of glory to another."[1] But it seemed that the recovery group at my church taught us that our sexual orientation wasn't going to transform at all. It was only something we could suppress.

After I was baptized with the Holy Spirit, I noticed many lust sources in my life. On social media, I was bombarded with sexy underwear ads. The TV shows I watched basically had softcore porn scenes, and the music I listened to had a lot of sexual themes. Although I used to enjoy all of it, suddenly, I hated it. It reminded me too much of porn. I realized that the things that once entertained me had normalized the hypersexuality that I once lived in. It reminded me too much of the darkness that God pulled me out of.

Yeshua was my only escape from the world's pornified culture. Everything that once entertained me now grieved me, but Yeshua became my source of joy. So I did my best to hide inappropriate ads from my social media, and I followed more people who shared things about God. I no longer watched certain TV shows or listened to certain music. Instead, I almost solely listened to worship music. I fell so in love with Yeshua that I no longer needed much of the world's stuff that once delighted me. My former sin was no longer as enticing as it once was.

Experiencing an overflow of power to overcome sin after the baptism in the Holy Spirit is not unique to my story. It seemed to be the typical Spirit-filled Christian testimony. In the recovery sessions, Pastor Andrew would invite people who had experienced sobriety for a certain period of time to share their stories in the main services. Week after week, I heard people share how God empowered them to overcome their sins.

One young woman stood up to share her testimony. She looked nervous as she fidgeted with her hands in front of her.

"Hi, I'm Jessica, a grateful believer in Jesus Christ, and I struggled with drug addiction," she said. "No matter how much I wanted to stop, I kept doing it. Until one day, when I was out of drugs, completely broke, and unable to buy food, I cried out to God for help. And it was like His Spirit came upon me."

I could see Jessica's eyes were welling up with tears, which she fought to hold back. It was as if we were watching her relive this moment right in front of us.

Jessica said through a slight laugh, "At first, I thought I was crazy, but I knew I wasn't because I could tell God was doing something inside of me." Her face lit up as she continued to speak. "I didn't want drugs anymore. In fact, since then, I've been clean for twelve months."

The auditorium erupted in applause. Pastor Andrew stepped over to give Jessica one of his big hugs. Then it was time for another person to share their testimony.

A large, older man went to the front. "I'm Dan, a grateful believer in Jesus Christ, and I struggled with alcoholism. I used to drink to self-medicate my depression and anxiety. It got to where I was drinking a quart of vodka a day. And I tried everything to stop—psychiatry, rehab—nothing helped for more than a couple of days or, at most, a week.

"Then one night, I got on my knees and prayed. At that moment, I knew that the Holy Spirit was filling me with power, and I had the faith to believe that He was delivering me from alcohol. The deliverance came with such an impact that it changed my life. I realized that Jesus is so much better than alcohol. I threw out all my liquor because the smell of it alone repulses me now."

I knew what Dan meant. Like him, I used to drink to numb myself from the life I had been living. Alcohol was a tool for me to dissociate from the trauma that was once normal to me. After the baptism in the Spirit, I was so full of God, so captured by Him, that I haven't been the same since. After the Spirit baptism, I stopped drinking. I no longer needed it. Like Dan, just the smell of alcohol causes me to gag now.

And I wasn't the only one to experience the power of God to overcome sex addiction. A young man with spikey hair and muscles bulging from his shirt stood up and went to the front.

"I'm James, a grateful believer in Jesus Christ, and I struggled with sex addiction."

I leaned forward in my seat.

"Women, please forgive me. I was raised thinking that to be a real man, I had to objectify women. I used to watch porn every night. I went to strip clubs regularly. And every weekend, I was the guy at the bar trying to get you in bed and then never text you back. But now, with Jesus, I've been waiting until marriage for the last two years."

James smiled as everyone clapped. His testimony reminded me of my own testimony, except that he was straight.

Then James began to preach, "If you're still struggling with any sin, look, all you need is the grace of God. Once you really understand God's love for you and the grace He has for you, you will be made totally free.

"What's interesting to me now is that porn has flashed before me since then. Like on the internet, I've stumbled upon hardcore porn a couple of times. It used to draw me in, but now, it's so disgusting to me. And today, because God's love is in my heart, I recognize that porn is degrading to women. It's so amazing to me just how much God's grace has changed my heart's desires. I don't even have the desire to look at porn anymore. I hate it."

James' testimony reminded me of something I had read in the Word of God.

> Delight yourself in the LORD, and He will give you the desires of your heart. Commit your way to the LORD; trust in Him, and he will act. He will bring forth your righteousness as the light, and your justice as the noonday.[2]

This passage means that God will give us *new* desires when we turn to Him. He will give us His desires. His Holy Spirit places righteous and just desires in our hearts,[3] and He will fulfill those desires.

Since knowing Yeshua, I experienced new desires. Like James, God took my hypersexualized heart and transformed me to have a higher value for myself and others. Unlike Mitch, who claimed to be ex-gay yet still was drawn to other men, I now felt no compulsion to go back to my former sin in porn. Instead, Yeshua's love compels me to love.

As I listened week after week to people testify about their triumph over sin by the grace of God, I imagined how I might tell my testimony. How could I tell mine? How would people react? Would they even be able to hear something like that? If they did listen, how would they respond? Would they celebrate the power of God? Would they doubt it was true because I'm gay? The best thing would be that people would repent from using porn, like James did.

AFTER MITCH preached about overcoming same-sex attraction, the guys in the SSA meeting spoke with their eyes glued to the floor, as if defeated in a massive fistfight between themselves and their same-sex attraction. They sighed in defeat at the revelation that their sexual orientation, the very thing they were seeking freedom from, would last the rest of their lives.

After church, some of the guys from the group and I went out to lunch at a 1950's-style diner. Mike, the older man who admitted to me that he was gay and affirming, came with us. Another guy who came, Eric, was about a decade older than me. I had only seen Eric in the SSA group once since I had been attending. I thought it was because he didn't need the group anymore since our church claimed that Eric had been delivered from same-sex attraction. Preston, like Ryder, was a leader in the SSA group. He was a talented musician on the church's worship team, and when he sang, a great passion poured from his heart. But it was fading.

"I've been really struggling with my faith," Preston admitted, pushing some of his eggs around with a fork. "From what I understand from Mitch, no one can change same-sex attraction. It won't turn into an attraction for women. They say it's like any other addiction that may be a lifelong disease, but drug addicts get hooked on a drug because they do the drug in the first place. I didn't do anything; no one did anything to cause me to be attracted to men. I don't get how we can compare same-sex attraction to addiction."

Since Preston was one of the SSA group leaders, it was startling for me to hear him say that.

Eric looked at Preston and made a similar confession. "That's why I haven't been going to the recovery group as much anymore. I can't stand going. It makes me too depressed."

"Wait! What?" I interrupted. "You're like their poster boy for freedom from SSA."

Since Eric had been a part of the SSA group the longest, our church claimed that Eric had recovered from same-sex attraction. In a special recovery service, the church leaders asked, and Eric agreed to hold up a sign saying, "Lost and lonely in homosexual addiction. Now found and alive in God's grace and truth. Nine months pure. Praying for a wife!"

Eric sighed, "I convinced myself that I was 'healed,' but Mitch is right. My SSA hasn't really changed, and I'm not really looking for a wife because I'm still not attracted to women."

Mike wrinkled his eyebrows. "It is interesting to me. Mitch's testimony seemed so different from the testimonies that people from the other recovery groups share."

"Yeah, I noticed that too," I said.

"Yeah." Preston looked up from his plate. "I'm not sure I believe any of this anymore. I'm not sure I even believe in God anymore."

The words came out of his mouth softly, but they hit my heart with a heavy thud that has stuck with me even today. After years of seeking Jesus for transformation, Eric and Preston were losing their love for God.

I sat silently and listened. I wanted to say something, but I wasn't sure anything I could say would help. I wished that I could take them back to the moment when I encountered God in my room. I wished that I could take them to the moment when I was filled with His Spirit. I wanted them to encounter the same living, tangible presence of the Almighty Who I knew. My experiences left me unable to deny His existence. I *know* God is real.

I SPENT a lot of time meditating on the difference between my transformation and what I heard from the SSA group. Often, when I meditated, I would go on a prayer hike through the Hollywood hills. On one particular occasion, I meditated on Yeshua's words, "You will recognize them by their fruits."[4]

Believers in Yeshua are like trees. As we grow, we repent; we allow Yeshua to prune off anything that would hinder our growth. Repentance isn't so much about behavior modification as it is about heart transformation. When following Yeshua, our hearts transform through His grace to bear the good fruit of *love* in our lives, and this love flows out of us in new behaviors.

Of course, even a non-believer can be loving, but the kind of love the Bible talks about is deeper than the world's common love. It is a love that is willing to lay down one's own life for the sake of others. It is a love that looks with compassion and mercy upon even those who hate and oppress us. It is a higher form of love that is sourced completely from the Almighty God.

The recovery group did provide some spiritual fruit for me because God used it to show me that I needed Him to heal me from the hypersexuality with which porn and rape had tarnished my heart. But there seemed to be a lack of fruit for everyone I knew when it came to freedom from same-sex attraction.

On my meditation hikes, there would often be other men on the trail hiking shirtless. Their muscles flexed with every step, their skin glistened with sweat, and my eyes were drawn to them. I didn't have lustful thoughts about them, though; I simply found them attractive.

As I noticed my attraction, I remembered when one of my straight friends and I visited a new church. At this church, a beautiful young woman led worship, and my friend was captivated by her beauty.

At one point, an older man worshiping next to my friend leaned over to him and said, "She's pretty, isn't she?"

"She is," he smiled. Then his smile faded, and he looked over at me. At that moment, my friend realized that although he could be open in church about his crushes, I and other gay Christians in the congregation could not.

For my straight friend, there was nothing wrong with his opposite-sex attraction. He wasn't looking at the woman to think lustful thoughts about her. He simply appreciated her beauty. His sexual orientation was seen as a good thing that would eventually lead to an even better thing—marriage.[5] And no one thinks it's wrong for him to desire marriage and the sexual intimacy that comes with it.

If my straight friend were married, his attraction to women still wouldn't be a bad thing. He could still find women beautiful as long as he didn't look at them with lust. If lust did creep into his heart, then he could shift his eyes to God, Who will give him holier desires. As a single man, my friend could lean on the hope of one day marrying a beautiful woman. When he is married, he could act on his sexual orientation through the intimacy he shares with his wife. My straight friend had an appropriate, loving outlet for his sexual orientation through marriage.

But if homosexuality is a sin, then there isn't a loving outlet for that sexual orientation. If homosexuality is a sin, then when I saw a man I was attracted to, I would need to flee from that attraction because there would be something inherently wrong with my desire for the same sex.

Of course, a same-sex attracted person could marry someone of the opposite sex, but that doesn't transform their desire for the same sex. Marrying the opposite sex would be a behavior modification, but not a heart transformation. A same-sex-attracted individual's heterosexual marriage does not take away their homosexual orientation. By even Mitch's own confession, same-sex attraction remains. And for me, the thought of the Church coercing same-sex-attracted people into marrying someone of the opposite sex seemed too much like what I experienced in prostitution: being groomed into having unwanted sex. People are worthy of marrying someone who wants to be with them.

Another option the modern Church has thrown at same-sex-attracted individuals is to remain celibate for life. It seemed that Christians with this view are teaching us to suppress the "temptation" to fall in love and start a family. We had to resist romantic love.

As I continued to hike up the Hollywood hills, I noticed a family. Two dads of two little boys hiking together. One of the dads picked up the littlest boy to carry him on his shoulders up a steep climb. They were a family, but if they went to most churches, they would be told they couldn't be a family.

I thought of my Christian high school teacher, her wife, and their kids. She had been sharing social media posts of their sons growing up. They had videos of the boys praying, worshiping, and reciting scripture. They were a family who loved God. My heart broke at the thought of their family going into a church and being told that they needed to divorce and dissolve their family. The thought seemed entirely unloving.

It echoed within me, *"You will recognize them by their fruit... The fruit of the Spirit is love... against such things there is no law."* [6]

There is no Biblical law against love.

Love is precisely why I know that porn is not what God wants for anyone. By its nature, I experienced no love in porn. I was treated like a piece of meat to be devoured, not a human worthy of love. When Yeshua touched my heart with His love, the hate and degradation inherent to porn became clear to me. Porn and prostitution are sinful because they fall short of the glory of God's love.

But sexual orientation is different from prostitution. The gay dads I saw on my hike were so different from porn. My former teacher's family is different from porn. They love each other, and there is no sin in love. A person's sexual orientation is an immutable trait that determines their capacity for romantic love. No matter how much I meditated and sought the Spirit about it, it seemed so wrong within my heart that the Church would forbid love for gay couples.

In my church, I was seeing what kind of fruit was born from forbidding love in a same-sex-attracted person's life. Everyone from the SSA group seemed to walk with such a heavy burden even though Yeshua promised that His burden is light.[7] All I could smell was the stench of rotting, dying fruit burning in my spiritual nostrils. Not only was the fruit bad, but many of the trees eventually died. Within that year, Eric, Preston, Ryder, and others left the SSA group, left the church, and left their faith. They didn't believe they could be Christian and gay at the same time. And since they couldn't stop being gay, they stopped being Christian. The church eventually had to stop offering the SSA group because no one attended it anymore.

Of course, someone leaving Christianity because they disagree with the teachings doesn't mean the teachings are necessarily wrong. But when someone truly seeks God to the point that they are willing to—as the Bible calls it—die to self and be a living sacrifice,[8] but they never experience the fruit of that sacrifice, it may be a sign that something is off. Good, healthy, Biblical teaching is supposed to bear the fruit of freedom, deliverance, and healing from sin. Yeshua's teaching turns us towards godly love, but the guys in the SSA group had the opposite experience.

While I attended the SSA group, I watched as Exodus International, the world's largest ex-gay ministry at the time, shut down because its slogan, "Change is Possible," was not possible. The president of the organization said, "The majority of people that I have met, and I would say the majority, meaning 99.9% of them, have not experienced a change in their orientation."[9]

National health associations warn against attempts to "cure" someone's sexual orientation.[10] The National Association of Social Workers states that someone's sexual orientation "cannot and will not change."[11] These organizations claim that conversion therapy, like the SSA group, cause "loss of sexual feeling, depression, suicidality, and anxiety."[12] That's not the good fruit born by turning to Yeshua. Those are bad fruits! It's almost as if these are the fruits born by attempting to heal something that doesn't need to be healed. To me, the bad fruit was sitting right in front of us, infested with maggots, but my church seemed to plug their noses and ignore it.

. . .

Pastor Pete preached, "We believe the Bible is the Word of God." I sat in a church room, taking a membership class. Pastor Pete paused and looked over his glasses at me. Although he spoke as if he were speaking to everyone, he locked his eyes directly on me.

"If you don't believe the Bible is the Word of God, then I would suggest finding a *different* church." After letting his statement sit on me for a moment, Pastor Pete turned to everyone else. "Everything we do is based on the Bible."

After seeing what the guys experienced in the SSA group, I decided to become more open about being gay at church. I wanted people to see that being gay doesn't necessarily mean promiscuity. Pastor Pete knew that I was openly gay, and it seemed that he assumed that because I'm gay, I must not believe the Bible.

But unlike my friends from SSA, I didn't feel that I had the option to deny that the Bible is the Word of God. I had heard God's voice, and He continued to speak to me through His Word. Even though people constantly used the Bible to explain why a homosexual orientation doesn't fit into the Kingdom of God, I couldn't deny its power. The voice of the Word sounded too much like the voice I heard, the voice Who said, "*I love you.*"

My experiences left me without a choice. God is real. The Bible is His Word. But there was so much bad fruit from the traditional teaching on same-sex attraction. There was only one other option. The traditional teaching on homosexuality *must* be wrong. I had to reexamine the clobber passages.

THIRTEEN

THE SPIRIT OF PORN

I N MY SOPHOMORE year of high school, my mom took me to
visit my aunt and uncle's church. It was a small congregation
that met in an old, white building. During service, I attended
the youth group meeting with seven other teenagers. We sat in a
small circle as Pastor Tami, a plump woman in her late thirties,
taught us from the Bible.

"God destroyed Sodom and Gomorrah because all the men
were homosexuals," she preached with a sweet, sing-song voice. If
someone wasn't paying attention to her words, they might have
thought she was preaching on Jesus' unending love for humanity.
"Lot offered up his daughters to appease the Sodomites' sexual
desires, but the men of Sodom were so homosexual that they
denied Lot's daughters because they wanted to have sex with men."

"Wait, I'm confused," a younger girl interrupted. "What
does that mean?"

An older girl laughed, "It means those guys were hot."

Pastor Tami continued, "What the men of Sodom were
and what they wanted is so clear that it is from this story that

we get the word 'sodomy.'"

I contorted my face to look as disgusted as I could. I was afraid that Pastor Tami or someone else might think that I might be attracted to other guys, and I wanted to hide the truth from even myself.

"What's sodomy?" the younger girl asked.

The older girl was still laughing. "Man-on-man action."

"Yes, that's right," Pastor Tami confirmed.

What wasn't correct is how she made it seem as if the word "sodomy" had been around for as long as the Bible. Actually, the first use of "sodomy" in English comes from around the thirteenth century, thousands of years after the Sodom story took place. People used the word to describe any non-procreative sexual activity, including oral sex.[1] It came from a less ancient interpretation of the story. I wish I had known that then.

"God destroyed Sodom and Gomorrah like He will destroy America if we embrace homosexuality," Pastor Tami said in a calm, matter-of-fact manner.

Although my church visits were infrequent as a child, this was my biggest takeaway: God is disgusted by gay people because they appease their sexual desires by sexually traumatizing other men. I carried this memory with me until I was raped, which solidified the idea and eventually led me to believe that selling myself was a normal part of being gay.

But in all the times that I'd heard a sermon on same-sex attraction or homosexuality, one thing that was never brought up is whether or not gay couples actually love each other. If love fulfills the Word of God, then sin is the opposite of love, and if being gay is a sin, then that would imply that gay couples do not really love each other. They do exactly what I saw them do in porn; they make hate to each other.

From my experience, churches that taught the traditional interpretation of the clobber passages seemed to—either consciously or subconsciously—assume some level of exploitation in their understanding of homosexuality. My church in Los Angeles invited Mitch to share his ex-gay testimony, but Mitch's story revolved around him being prostituted. It seemed his perspective implied that prostitution is a part of being gay.

A female friend of mine, who was also formerly prostituted in porn, claimed to be "ex-gay." When she was a child, she was molested by a teenage girl. Then as an adult in the porn industry, she was gay-for-pay. She was never attracted to women, but in her eyes, her childhood rape and being gay-for-pay was enough to say that she used to be gay, even though, by definition, she never really was. The situations of Mitch and my ex-gay-for-pay friend were clearly exploitative, but they weren't in loving relationships with someone of the same sex. Those with the traditional view seemed to have an inability to divorce a homosexual orientation from sexual exploitation.

When I opened my Bible and grappled with the clobber passages, I grew nauseated by how these stories are taught today. I saw clearly why the modern Church might struggle with separating homosexuality from exploitation. All of the clobber passages have more to do with pornography and prostitution than with being gay.

SEVERAL PEOPLE from my church were interested in the clobber passages, so I decided to organize a little Bible study to talk through them. My church would never allow us to meet in their building, but a friend's church welcomed us to study the Word in one of their classrooms. We had a nice-sized little group going. Mike, the older man from the SSA group, joined. I was still pretty new to the faith, so I thought it was great to have him around since he was older and more experienced. A new friend of mine named Barnabas also joined. He was a decade older than me, and he was familiar with the LGBTQ-affirming Christian movement. He and I were different in many ways, but he loved God with similar exuberance.

At first, I tried to conduct the Bible study like a discussion, but no one else really spoke, except for Mike, Barnabas, and me. When we discussed the clobber passages, I ended up essentially teaching. I stood in front of everyone with a dry-erase board.

"First of all," I said, "I want to be absolutely, one-hundred percent clear. I believe, like the Bible says, 'All Scripture is breathed out by God and profitable for teaching, for reproof, for correction, and for training in righteousness.'[2] This includes the clobber passages."

Mike nodded his head in agreement.

"However, I also believe that these passages cannot be about LGBT+ people. But instead of talking about what these passages are *not* about, I'd like to take a look at what they *are* about."

I picked up a marker to begin to write on the board.

I said, "There are twelve verses in the Bible that reference same-sex sexual activity."

"Wait! There's only like six clobber passages," Barnabas interrupted.

"Well, there are twelve times that some form of same-sex sex is addressed throughout the entire Bible. Seven of them have clear contexts. Five of them are a little bit more ambiguous. I want to look at all of these because I believe we must let scripture interpret scripture. If we look at the five vague verses in light of the clearer seven, we can understand them better."

I wrote on the board:

Genesis 19, Judges 19:22-26, Deuteronomy 23:17-18,
1 Kings 14:24, 1 Kings 15:12, 1 Kings 22:46, 2 Kings 23:7

"These are the clear seven verses," I said. "The first two—Genesis and Judges—are about a group of men attempting to gang-rape other men. These other five verses—Deuteronomy and 1 and 2 Kings—are about male prostitutes."

When I was studying these passages in my private time, it struck me as wrong that the modern Church had consistently compared Sodom to gay people. Just because the men of Sodom wanted to rape men doesn't mean they were homosexuals. Rape is not about attraction; it's usually about asserting violent power. In prison and in the military, straight men often rape other men to assert dominance. In porn, straight men performed rape scenes on me because, even in the gay community, being straight or "straight acting" is seen as being more dominant. Even in ancient times, rape was often used to assert superiority. In the case of both Genesis 19 and Judges 19:22-26, rape was used to demonstrate just how inferior the people believed foreigners were. For the Church to say that gay people are like the men of Sodom, it says that many people in the Church might believe—either consciously or subconsciously—that gay men are rapists.

And coming from gay porn, the passages about prostituted men really stuck out to me.

"Okay, but other than Sodom and Gomorrah, no one says that these passages are about gay people," one woman argued.

"Well, some Christians do say that these are about gay people because some Bible translations, like the King James Version, use the word 'sodomites' instead of 'male prostitutes.' So some Christians have confused these verses to be about gay people. To me, this confusion between homosexuality and prostitution shows that many modern Christians maybe don't fully understand the Biblical context of the clobber passages, or the nature of prostitution, or what it means for a person to have a homosexual orientation."

I pointed to the references written on the board, saying, "These seven passages paint a picture of the common circumstances in which ancient believers saw same-sex sexual activity. From what I understand, if the Bible is sufficient to interpret itself, then we have to understand these seven passages to truly understand the other passages that are supposedly about gay people."

I wrote on the board:

"You shall not lie with a male as with a woman; it is an abomination." (Leviticus 18:22)

"If a man lies with a male as with a woman, both of them have committed an abomination; they shall surely be put to death; their blood is upon them." (Leviticus 20:13)

As I wrote it, the same woman who interrupted earlier blurted out, "See! Isn't that clear?"

I turned to face her. "But we have to look at the rest of the Bible to understand the world in which ancient believers described this idea. For most laws in the Bible, there are specific examples of that law being broken somewhere else in the rest of the Word. When it comes to these two, the *only* examples that exist are rape and prostitution, which tells me that when the ancient people heard about a 'man lying with a male,' they most likely thought about rape and prostitution."

The woman squinted her eyes as if she was thinking really hard about it.

"Okay, look at this," I said. "In Deuteronomy 23:17-18, the Word says that none of the sons or daughters of Israel shall be prostitutes. And it says not to bring the wages of prostitution, neither male nor female, into the house of God because *prostitution* is an abomination. It uses the same language as Leviticus 18:22."

Some people seemed to nod their heads as if they understood, but the woman still looked confused.

"And," I continued, "1 Kings 14:24 also uses the same language as Leviticus. It calls male prostitution an abomination, and it even says that male prostitution was a behavior that the people did in the land of Israel before the Israelites lived there."

Barnabas cocked his head to the side. "Why does that matter?"

"Because look at Leviticus 18. The entire chapter is bookended with the idea that the Israelites should not do what the people did in the land before them. The entire purpose of chapter 18 is to make Israel a nation that looks different and set apart from other cultures around them. According to the Bible, the people around Israel used prostituted males. In ancient times, prostitution was used as a form of idol worship. Having sex with a prostituted person in a pagan temple was a way to get intimate with a pagan god or goddess.[3] That idolatry is an abomination, but there is not a single example of a same-sex relationship throughout the Bible.[c] It doesn't say anything about same-sex couples in romantic relationships, living together, and raising a family. We don't see that. We do see male-on-male rape and male prostitution. Those are the *only* specific examples we have of a man lying with a male."

When I was studying the clobber passages, I thought that if the Church took such a strong stance against gay couples, then there must be some example of a gay couple in the Bible being condemned. But there wasn't. The lack of a same-sex couple in the Bible is precisely because this type of relationship was mostly unheard of for people at the time. If gay couples had been so common, surely they would have been referenced at some point in scripture. But in fact, the Bible was written at a time when there was no understanding of sexual orientation.[4]

Sexual orientation first began to be understood by psychiatrists starting in the late nineteenth century, and the mainstream culture didn't widely understand the concept until the last few decades. In ancient times, people assumed that any man, regardless of his actual orientation, could be inclined to have sex with other men due to excessive, unquenchable lust. Typically, same-sex sex happened in exploitative circumstances like rape, prostitution, and pederasty.[5] But these clobber passages say nothing about "same-sex attraction" nor loving same-sex relationships.

"What about Romans 1?" one of the other guys asked.

---

[c] Some argue that David and Jonathan, Ruth and Naomi, or the centurion and his servant from Matthew 8:5-13 were in romantic relationships. Reading these relationships as gay seems a bit too farfetched for me. The Bible does not mention romance in these relationships.

"Great segue," I laughed. "Romans 1:26-27 starts with the phrase, 'For this reason…' Well, what was the reason?"

"Idol worship," Barnabas answered in a tone that let me know that he knew where I was going.

"Right! In Romans 1, Paul speaks about how humans 'exchanged the glory of the immortal God for images resembling mortal men and birds and animals and creeping things.'[6] That's idol worship! Everything Paul describes in Romans 1 takes place within the context of ancient Roman paganism, and prostitution was a part of that, just like it was in 1 and 2 Kings."

When I researched the ancient world, I saw a lot of similarities with the modern world. In the decadent, first-century Roman culture, men sexually used anyone of lower social status— his female and male slaves, female and male prostitutes, and children.[7] Regardless of the sex of the person they penetrated, Roman men exploited the most vulnerable in their society for their own sexual gratification. This power dynamic of the superior exploiting the inferior reminds me of the spirit behind prostitution; in prostitution, marginalized people are degraded as sex objects.

I continued, "When Roman men had sex with prostituted men, male slaves, or men of a lower class, they were 'men committing shameless acts with men.' Even if it were in the context of pederasty where an adult man had sex with a boy, which was common in ancient times, I would consider that a form of prostitution. By today's legal standards, it'd be considered rape or sex trafficking. To the ancient Romans, it was acceptable as long as the adult citizen was the penetrator because he could use sexual penetration to assert his dominance over socially inferior males. Still, it had nothing to do with his sexual orientation.

"And many argue that this passage refers to gay women, but that's unlikely because female same-sex activity was very rarely discussed in ancient times.[8] Within the context of idol worship, Paul more likely refers to women having promiscuous, excessive sex, as they would be expected to have as prostituted women."

When I first read Romans 1, one of the biggest things that stood out to me was Paul using the word "unnatural." Many assume that same-sex activity is what Paul calls "unnatural," but for me, coming from prostitution, I can think of nothing more unnatural than exchanging money for sex. It is utterly unnatural to take something as natural as sexual intimacy and exchange it for human-made money. That unnatural exchange was a common way that sex between men happened in the ancient world. The lust-filled language of Romans 1 reminds me too much of all forms of sexual exploitation, but it doesn't say anything about gay couples in love.

"And now to my favorite passages on this topic because they make it so obvious to me," I said. I erased everything I had written on the board, and I wrote:

1 Corinthians 6:9–10, 1 Timothy 1:10
malakoi, arsenokoitai

1 Corinthians 6:9-10 was the first verse I read when I first got my Bible. It was the verse right before I read that I was bought with a price.

I said, "1 Corinthians 6 tells us that the unrighteous will not inherit the Kingdom of God. Then it lists several types of unrighteous people. On that list, in my ESV Bible, is 'men who practice homosexuality.'"

I pointed on the board where I wrote the two Greek terms. "'Men who practice homosexuality' is a combined translation of these two words. But what's interesting is that translators never translated these words to mean homosexual men until the Revised Standard Version (RSV) translated the terms to 'homosexuals' in 1946, during a time when sexual orientation was still not well understood. Then, later translations, like my ESV, followed the RSV's example."

I picked up another Bible that I had.

"This is my New Revised Standard Version (NRSV) Bible, an updated RSV. It translates the words to 'male prostitutes' and 'sodomites,' which makes more sense within the historical context."

I opened my NRSV Bible and turned to 1 Corinthians 6:9-10.

"Listen to this footnote." I read, "'*Male prostitutes* ("malakoi"), literally, "soft," referring to moral and physical weakness, and perhaps also to being sexually submissive or coerced; *sodomites* ("arsenokoitai," a term of uncertain meaning combining "male" and "bed"), perhaps those guilty of coercing others sexually.' Look at what this footnote says about this translation. 'The translation is not a good one since the original reference has nothing to do with Sodom...'"9

Some of the people listening seemed to lean forward in their seats.

"Hold that thought as we look at 1 Timothy 1:10," I said.

I turned back to the board, and I wrote:

1) The lawless and disobedient, the ungodly and sinners, the unholy and profane
2) Father strikers, mother strikers, murderers
3) Sexually immoral, arsenokoitai, enslavers
4) Liars, perjurers, whatever else is contrary to sound doctrine

"1 Timothy says that the Biblical Law is not laid down for the just but for these people. I wrote these on the board because I want you guys to see that Paul uses a pattern in this list.

"The first category is general sinfulness. The second category is actually about murder. Father and mother strikers specifically refer to those who *murder* their parents. Apparently, that was a thing back in the first century. The third category is about sexual sin. And the final category is about general falsehood.

"But do you guys notice the break in the pattern?"

Everyone stared at the board for a moment.

"I'll give you a hint," I said, pointing to the board. "It's in this third section."

Everyone continued to look at the board.

A man laughed, "Maybe you should just tell us."

I circled the word "enslavers" and asked, "What do enslavers have to do with sexual sin?"

"Oh," everyone seemed to say in unison.

"What we have in this section is 'sexually immoral,' which comes from the original word '*pornois.*' This word also translates to both male and female prostitutes.[10] It's from *pornois* that we get the word 'pornography' because porn is documented prostitution. If someone had sex outside of marriage, they were also generally referred to as *pornois*; they were just *pornois* who didn't receive payment.[d]

"Then we have '*arsenokoitai*' followed by 'enslavers.' The word for 'enslavers' could also be translated to 'kidnappers.'[11] It refers

---

[d] In Ezekiel 16:31-34, God compared Jerusalem to a prostitute who doesn't receive payment. In God's eyes, even if someone is not paid, they can still act like a prostituted person by devaluing themselves through uncommitted sex.

specifically to those who steal and sell people into slavery, but in this context, Paul is talking about sex-traffickers, pimps, and sex-sellers."

Again, the room seemed to give a unified, "Oh."

"In 1 Timothy, Paul addresses the entire system of prostitution. He mentions people who submit their bodies and their pimps, so what's missing to fill in the gap for *aresenokoitai*?"

One smart guy spoke for the first time, "People who have sex with prostitutes?"

"Yes!" I exclaimed. "Sex-buyers. *Arsenokoitai* are sex-buyers. This passage could just as easily be translated as 'prostitutes, sex-buyers, and pimps.'"

It makes so much sense to me. If *malakoi* are male prostitutes, then *arsenokoitai* are the men who rent them. Today, *arsenokoitai* applies to those who rent prostituted people, those who watch pornography, those who go to strip clubs, rapists, child rapists, and any other situation in which sex is bought, coerced, and/or taken by force. But Paul did not have in mind loving, same-sex marriages because that was a foreign concept to him.

The clobber passages may not be about LGBT+ people, but they do have a lot to tell us about the world today. Because I was prostituted, I am familiar with the spirit of prostitution. Temple prostitution may not be as common today as it was in the ancient world. Still, the same spirit present in ancient temple prostitution is in modern prostitution and porn. The spirit of porn seduces this generation, just like temple prostitution seduced ancient generations. Porn is as normalized today as temple prostitution was back then. Porn is the same spirit, just evolved for a new generation.

Coming from prostitution, I see the problems the traditional interpretation creates for the Church. There are countless prostituted men, but the Church's main resources for prostituted people are focused mostly on women. Of course, in our patriarchal society, women make up the vast majority of prostituted people, but men can also be prostituted. Women in prostitution are seen as exploited, but because the modern Church fails to see sexual exploitation in the clobber passages, they also mistake prostituted men for same-sex-attracted men. If those verses are about homosexuality, then a homosexual orientation is the problem, not prostitution. So the Church misses out on saving and offering discipleship to a whole demographic of men who need healing from prostitution, not their sexual orientation.

Even though I went to church only a few times as a youth, the traditional interpretation of these passages messed up my perspective on what it means to be gay. The Church groomed me to associate my sexual orientation with exploitation. By saying the clobber passages are about same-sex couples, the modern Church—either consciously or subconsciously—marries the LGBT+ community to a pornographic spirit. By inviting ex-gays to talk about their rape and prostitution, as if that is what it means to be LGBT+, the modern Church marries the LGBT+ experience to a pornographic spirit. By considering all same-sex acts as gay regardless of an exploitative context, the modern Church marries LGBT+ love to a pornographic spirit. What we speak produces either life or death,[12] and what the modern Church has traditionally spoken over my community has bound many of us to a pornographic spirit.

In much the same way that pornography exposes children to unhealthy sexuality and grooms them into traumatic experiences, the modern Church's teachings on what it means to be LGBT+ cause LGBT+ children to have unhealthy views of their sexuality. It traumatizes gay kids. It happened to me, and I know I'm not alone in that experience.

After the Bible study was over, I wanted to share my personal testimony with these friends. It seemed to be the best way to explain where this interpretation came from, but I chose not to tell them yet. The trauma of prostitution was still too fresh. I wasn't ready to relive it by talking about it. Since mostly everyone seemed to agree that the clobber passages were more about sexual exploitation than gay people, I assumed they understood that porn and prostitution are unloving. But I couldn't tell them about me yet. I needed a little bit more time.

FOURTEEN

EUNUCHS

A NEW WOMAN began to attend my church, and many congregants assumed she was a transgender woman. When she joined in the worship, some people raised their eyebrows and requested that leadership rebuke transgender identity. The only problem was that Rachel is not a transgender woman. She's *intersex*. Intersex is an umbrella term to describe atypical sex traits or reproductive anatomy. While uncommon, intersex is not as rare as it may sound. According to InterACT, an advocacy group for intersex youth, about 1.7% of people are born intersex, and 1 in 2,000 babies are born with noticeable genital ambiguities.[1]

When an intersex child is born, many doctors recommend performing surgery to "normalize" the child's genitals. However, this is a procedure that InterACT does not recommend doing at birth because the child may be assigned a gender with which they do not identify later in life. That's exactly what happened to Rachel.

Rachel and I became friends while we attended our church. She explained that when she was born, her parents allowed the doctor to change her genitals and make her into a boy. But when

Rachel grew older, she struggled with the gender the doctor had assigned to her. As a teenager, she thought she might be gay, and then she was curious that she might be transgender. It wasn't until later in life that she discovered she was born intersex and had been incorrectly assigned a male gender. Then Rachel realized that she was not a man; she is a woman. At which point, she changed her name and began to live as the person she always knew she was: Rachel.

Similar to how I came out to my church's leadership team, Rachel came out as intersex. When Rachel wanted to serve on the worship team, she was given the "Standards of Ministry" to sign. She didn't sign it because the church expected unmarried people to have only same-sex roommates. Rachel had two roommates, a man and a woman, so this complicated things for her.

I thank God for Rachel's presence at my church at that time because her existence got me to look even further into the Word of God to understand the situation for sexual minorities.

As I got to know Rachel, a question burned in my heart. *Are intersex people in the Bible?* For that matter, if the clobber passages aren't about gay people, then *are there any gay people in the Bible?* If intersex people and gay people are a part of God's creation, clearly, we aren't a surprise to Him. If God inspired the Bible, and I believe He did, where are LGBTQIA people in His Word?

For some affirming Christians, saying the Bible says nothing about sexual orientation is enough to say God approves of same-sex marriage. Still, for me, I couldn't assume a mere lack of a mention is God's acceptance. After all, the idea of internet pornography is not mentioned specifically in the Bible. The early Church would never have imagined that every possible sexual experience would be accessible to everyone through a little screen that fits in their pocket. If porn isn't specifically mentioned, does that mean it's okay? *No!* I know first-hand that prostitution and porn are unloving, so they are sins.

But what about being gay? Or intersex? How could an entire demographic—the entire community of sexual minorities—be missing from the Word of God?

As I prayed about it, God showed me something that I hadn't noticed before.

"I HAVE a question," I said as I sat down to talk with Pastor Andrew.

He smiled as he always did. "Okay. I might have an answer."

Pastor Andrew knew Rachel, so I wondered what he would think of what I saw in the Word.

I said, "So in Matthew 19, Jesus was asked about divorce, and He's like, *'Divorce is not cool because the two become one.'* And He quotes from Genesis that God created us male and female, and the two become one in marriage."

Pastor Andrew leaned forward in his chair with a big grin on his face, like he expected that I was about to announce that I'm no longer gay or something.

I continued, "But Jesus' disciples said if that is the case with a man and his wife, maybe it's better not to marry. Then Jesus says, *'Not everyone can receive this because there are eunuchs. Some eunuchs are born that way, some eunuchs have been made that way, and some eunuchs choose to be eunuchs for the sake of the Kingdom of God.'"*[2]

Pastor Andrew's eyebrows wrinkled as he tried to follow along.

"Obviously, eunuchs for the sake of the Kingdom of God are those who choose to be celibate to focus all of their attention on ministry. Those who are made eunuchs are those who are castrated. But who are the eunuchs who are born that way?"

I waited for a moment to see if Pastor Andrew had an answer, but he leaned back in his seat. His smile seemed to fade to a half-smile, and his eyes seemed concerned with confusion.

I asked, "Is it possible that Jesus had sexual minorities in mind?"

"Sexual minorities? Like who?"

"Like intersex people? They aren't specifically mentioned in the Bible, but could Jesus have had them in mind when He talked about eunuchs who are born that way?"[3]

"Hm, maybe." Pastor Andrew shrugged.

"Okay, but even if intersex people aren't literally born eunuchs, at least eunuchs are a close representation, right? Like could eunuchs be an example of sexual minorities in general?"

I paused to see if Pastor Andrew would say anything. He sat stoically, with a half-smile frozen on his face.

I continued, "I read somewhere that Jesus mentioned eunuchs as a group of people who can't get married, but Jesus doesn't specifically say that. Even if an intersex person is a born eunuch, surely, they can get married, right?"

"We don't teach that intersex people can't get married," Pastor Andrew said.

"Right. But *to whom?*"

He furrowed his eyebrows again.

I continued to press the question. "If the Church's stance is that marriage is between a *biological* man and a woman, then how do we determine which biological sex an intersex person is allowed to marry?"

His half-smile faded to the straightest face I had ever seen him wear. "Um," he stammered, "I guess based on whichever sex they identify as."

"But how do we know that they aren't transgender? Or gay? And if the Church is against same-sex marriage, how do you handle that in an intersex person's case?"

He thought about it for a moment with the same concern on his face.

I asked, "Is it possible that Jesus mentioned eunuchs because—being God—He knows everything and knows about sexual minorities? The Word says Jesus knew all people, and He knew what was in humans.[4] Could He maybe have just been saying to His disciples, *'If you don't want to stay married, there are people who aren't suited for marriage with a wife: castrated people, celibate people, and people who are born differently'*? And to His straight disciples, those options clearly weren't great compared to getting married to a woman and having sex.

"And what if being gay or trans is kind-of-sort-of like a type of intersex that manifests in sexual attraction or identity, like in our brains or something? Like, in my head, if eunuchs were as common today, they would fall under the LGBT+ category. Is it possible that Jesus—being God and knowing all things—knew about LGBTQIA people when He mentioned eunuchs who are born that way?"

Pastor Andrew stared at me silently. He didn't blink. I tried to read his face, but I couldn't understand it. He looked at the floor and then back at me. For a second, he looked like he was about to say something, but then he stopped himself.

"I'm just asking," I said, shrugging.

He looked back to the floor as he thought, and then finally he looked up at me, put on his normal smile, and confessed, "You know what, I don't know. That's very interesting to think about. Let me look into it and get back to you."

BOUGHT WITH A PRICE

. . .

As I CONTINUED to meditate on sexuality in the Bible, I kept coming back to a specific story in Acts 8:26-38. The Spirit of God led Evangelist Philip into a desert place. Off in the distance, he could see a chariot, which the Spirit led him to approach. When Philip arrived at the chariot, he met an Ethiopian eunuch who was reading the Word of God. The eunuch was on his way back to Ethiopia from Jerusalem, where he had gone to worship.

Philip asked, "Do you understand what you are reading?"

"How can I," the eunuch answered, "Unless someone guides me?"

Because the religious people back in the first century misunderstood a couple of scriptures, they excluded eunuchs from worship,[5] much like LGBT+ people are often forbidden from certain membership levels in churches today.

How can I unless someone guides me?

The eunuch was reading from Isaiah 53:7-8, a prophecy about how the Messiah would be killed like a lamb led to the slaughter. He asked Philip, "About whom does the prophet say this, about himself or about someone else?"

Philip joined the eunuch in his chariot as they continued on the journey. As Philip shared that Yeshua fulfilled the prophecy, like a miracle in the middle of the desert, the chariot approached an oasis.

"See, here is water! What prevents me from being baptized?" the eunuch asked.

This was controversial! There may have been scriptures that seemed to say the eunuch could only come so close, but the Holy Spirit showed Philip that it would be wrong if he didn't fully include the eunuch.

150

"If you believe with all your heart, you may," Philip answered.
The eunuch confessed, "I believe that Jesus Christ is the Son of God."

Philip baptized the eunuch. He fully included a sexual minority in the family of God.

I'm not saying that there's no such thing as men and women, or male and female, but I am saying that sometimes creation can blur the distinctions. And just as the Holy Spirit did, the Church needs to understand and acknowledge these blurred distinctions in human sexual diversity.

Sexual orientation may not have been understood in the first century when the New Testament was written. Still, the modern understanding of sexual orientation does find its place in the Spirit of the Word. It actually comes right after the "you were bought with a price" passage from 1 Corinthians 6.

After Paul says that believers should not engage in prostitution, he reminds us, "Glorify God in your body."[6] He then talks about marriage, implying that marriage is how we can glorify God with our sexualities. Of course, Paul uses language that is focused on a man with a woman because that's the situation for the overwhelming majority of humanity. But then Paul says, "If they cannot exercise self-control, they should marry. For it is better to marry than to burn with passion."[7]

When I first read this, I applied it to my life. I used to sell myself to the highest bidder, but God Himself paid the highest price through Yeshua's life on the cross. He cleansed me of my prostitution and gave me true value. Now, I live my life for Him. However, I still have my sexual orientation, this part of me that desires a loving, romantic relationship with a man.

"It is better to marry than to burn with passion."

This verse told me that if a believer has a sexual orientation—a sexual desire or passion—they should seek an appropriate marriage. Marriage is the only place to express a sexual orientation in love. Not prostitution. Not porn. Not casual hookups. Not having sex while dating. *Marriage.* Whether a person has a heterosexual, homosexual, or bisexual orientation, whether the person is cisgender, transgender, or intersex, the Word of God seems to paint marriage as the most loving expression for sex, and there is nothing in the Word of God against love.

AFTER ONE Bible study, I brought up my idea about intersex people, eunuchs, and LGBT+ people's place within marriage. Some of the guys were just as interested in it as I was.

One person suggested, "Maybe an intersex person should go by their genes."

Barnabas replied, "What if they have Swyer syndrome? That's when a person has typical female anatomy but male genes.[8] If they married a man and if marriage is based on genes, wouldn't that be a same-sex marriage?"

As we continued to talk, my friends suggested that I reach back out to Pastor Andrew because they wanted to know his answer. A month after my conversation with Pastor Andrew, he still hadn't got back to me, and I really wanted to know what he was thinking. Finally, I texted him.

ME

Hey Pastor Andrew! I was wondering if you had found an answer to what we talked about in our last meeting.

ANDREW

> Hey, Aaron. Honestly, I don't know how to answer your question.

When Pastor Andrew didn't answer my questions, I wondered if my lead pastor, Pastor Pete, might have some thoughts. He seemed to think that because I'm gay, I must not believe the Bible. But maybe if I asked him questions about the Bible, it would show Pastor Pete that I am concerned about what the Word of God says. I hoped he would see that.

FIFTEEN

UNLESS SOMEONE GUIDES ME

//"T HE LORD IS showing me that someone on this side
of the room has suffered severe stomach problems for
several years," Pastor Pete proclaimed at the end of a
Sunday night worship service. "And the Lord says He wants to
heal you right now. If that's you, please come forward so that
we can pray for you."

No response. The only sound came from the keyboardist
playing a soft melody to set the atmosphere in reverence to God.
There may have also been a cough from somewhere.

Pastor Pete was attempting something that he hadn't done at
least since I had been a part of the church, which was a year and
a few months at this point. After a lingering lack of reaction from
the congregation, he moved on.

"I also sense in my spirit that there's someone who has had
problems in their back." He placed his hands on his lower back to
pinpoint where he sensed the person's pain. No one stirred.

I actually had a dull ache in my back from straining during
a prayer hike. It wasn't exactly where Pastor Pete explained, but

I thought it might be for me since no one else responded. I was already standing at the front altar with several others, so I raised my hand. Pastor Pete looked directly at me and stared for a moment before moving on to call out another ailment that he said he sensed in his spirit. He looked right at me, but I assumed he thought I had my hand raised in worship.

Pastor Pete sensed different pains and illnesses for what felt like hours but was probably only ten or fifteen minutes. Now and then, he would call out something generic, like a headache, and a few people would raise their hands so that the leaders could go to them and pray. Though for the most part, he would call out something, and there would be no response—just the keyboard on stage, a sneeze, a cough, a baby crying as the mother rushed them out of the auditorium. The awkwardness was deafening.

One sound was clearly missing, a sound that would break the discomfort that flooded that evening's service. We desperately needed prayer to lift our pastor as he stepped out in faith for healing and signs and wonders.

Still at the altar, I got on my knees and bowed my face to the ground. As discreetly as I could, under my breath and to the floor, I prayed, "Lord, thank You for the boldness of Pastor Pete. Give everyone else boldness to step forward when their situation is called out so that You can heal them and be glorified." I prayed in tongues when I wasn't sure what else to pray.

In the corner of my eye, I saw a couple of other people join me in kneeling at the altar. Pastor Pete continued to call out various ailments and conditions, hoping that someone would respond in faith to be healed, but very little happened. I continued to whisper my prayer.

As he continued to call out various things to no response, I could sense his frustration. The light keyboard synthesizing melodic chords in the background and the few of us praying on the floor were the only responses he got.

"Stop praying!" Pastor Pete commanded from the pulpit.

I stopped for a moment, thinking, *Surely, he's talking to someone next to him on stage. There's no way he can hear us praying from where he is.*

I looked up. Pastor Pete glared straight at me. The other people praying around me weren't sure if they should stop too. They kind of fizzled out. Some continued to murmur lightly. When he saw that I stopped praying, Pastor Pete continued to pace the stage calling for healing miracles. Some people in the back began to leave the auditorium.

Then Pastor Pete came back to my direction, stopped right over me, and extended his right hand in my general direction. With eyes closed, he said, "The Lord is showing me that a young man has struggled with homosexual addiction since the time he was molested as a young boy. The Lord says, 'Be healed and set free from that addiction!'"

Homosexual addiction? What does that even mean? Someone's addicted to homosexuals?

I wanted to believe that he was just speaking generically, but I also knew it was too obvious. He was referring to me. Either way, it was clear that Pastor Pete believed that my being gay resulted from some imagined childhood sexual abuse.

In the same-sex attraction recovery group, some of the guys had mentioned that ex-gay ministries had told them that their childhood sexual abuse or dysfunctional relationships with their parents caused them to experience SSA. But they struggled with this idea because most of them were not molested and had great relationships with their parents.

I also struggled with this idea when I heard it from my church. When Mitch told his ex-gay testimony, he said he noticed that most same-sex attracted boys came from single-mother households. As a gay man who came from a single-mother household, I began to wonder if my upbringing might have influenced me to be gay. Still, as I think back on all the LGBT+ people I had ever known, I find my upbringing is in the minority.

Also, I wasn't molested as a child. I was exposed to porn at an early age, which could be considered childhood sexual abuse, but my porn exposure was about the average age for most children today. Although porn can influence someone's sexual behavior, porn exposure doesn't change someone's sexual orientation. I was raped in college, but given the devastating frequency of rape on college campuses, it's clear that rape doesn't cause someone to become gay either. These things definitely contributed to me normalizing porn and sexual abuse to the point that I was prostituted, but these situations are not why I'm gay. And medically, the idea that childhood molestation, single mothers, or any specific childhood upbringing can make someone gay is completely unfounded.

Although scientists and medical experts favor biology as establishing sexual orientation, there is no consensus yet on what determines someone's orientation. Still, the American Academy of Pediatrics has stated, "…there is no scientific evidence that abnormal parenting, sexual abuse, or other adverse life events influence sexual orientation."[1]

After Pastor Pete's awkward healing service, I realized that he did not know me. He knew that I was gay. That came with all kinds of assumptions that he believed about me, but he didn't really know me. And I wanted him to know me, especially if he believed that I was gay due to sexual abuse.

Because I could not get a successful dialogue with Pastor Andrew about my ideas on eunuchs, and because I was eager to discuss my ideas with some leader in my church, I hoped that maybe I could talk directly to Pastor Pete about it. Maybe if we had the chance to speak, he would see that I actually love the Word of God.

After service the next Sunday, I planned to give Pastor Pete a greeting card to invite him and his wife to dinner sometime. At one point in the card, I wrote, "I may be gay, but I'm not what you think I am."

After the service, when I planned to give him the card, I couldn't find Pastor Pete, but his wife was still in the auditorium.

"Hi, Pastor Hailey," I said when I was able to get her attention. "I wanted to give this card to you and your husband."

"Oh, you're so sweet," she said, taking the card with a bright smile.

"I also wanted to invite you and Pastor Pete to dinner sometime. Is there a way to set that up?"

Pastor Hailey grabbed me by the shoulders, squeezed, and gave me a little shake with excitement. "Wow! How sweet of you!" She released me. "If you would email our assistant, that would be the easiest way to set up a time. And thank you. I really look forward to that."

When I got home, I shot an email to Pastor Pete's assistant.

I was hoping to schedule a meeting with Pastor Pete and Pastor Hailey, so they can get to know me better. I'd like to tell them my testimony. Do they have a time that we can meet for dinner to discuss homosexuality in the Bible?

Her response was simple,

Pastor Pete and Hailey's schedule will not allow for it at this time. They care about you and everyone at the church, so they have a pastoral care team available if you would like to meet with someone from our team.

By "pastoral care," she meant someone like Pastor Andrew, but Pastor Andrew couldn't answer my questions. I replied,

I totally understand that their schedule is pretty busy. Is it possible to invite them for dinner in the distant future, even if it has to be two years in the future?

She continued with the same story.

I'm sorry, but as we discussed, their schedule won't allow it.

I was still a fairly new believer, so I didn't fully understand how churches operated. My church was pretty large, so today, I can see how my pastor's schedule could be packed. I grant him grace for not meeting with me, and I grant myself grace for being so naive to think that he could or would.

WITHIN A WEEK of sending that email to Pastor Pete's assistant, I got a text message from Pastor Andrew to have another chat with him before the next Sunday night worship service. When we met up, he greeted me with his typical smile and a hug before talking.

"What's going on?" I asked.

"Aaron, did you reach out to Pastor Pete's assistant to set up a time to talk to him about you being gay?"

"Yes. I was hoping he could get to know me a little bit more. I want to tell him my testimony. I think it could help him gain a better understanding of how to talk to gay people if he knew a gay person."

Pastor Andrew sighed a bit through a half-smile. "I told Pastor Pete that you were probably just wanting to get to know him more. I told him you're a kind, sweet guy, but he asked me, 'Does Aaron believe what we do?' And I had to tell him that no, you don't."

"Okay, but is that a problem?"

Since I had been a part of this church, their understanding of LGBT+ people had been the only thing that seemed off to me, but that didn't mean I wasn't willing to have my mind changed. That's why I was so desperate to speak to leadership.

"Well," Pastor Andrew hesitated, smiling nervously. "Pastor Pete said if that's the case, he has no reason to meet with you."

The words pierced my heart like a spear. It was one thing to believe that my pastor was just too busy, but it was a whole different pain to know that he had no interest in ever getting to know me because I'm gay. It's uniquely painful to feel rejection from someone who represents Yeshua as a church leader.

"I don't understand," I said through a lump in my throat as I fought the urge to cry.

"Aaron, I need you to please stay away from Pastor Pete." As Pastor Andrew spoke, I sank deeper into my seat. "Stay away from him, his wife, and his assistant. Give him space. In fact, we'd like to ask you to stop worshiping at the front altar until further notice. Please stay by your seat during worship."

When I first worshiped at the front, there were only a few of us: me, the other young man, and some other people here and there. A year since I first stepped up to worship at the altar, the worship team made an effort to invite everyone to the front. So then, there were a lot more people at the altar. I became just a speck in a sea of worshipers, but somehow, I was still noticeable to my pastors.

"I mean, think about it, Aaron," Pastor Andrew motioned to my left wrist where I wore a gay pride rainbow bracelet. "If people see someone worshiping at the front with a bracelet like that, they might think that we approve of the gay lifestyle."

That word. *Lifestyle.* Like being gay is all that defines me and who I am. Like I chose to be gay. When he said that, I lost the battle with the tears warring in my eyes. Once the first droplet broke free, the rest followed like an enemy army rushing downhill for the attack. I had fought back these tears since the moment I read in the "Standards of Ministry" that I had to "live by God's standard of a heterosexual, monogamous marriage." It seemed like my entire relationship with God was nothing to them. Like I must have no other reason to worship God except to start some controversy over being gay. They refused to get to know me, so they didn't know that I loved Yeshua so much because He forgave me of so much.

"What if you guys are wrong?" I cried. "What if you are treating me like churches in the past have treated women and people of color?"

Pastor Andrew was Black. His smile evaporated, and his eyebrows rose to make the most intense face I had ever seen him make. "I would never even go to a church that taught that. It wouldn't be safe for my family or me." His look seemed to ask, "Do you get the hint?"

Tears continued to run down my cheeks. "Please, let me worship. I'll take off the bracelet." I began to pull the rainbow bracelet off my wrist.

Pastor Andrew sat back in his seat, and his face took on a softer aspect. He said, "Let's make a deal. If you can worship at the far side of the altar against the wall and stay as far away from Pastor Pete as you can, then we may be able to allow you to worship as usual."

I promised to follow his directions. But that deal was short-lived. After service, I emailed Pastor Andrew.

> Thank you for letting me worship at the altar. I'm grateful that you understand that I really have no malicious intent, and I agree that maybe I should give Pastor Pete some space. I want to apologize to him, but because of your idea to stay away from him for a bit, I wondered if you might tell him that I am sorry. I don't want to come off as a problem.

Pastor Andrew replied,

> I will make sure your sentiments get communicated to leadership. I left the church after our talk on Sunday, so I did not attend the worship experience. After speaking to leadership, I received the note that your movements drew attention to yourself in a distracting way during praise and worship. I need to ask you to stand in front of your seat during praise and worship and not come down to the front altar.

I couldn't think of why someone would have told Pastor Andrew that I was distracting. I worshiped up against the wall with a crowd of worshipers between Pastor Pete and me, and I didn't worship any differently than the people around me. My worship style was birthed from watching others in this church. I didn't realize that I was doing anything different. I couldn't figure out what I was doing wrong.

When I pressed the issue with Pastor Andrew the next time I saw him, he let me worship again at the front, but he stood right in front of me the whole time to where I couldn't even see the TV screens with the worship lyrics. At one point of energetic praise where the audio speakers in front of us shook the floor and walls around us, I heard two young women beside me praying in tongues. I joined their prayer until Pastor Andrew turned around, grabbed me painfully by my shoulder, and leaned into my ear.

"Shh."

After worship, he pulled me to the side. Before he could say anything, I argued, "Pastor Andrew, at first you said I couldn't worship at the altar because I need to stay away from Pastor Pete. Then you mentioned my rainbow bracelet. Then you said that my movements are too distracting. Now, I'm expecting you to say that I pray too loud or something. You keep changing the reason. If my prayer is distracting, why keep me in my seat where people around me can hear me? Why didn't you stop the ladies praying next to me? Why am I the only one in this church not allowed to worship at the altar?"

"I didn't hear those women praying. I heard *you*," he snapped. "You need to worship at your seat. This is what leadership is asking of you, Aaron. Will you please follow directions?"

I sighed, looking at the floor.

I did submit to Pastor Andrew's direction, but it took much prayer and great pain. The Word of God talks about the importance of submitting to and honoring leadership in the Church. "Obey your leaders and submit to them, for they are keeping watch over your souls, as those who will have to give an account."[2] I submitted to leadership because if they were wrong, then they will have to give an account to God, not me. But if I did not submit, even if I worshiped with everything else in me, I would have to give an account for not honoring my church's leadership, and I couldn't worship like that. How could I stand before God and say that I yielded when I couldn't yield to the direction of my church's pastors?

I wanted to worship from a place of yielding, and for me, that place of yielding means giving God everything. I used to go all out at the clubs when I was a sinner. Now, as a saint, I wanted to give God more than that. Worshiping at my seat was too constricting. I tried to always sit on the aisle seat so that I had a little bit of extra room, but when I lifted my hands, I still ended up smacking people a couple of times. And then, when people came in late, the ushers would ask us to move in so that the new people could squeeze into their seats. To me, my worship was being distracted by not worshiping at the altar.

It made me wonder if maybe this wasn't the right church for me. I wondered if it was their plan all along to get me to leave. Like Pastor Andrew mentioned, he wouldn't go to a church that taught against his skin color. Pastor Pete even hinted in the membership class that I should maybe find another church. It seemed like they wanted me to leave.

But this was the only church I had known since leaving prostitution. I wanted to keep it if I could, but it was starting to feel like, in their eyes, there was nothing about me that truly loved God. If I'm gay, I must be some pervert who just wants to flaunt my obscene sexuality in front of everyone, and what fun it must be to flaunt my sexuality in a church. It's like they saw me as the person I used to be before I knew the Lord.

I would have loved to talk to leadership and maybe get them to see me as more than some sexually broken mess. And if they changed their theology, that would be cool, but that wasn't why I went to that church. I came to the church to grow in faith.

Though I was still a young tree, I could feel my roots were crowding in a pot that was much too small. My trunk wanted to grow to great heights, but the proper space was lacking. I was able to grow only within the limits of the shallow, narrow pot I found myself in. I was unable to bear the full yield of fruit that I was created to bear.

Everyone else in that church was invited to go to the altar to worship and pray, but leadership told me to stay at my seat. Everyone else in that church was asked to step up and serve in the various ministry opportunities that the church offered, but I was told that I could only attend worship, SSA recovery, and do community service. Everyone else was asked to submit to an authority who would help them grow in their personal ministry, but I was asked to submit to an authority who told me not to move from my spot. Everyone else got to grow, but leadership told me to stay.

This must have been what the Ethiopian eunuch felt like to seek God, only to be told that he could only come so far. He was forced instead to watch others grow and be able to go where he was not allowed. I understood his cry.

"How can I unless someone guides me?"

The Lord said, "Let not the eunuch say, 'Behold, I am a dry tree.'"[3] But in this church, I was becoming a dry tree. I was unable to branch out and produce fruit. I wanted to be a nourished tree, but *how can I, unless someone guides me?*

After our last exchange, Pastor Andrew referred me to his leader, Pastor Adam. He was more stern and severe; he didn't even try to fake a smile. After one Sunday service, Pastor Adam followed me out of the auditorium to talk with me.

I said, "Pastor Adam, I feel like I'm being asked to stay at my seat during worship because I'm gay."

"We're asking you to worship from your seat because we want to know if you'll submit to leadership."

I looked at the ground to hide the frustration that rushed across my face. I had done everything I could to show them that I submitted to them. I showed up to every service that I could.

I served in the limited places that I could. I even went to the SSA group because Pastor Andrew suggested it. And now, I was worshiping from my seat.

"You guys keep changing the reason for why you're asking me to do this. Now it's because you want to see if I'll submit to leadership?"

"I'm telling you that it is because we want to see if you'll submit to leadership."

How can I, unless someone guides me?

"I got to tell you, man," I replied, "I feel like you guys won't let me grow."

Pastor Adam responded, "Homosexuals don't grow much in this church."

I did a slight double-take. His response was cold. His face, hard and unmoving. His confession revealed that there would be no more fruit born for me if I continued to worship here. I sighed as I realized that it was time for me to find a new house of worship. It seems so obvious to me now that it was unhealthy for my spirit to try to fit into a body of believers who taught that my very personhood was wrong. I had to leave that church, but the problem was that I didn't know where else to go.

SIXTEEN

LONELY

W HILE AT WORK, I got a notification from OkCupid, a
dating app I had been using. I opened the app to see
a message from a guy.

HIM

> Are you seriously a Christian? And you're really
> waiting until marriage to have sex? No one
> wants to marry a prude. XD LOL

I could never understand what it was about setting personal
boundaries that made people think a person is a prude. If only he
knew where I came from.

By this point, I was familiar with this reaction. I turned
off my phone and continued working. Since I had quit using
hookup apps, I signed up on several not-so-hookup-oriented
dating sites, like OkCupid. Still, even on traditional dating
apps, I wasn't having much luck finding a boyfriend. Even

when guys said that they were Christian and waiting until marriage, it often turned out not to be true when I met them. I began to lose hope that I would ever meet anyone who met my uncompromisable standards.

"Come on," my co-worker, Greg, would say when we discussed my ideal spouse. "You mean to tell me that if you were given the opportunity, you wouldn't want to *get it in*—or whatever gay guys do?"

"I mean, I want to," I laughed, "But I want it to be for the right reasons."

"There's never not a right reason, Aaron," Greg laughed. He was not a Christian, and I didn't want to get into an argument at work about all the not-right reasons for sex. "What kind of guy are you looking for?"

"Well, they need to be Christian—"

"No, I mean, like, what should he *look* like?"

"Oh. I mean, I guess someone around my age, not too much taller or bigger…"

"Oh!" Greg turned to his computer to search on his social media page. "I have a gay friend who I think you would like, but his name is also Aaron. Would you ever date someone with your own name?"

He pulled up his friend's profile. This Aaron was cute, but as we scrolled down his social media page, under "Religious Views," he labeled himself "Agnostic." It was crucial to me that anyone I dated should also be a Christian. I wanted to date with the intent to marry, and I didn't want to marry someone who didn't know Yeshua like I knew Yeshua.

"No," I said. "I could never date someone with my own name. That would be weird."

. . .

EACH NIGHT, as I lay in bed, the awareness of my loneliness sat heavily upon my chest. No one was beside me. I had gay Christian friends because of our Bible study, but I was beginning to realize that many of my friends didn't believe some of the most critical parts of my faith.

After one Bible study, two of the guys were acting weird around each other. They avoided each other's presence and wouldn't talk to each other the way they used to.

After a while, I whispered to one of them, "What's going on between you two?"

He said, "I think he's acting weird because we hooked up last weekend."

My heart sank. My friend said it so casually as if this was a typical thing, as if it's normal to hook up with a friend and then be weird around each other. It was very alienating for me to realize that, except for my older friends, Mike and Barnabas, many of my friends did not believe waiting until marriage was necessary for Christians.

The hardest part for me was that many of them would hook up and share porn. It was normal for them. It further drove me to want to tell them my testimony, but since I knew that they were okay with porn, I also didn't feel safe to tell them. And by not telling them, I felt like none of my friends really knew me.

I could barely find friends who were willing to wait until marriage, so it was tough to find a boyfriend with the same commitment. After what happened to me at my first church, I felt like I was alone in my own little bubble, but I knew God was always there, even on my loneliest days.

My primary place of worship became my bedroom. I would play worship music from my computer and have my own little church service complete with dancing, singing, and lifting my hands in the air like a little child wanting to be picked up. But even though I knew God was there with me, I longed for someone to share His Presence with. It echoed in my spirit that when God created the world, although He was with Adam, God said that it was *not good* that Adam was alone, so He created a helpmate suitable for Adam, Eve.[1]

Every night, as I got into my bed, I prayed, "Lord, in Yeshua's name, please, bring a suitable helpmate into my life. Amen."

The Lord would reply, "*Seek first the kingdom of God and His righteousness, and all these things will be added to you.*"[2]

"Lord, I *do* seek You first."

"*Delight yourself in the* LORD, *and He will give you the desires of your heart.*"[3]

"Father, I *do* delight in You above all things."

I wasn't getting the hint.

Then one night, during a time that I had planned to worship the Lord, I found myself instead fixated on OkCupid. Even though I had worship music playing, even though I had my Bible opened in front of me, I was chatting with guys online. I caught myself and realized that maybe I had allowed myself to get a little too distracted with looking for a spouse. Maybe I wasn't seeking God absolutely first, and if I wasn't seeking God first, then maybe what I was seeking had become an idol in my life.

Anything can become an idol: money, work, friends, entertainment, porn, boyfriends, girlfriends, *anything*. If it can take away our joy because we don't have it, or if it distracts us from God, then that thing is our false god. For believers, God is supposed to be our source of joy because only in His Presence is there true fullness of joy that the world can never take away.[4] Only in Him is there peace that surpasses human understanding.[5]

Idolizing my desire for a husband was not spiritually healthy because if I got a husband, he would have become my source of joy instead of God, and I would end up relying on him to satisfy my life. It became clear to me that there was an area of my heart that I still needed to give to God.

After being rejected by my first church, I realized that a part of me still desperately desired human approval, and its absence—from my church and from not finding a boyfriend—caused me to doubt my worth. My unhealthy need for human approval meant that I still didn't completely love myself, and this lack of love for myself left me *thirsty*. Instead of focusing on God, I was focused on finding a husband to love me. It took me a while to learn that my thirst for approval could only be satisfied by the approval of God.

Needing a spouse to this degree is unhealthy because if something happened to my future husband, like if he left me or died, it would mean that my life would be over. Of course, the situation would be sad, but if I could fully set my heart on God, I would walk through life satisfied in Him even in the worst situations. I needed to be content with myself and the Presence of God before I could be in a healthy romantic relationship. Otherwise, my lack of love for myself would build the foundation for my relationship, and my husband would be forced to play a role that should only be given to God.

At that moment in my room, I remembered what I already knew: all I need is Yeshua. When He is all we need, we don't *need* a spouse; we get to *choose* a spouse.

I closed OkCupid and put my phone down. I got on my knees and lifted my hands to God.

"Father, forgive me for putting dating ahead of You. Forgive me that I have not sought You first in everything. Thank You for shedding Your blood to forgive me. I'm turning off my dating apps and turning to You right now. I delight in You, and I seek You first above all things. Only You satisfy me. I will trust Your timing and believe that You will introduce me to my spouse when I am ready. Until then, You're all I need."

The rush of the Spirit embraced my heart, and I began to pray in tongues. I jumped to my feet and danced and sang to God.

"Lord, if I'm supposed to be like Apostle Paul and be celibate forever, I don't mind because all I need is You."

I worshiped so much that night I didn't even notice I received a message from a new guy on OkCupid, and I didn't care. I pledged to God that I wouldn't check the messages for at least a week because all I wanted to do was worship Him.

THE NEXT TIME I was in a church, the worship music washed over me like a cool ocean wave. I jumped to my feet, and with a new rush of freedom, I found myself at the front altar. I was not at my church, my *old* church. I was visiting an LGBT+ affirming church where my friend Barnabas had invited me to hear one of his friends preach.

Barnabas had been a Christian since long before I was born-again. He knew many influential voices in the LGBT+ affirming movement, and he introduced me to the community.

As worship played, I raised my hands, jumped for joy, danced at the altar, swayed with the melodies, sang like I was alone in the shower, and prayed as the Spirit of God led me. It was a freedom that I had not been allowed to move in for several months at my old church. I was so glad to get to express worship without boundaries finally!

After the service, I looked around the auditorium as people chatted. At the altar, the guest speaker was consoling an older man who seemed to be crying. I was too far away to hear what they were saying, but the crying man looked up and pointed at me with tears dripping off his chin.

Oh no. What did I do now?

This was the first time I had ever seen this man, so I had no idea what his problem could have been with me.

"Go to them," the Lord said.

Before I could even argue with the Holy Spirit, my feet stepped towards them, yet my heart pounded in my chest as if trying to push me in the opposite direction.

I was too distracting. I ruined his worship experience. They're going to tell me that I should worship at my seat next time.

I crept closer to them as the guest speaker rubbed the crying man's back. She handed him a tissue and whispered something in his ear, comforting him from whatever I had done. When I finally arrived at the man's side, I heard him say, "It was so powerful."

I asked, "Is everything okay?"

When he noticed that I was next to him, the man sobbed into his hands. The guest speaker gave me a proud, reassuring smile like that of a mother looking upon her child who has just done something right.

She said, "For many years, I have been trying to explain to him that it is okay to be gay and Christian, but he was taught his whole life that he couldn't be. So it's been hard for him to believe it."

The man wiped his eyes and blew his nose with the tissue in his hands as the guest speaker continued. "But today, he saw you worshiping and felt the love of God—"

"For the first time in decades," the man interrupted. He looked at me as he tried to compose himself. "You're so full of joy, and you clearly love Jesus. I want what you have." He broke down sobbing again as I hugged him. After running from God for years because he thought he couldn't come to Jesus, he was now ready to turn to Him.

This was fruit! This man experienced repentance because I was allowed to share my love for God without shame. The tree of my faith had been in too small a pot for too long, but I could feel my roots stretching out and shattering the pot around me. My roots now burrowed into the soil beneath me, allowing me to absorb nourishment from the Living Water of God. Now I can grow as bounteous as possible. Now I can bear ripe, healthy fruit, which others could "taste and see that the Lord is good."[6] And having consumed the seed of faith, they could go on to bear the same holy fruit, passing on Yeshua's Word and love to infinitely more people.

I CONSIDERED attending Barnabas' church regularly, but it was too far from where I lived. I attended a few times when I was able to make the drive. Still on the hunt for a church home, I found a conference that taught the Biblically-based inclusion of LGBT+ people. Although it was not a church, I thought it would be a great place to meet other affirming Christians, especially leaders, and maybe, eventually, find my spiritual family.

The conference application alone filled me with hope because it asked us to explain our beliefs on sexual ethics. If they were so concerned with sexuality to ask about it on the application, this must be a group of people who would understand me and where I came from. I imagined being surrounded by other like-minded LGBT+ affirming Christians who sought to live holy lives even with their sexual orientation. Because this was a community that we needed, I encouraged Barnabas to sign up as well.

It had been a year and a half since I had left porn, and I hadn't told any other Christians about my testimony. Most people who knew me before my conversion were aware of my past, which was public knowledge. With my new Christian friends, no one was aware as far as I knew.

I thought, *If just my worship caused that man to turn to God, what would happen if he had known the testimony behind that worship?*

But too many of my new Christian friends were okay with porn and casual sex. They treated porn like it was cool, and every time I heard it mentioned casually, a rush of memories pulsed through my mind. There was an urgency on my tongue to speak about it, but a panic sealed my lips. I couldn't say it. I wanted to, but the words wouldn't come out. I didn't feel safe enough to speak.

In the months before the affirming conference, all the attendees spent time on social media getting to know each other. There seemed to be an understanding that the clobber passages were about exploitation, so I assumed that all the attendees understood that prostitution and porn were unloving. I assumed that the attendees would be excited about how God rescued me from prostitution, so I assumed they would be a safe group to tell my testimony.

Because the testimonies that were shared regularly at my old church seemed to impact people and encourage them that God could transform any life, I wanted to share my experience so that

God could work through my story as well. A testimony is a weapon. We are in a spiritual war against the kingdom of darkness. The Word says, "They have conquered [the enemy] by the blood of the Lamb and by the word of their testimony, for they loved not their lives even unto death."[7] Prostitution is an enemy of God—not the people in it, but the institution and the spirit behind it—because it is the selling and purchasing of human beings, the image of God, to be used as sex toys. My testimony could be the sword needed to slay the dark beast of sexual immorality that has gripped so many people. If I could tell people what really goes on behind the cameras on porn sets, maybe I could lower the demand for prostitution.

While getting to know people online from the LGBT+ Christian conference, I allowed myself to get vulnerable. I wrote everything in a blog, which I published publicly but shared specifically with the attendees of the conference. I wrote about being raped, my time in prostitution, the STIs, my suicide attempts, hearing God say, "I love you." Everything.

It was healing to release my voice to speak about it because I had remained silent about it after leaving porn. Because of the shame that latches onto victims of sexual abuse, it's common for survivors to not speak about it, but speaking it out was my way of showing that it no longer had power over me. Porn, shame, and trauma couldn't silence me anymore. I decided I was going to use what happened to me to tell my friends the truth. Even if some of my friends thought porn was normal, writing it out and sharing the blog meant that people would finally get to know this part of me. By knowing where I came from, maybe they would see how harmful porn truly is. And even if not, I would find safety among the people at this conference, who seemed to be the type of people who would understand.

For the most part, the response from the conference attendees stirred my spirit even more. Several people reached out to say my story moved them. It seemed that I was finally going to meet other affirming believers who understood that sexual exploitation is neither a part of being gay nor Christian. That's what it seemed like—at first.

SEVENTEEN

DIGNITY

T HE SAME DAY I published the blog with my testimony, I got
a social media message from an older straight man I knew
from my old, non-affirming church.

HIM

> Hi, Aaron. A few minutes ago, I saw your porn
> videos. Not to be rude or anything, but I thought,
> "Wow!" That is some hardcore stuff. I imagine
> it's embarrassing for you to have that out there.
> I just wanted to say that I'm here for you if you
> need anything.

I read the message with my mouth agape. Each word sent a
rush of hot blood to my face. My ears burst with the sound of my
heart pounding inside my chest.

*Why would you watch that porn? Why would you willingly
look it up?*

I didn't know how to respond. I couldn't understand why a straight Christian man from a non-affirming church thought it was okay to watch videos of me in inappropriate situations. This man clearly thought he was reaching out and doing a service to help me. But he had willingly participated in my trauma and exploitation, and he didn't even recognize it.

The hardest part for me was that this man was a Christian from my first church. When I was a part of that non-affirming church, they never preached about pornography. I heard James from the recovery service testify about overcoming temptations from porn, but other than that, leadership was silent. I heard them preach against homosexuality at least every other month. I heard once, maybe twice, about sex being reserved for marriage, but porn was never specifically addressed. I thought that maybe no one addressed porn because it was so obviously unloving and sinful.

When I left prostitution, I ran to the Church because I thought it would be a refuge from the trauma I experienced in the pornified world. However, I was naive about the sin that still enslaved most Christians. Two-thirds of Christian men and one-third of Christian women watch porn regularly; it is so normal among Christians that even one in five youth pastors and one in seven lead pastors watch porn regularly.[1] Over half of the Church engages in renting human beings through porn, yet most churches are silent about it. They'll talk about gay people, a small minority, but they won't address the actual sexual sin from which most of their congregation has not yet been freed.

When this man messaged me, I thought I had divulged too much information in my blog. The Church wasn't ready for it. I edited my story to make it extra clear that I was not proud of being in porn. I clarified that I shared my testimony to glorify God for what He has done for me and to help people who may struggle with porn.

AFTER EVERY Bible study that I had with my gay Christian friends, we asked for prayer requests.

"I really need your prayers, guys," I said when it was my turn. "Since sharing my testimony, I've had some people reach out to tell me that they've looked up the porn I was in, and they seem completely unaware that they hurt me by doing that."

Barnabas' eyebrows raised. Some of the other guys cocked their heads to the side as if trying to understand what I had just said.

"Honest question," one of them replied, "How does it hurt you for someone to watch your porn?"

At first, I couldn't tell if he was serious. I looked around the room and noticed everyone seemed to have their ears perked up, all wanting to know. They really didn't understand. Like my friend said, it was an honest question. Porn was completely normal to them, so they didn't see anything wrong with it. When you're involved in it, it's hard to see that the system encourages all of us to sexually exploit other people. I thought my testimony alone would be enough to make it clear to them, but they really didn't get it. To me, the answer was obvious: I didn't want my friends to see me naked.

"Think of it this way," I finally said. "What is the first thing you do if someone walks in on you naked?" I waited. No response. "You cover yourself, right?

"When someone goes out and watches the porn videos of me, they take away my power to cover myself. By watching those videos, they deny me my choice in who can see me naked.

"I only signed the line saying that I consent to be in porn because I was pressured by needing to pay bills, feed myself, and to make the producers happy. I did it after I experienced sexual assault, so I wasn't even in my right mind. I wasn't thinking that I was giving away my freedom to choose who could see me naked.

"Back then, I may have signed a paper saying that I consented, but consent, by definition, can be withdrawn even if someone has previously given it. If a couple is having consensual sex, but then one of them says, 'Never mind,' then there is no longer consent. The internet has been having sex with me through those porn videos, and I'm asking it to stop. I clearly do not give consent for the world to see me naked anymore. I withdraw that consent. If the exchange of money negates my ability to withdraw consent, then the exchange of money negates the possibility that there ever was true consent in the first place."

My heart pounded with every syllable that fell from my mouth. The words flowed out like a river. I barely breathed because my mouth was too busy talking.

"As a Christian, I now have more dignity and self-respect and love for myself, so I do not want everyone, especially my friends, to see me naked. I want to be given the same respect as everyone else. We don't go around pulling each other's clothes off, do we? Just because I used to do porn, does that give everyone the right to expose my body? You guys, watching porn steals a person's dignity."

Someone gulped.

"I want to reserve myself for someone who has given me their love. I'm not giving myself away cheaply anymore. And now that I realize that I was giving myself away cheaply in porn, I also realize that when people watch the porn I was in, they violate me!"

After I let it sink in for a moment, I caught my breath.

Lord, please help them get it.

After the Bible study was over, the friend who asked the question admitted to me privately that he disagreed with how I feel about people watching those porn videos.

"I don't think that's fair. I haven't stolen anyone's dignity at all."

"Okay. But I'm telling you, when I hear someone has seen those videos, especially after they know that I would rather they didn't watch them, I feel like they have stolen my dignity. I feel like they've raped me."

THE GUYS in the Bible study were my brothers in Christ, so I thought they loved me. But after that Bible study, I discerned that some of them may have looked up the porn I was in, and not by accident. Before I was a Christian, I expected people to see the porn, and I know that many did. But I couldn't believe Christian friends who loved me would watch it. I expected it from non-believing people, but I couldn't wrap my head around Christian brothers willingly looking it up. It was too hard to believe that people who loved me would do that.

My mother loves me, and when she found out about me being in porn, I know that she did not look up the videos. I told her about my past when I visited home during the holidays.

Before I knew the Lord, my relationship with my mom was a bit strained, but since knowing the Lord, I sought to honor her as much as I could. A part of honoring her would be telling her the truth that everyone else had known by this point.

We had spent the day together, and as I was dropping her off at my aunt's house, I told her. "Mom, I really want you to know something before it gets to you by someone else."

"Okay?" she said, visibly bracing herself.

"For a bit during and after college, I did porn."

Silence. Her face was frozen. Then she turned her eyes to the ground. I noticed tears developing in the corner of her eyes, but she was clearly trying to hide them from me. Finally, she looked back up at me.

"You were filmed naked, having sex?"

"Yes, but Jesus saved me from all of that. I don't do that anymore."

She looked back to the ground. Tears continued to well up in her eyes. She turned around for a moment and wiped her face. Seeing her face like that broke my heart. My mom hardly ever showed an emotional side. The only other time I can remember her crying is when my father gave up his parental rights and left my mom as a single mother when I was only four or five years old. But it was clear that hearing that her youngest son had been in porn was just as heavy a blow. She finally turned back to me.

"Well, the Bible says, 'The old has passed away, the new has come,'"[2] she said before I hugged her goodnight.

I might not expect this exact response from everyone who loves me, but I did expect my friends to re-humanize the people in porn. To see the face of a person they knew and loved when they thought about porn. To recognize the degradation. To honor my dignity as a human being.

On the internet, every single click a person makes tells websites what we want. By clicking on videos of people who are being degraded and exploited, porn users tell websites they want more of that. By clicking on the porn videos that I was in, people told the internet that they want to see me degraded and exploited. That told me that they did not honor my dignity.

To honor someone's dignity is to honor that person's true value. They've been bought with a price. I used to be given a couple hundred bucks for access to my body. To my buyers, to anyone who clicks on the videos I appeared in and justifies it because I was paid, I am only worth money. When I didn't know my worth, I believed that was my value too.

Then God showed me that, to Him, I am worth dying for. When Yeshua opened my eyes to that truth, I decided that if anyone wanted access to my body, then they would need to value me with the same value that God gave me.

"You are not your own for you were bought with a price. So glorify God in your body."

By coming to the earth to die on the cross, Yeshua told all of humanity that we are worth dying for. Our sin deserved the worst punishment possible, and He was willing to bear it in our place because we are worth it to Him. The value God gives us is one reason why, throughout His Word, He compares our relationship with Him to marriage. If His love for us is like the love in a marriage, and He showed us that kind of love by laying His life down for us, then we also are called to love our spouses by laying our lives down for them.[3]

Laying our lives down means that our lives are not our own anymore. We give ourselves to our spouse—after the Lord, of course. By being willing to give ourselves to a spouse, we show them that we have the highest value and love for them!

Sex is the most vulnerable and intimate act that a human being can engage in with another human. Everyone else can only come so close as to embrace us, but in sex, we let someone come into us, or we go into them for mutual pleasure. That's intimate!

That's why the Bible often calls sex *knowing* someone.

Unlike the marriage relationship, hookups, porn, casual sex, and even sex in impermanent, long-term relationships are expressions of devaluing a person's inherent worth. While uncommitted sex says, "You are worth a few years, a few months, a couple of days, a passing moment, a couple of dollars, and then I'm done with you," marriage says, "You are worth my life." The sacrificial love offered by consenting adults in marriage echoes the sacrificial love of Yeshua for the Church.

Unfortunately, many believers who were raised in the Church have been damaged by messages that seem to say that people lose their value if they don't wait until marriage. But waiting until marriage does not determine someone's value. Waiting until marriage is about recognizing one's own value and the value of others *already* given by God. Waiting until marriage is about displaying Yeshua's love to a spouse, and His love is not determined by virginity. If someone has lived like I used to live, God's grace covers the past. All anyone in that situation needs to do is repent and start living like they were bought with a price.

If God is our example of the highest, most perfect love, then marriage sounds like a higher, more perfect love than casual sex. If we are truly bought with a price, then we shouldn't allow anyone to have us for any lower price than the price that the Almighty paid for us. Every human is worthy of real, true love, and we should expect that inherent dignity to be honored.

The best and only way to honor someone's true dignity in sex is to marry them. In marriage, we tell our spouse, "I give you my life. I lay my life down for you." It says, "You are worth dying for."

I've been asked before, "But don't you want to test-drive the car before buying it? Don't you want to sample the burger?"

With sex, we are talking about human beings, not a car or a piece of meat. Requiring a test-drive comes from a consumer mindset that has already objectified and commercialized humanity for one's own sexual gratification. This sounds too much like prostitution to me.

In our culture, we are told, "We *must* have sex. We're only human. We have no control."

But God's grace is *power!* If someone realizes that they struggle with sexual sin, His grace is so accessible because of the shed blood of Yeshua, and His grace empowers our hearts to transform into His perfect love. After all, self-control is a fruit of the Spirit.[4] If someone struggles with sexual sin and finds themselves unable to value others in this way, then all they need to do is repent, turn to God, and trust that His grace is transforming their heart.

I SHARED my testimony because the people in the LGBT+ Christian conference seemed to recognize the exploitation inherent to the clobber passages. Their responses to my testimony encouraged me, but I still only knew them online. I looked forward to meeting them in person because I now struggled with trusting some of my friends. I looked forward to being around Christians who would stand beside me and love me if I continued to step out and fight the enemy by telling my story. But in the meantime, I needed a distraction from the people around me who—from what it seemed—had willingly dishonored my dignity.

I remembered that I had messages waiting for me on OkCupid. I hadn't opened the app since I had promised God I would seek

Him first. It was well over the one-week wait I had given myself. When I opened the app, most of the messages I had missed were typical. Someone tried to hookup, and someone argued that I couldn't be gay and Christian. But there was one that stood out.

HIM

> Hi. I was looking at your profile, and I think it's nice everything on your page is about Jesus. I'm so glad that you're waiting until marriage. I'm a Christian waiting until marriage too. I'm planning to move to the Los Angeles area from New Mexico soon, so I'm mostly looking for friends. I wanted to ask you how your journey towards believing homosexuality is blessed by God has gone and how you've come to what you believe now.

I reread it to make sure I read it correctly. He was a gay Christian who seemed serious about waiting until marriage! I went to his profile and saw that he was a cute guy. He reminded me of Logan Lerman from *The Perks of Being a Wallflower* with his bright, greenish-blue eyes and sweet smile. I read his message a third time because I couldn't believe it. Then I noticed his name: Aaron Michael.

My own words echoed in my head, *"I could never date someone with my own name. That would be weird."* I had said that to my co-worker about his agnostic, gay friend also named Aaron, but this Aaron on OkCupid was a Christian who was waiting until marriage.

But Aaron Michael was not asking to date. He said he was simply looking for friends, and he wanted to know how I reconciled being a Christian with being gay. I decided I needed to see how serious this guy was about his faith. I copy-and-pasted the link to my testimony and replied.

ME

> Wait! So your name is also Aaron? That's my name too!! LOL. I'm so glad to hear that you're a gay Christian who is also waiting until marriage. Sometimes, it seems like that's so hard to find, so thanks for giving me hope. :) It's kind of a long story how I reconcile my faith with being gay, but I'll share with you a blog I recently wrote. It's just an easier way to answer that question because there's a lot that I feel required to say when I'm asked that. Check this out.

Send.

Right from the start, I let Aaron Michael know that I was prostituted in porn because if he was okay with getting to know someone with a past like mine without degrading me, then I would be willing to see where a friendship with him could go. But if he couldn't, that was fine too. I had already decided I'm going after God first, and if someone can't keep up, then they aren't meant for me.

I'd be lying if I said I wasn't eager for his response. Before I had promised God to seek Him first, my days would be consumed with waiting for guys to respond to me on OkCupid. After I had prayed to seek God first, though, I was more chill and willing to let whatever happened happen as long as God was the one behind the scenes piecing everything together. Otherwise, my focus was on the Lord, and I wanted nothing and no one else to distract me. The next day, Aaron Michael responded.

AARON MICHAEL

> Wow! Your story is so powerful. I can't express how grateful I am that you shared that. I want to cry because you went through all of that, but I know this story isn't a sad one. It's a victorious one because Jesus found you. This is gonna help a lot of people! Even me. I struggled a lot with porn in middle school and high school. And to be honest, sometimes I have trouble watching it still. But this really helps. You have no idea. I don't think I'll be able to watch porn again now. Thank you.

You know that feeling when you're going up a rollercoaster, and you reach the first main drop that gives the cart enough momentum to push through the rest of the ride? The feeling that your stomach is being lifted inside of you? That's what it felt like when I read Aaron Michael's reply. When he said that my story helped him and that he couldn't watch porn again after reading it, it was the first time I had a sense of being truly heard and truly seen. My conversation with Aaron Michael was one of the first times I saw the fruit that could be born from sharing my testimony. His response gave me hope that God could use my story to end the demand for pornography, and with God's grace, to help people repent of sexual sin.

As Aaron Michael and I continued to connect, I told him about the LGBT+ conference I was planning to go to. I held onto the hope that the conference would be a key part in helping me share my testimony. I desperately wanted to find a safe place with safe people who would give me the support I needed as I went forward to fight back against this enemy of God's love.

EIGHTEEN

GLORIFY GOD IN YOUR BODY

B EFORE THE CONFERENCE, most of us hung around the hotel's
lobby, getting to know each other. Barnabas and I bounced
from group to group, chatting with everyone we could. The
last person I spoke with was an older man named Bill, whose eyes
were half opened and glazed over. He was holding a glass of wine
in his hand, and his speech slurred as he spoke.

After a quick chat, I said, "Alright, Bill. Since we all have to
get up early tomorrow, I'm going to head to bed."

I reached up to give him a friendly hug, but as I tried to
pull away, his hand slid down to my butt, and he pulled me up
against his body to where I had to balance on tiptoe. I pushed
my forearms against his chest to try to break his hold, but he
held me firmly. He brought his face so close to mine that I
thought he might kiss me. The alcohol on his breath burned in
my nostrils. I held my face as far away as possible and looked
around, attempting to make eye contact with anyone who
would notice. I locked eyes with Barnabas, who was talking to
a group nearby. I gave him a look that said, "Please, help me."

I could tell from his face that he knew I was uncomfortable, but he didn't know how to respond.

Bill breathed, "I read your testimony. I just wanted to say that's really good for you."

Each word reeked of sour wine. My skin crawled. I flashed back to college, and the older man is on top of me, pinning my body down as he rapes me. I flashed back to sitting on the lap of one of my sex-buyers, shifting uncomfortably as I try to make it seem like I'm having fun, so I can afford to eat—Bill drones on much like my sex-buyers. I flashed back to a porn shoot where my body is being invaded as everyone in the room looks on. I act as if I enjoy it—business as usual. And now, I'm trapped in Bill's uncomfortable clutches, frozen, unsure what to do, hoping to escape.

I hung in Bill's grasp, petrified. A sexual violation doesn't only happen in the act of sex. It can come from an uncomfortable touch. A lustful look. A word. There were people all around. I wished one of them would say something. Maybe they didn't notice where Bill's hand was. Maybe they thought he was being friendly, but I also feared that maybe Bill thought I would be easy to sleep with because of my story. Either way, I didn't want to be held against his body.

"I-I'm going to bed now," I stuttered.

He finally let me go, but I could still feel his fingers on my skin, like little bugs crawling all over me. Barnabas continued chatting in a group near me. I pulled him to the side and asked, "What do I do? I don't feel safe around Bill. Should I tell a leader or someone?"

Barnabas, please tell me I need to tell someone. Tell me to talk to a leader. Tell me you're going to make sure this doesn't happen again.

"Just leave it alone for now. Bill is clearly drunk," Barnabas said. "If you don't feel safe, just stay away from him."

If Bill was too drunk to realize how inappropriate he was, then Bill was *too* drunk. The harassment I experienced is exactly why the Word says that drunkenness is debauchery.[1]

"Yeah, maybe I should just let it go." I didn't know how else to respond. I looked at the ground reeling beneath me. "Maybe I'm thinking too much into it."

"Aaron, I wouldn't be surprised if some people here looked up your stuff."

Everything in me froze—my heart, my breath, everything—like I was back in Bill's grasp. "What do you mean?" I knew what he meant; I just didn't want to believe it.

"Your blog. I'm pretty sure some people looked up your porn." Barnabas then mentioned that a friend of ours from the Bible study had admitted to him to searching for the videos. It validated my suspicion that some of my friends had viewed my naked image, even though I didn't want them to.

The places on my body where Bill had touched became colder, tighter. I was walking around naked. The spinning floor beneath me cracked open and swallowed me whole.

Did Bill see me naked in porn and get some kind of kink by holding me against him? Who else at this conference has seen those videos?

"Can you blame them?" Barnabas asked. "Not everyone knows a porn star, and now they do. Reading your testimony just gave them some curiosity."

It's my fault?

I wanted to say, "But I'm not a porn star. Why didn't you stick up for me when you found all this out?" Instead, I said nothing.

I hate that term, "porn star." It implies glitz and glamor, as if porn is just like any other part of the film and TV industry. Of course, that's what the porn industry wants people to think, but there is nothing glamorous about porn. It's like any other form of prostitution, except there's a camera. The camera prolongs the degrading experience as people continue to see you as nothing more than a "porn star."

I stood there silently as I tried to grasp the reality that people were using my testimony as an excuse to see me naked. Whether by curiosity or arousal, they were violating a sacred boundary that they respected for every other person. The Word says that we conquer the kingdom of darkness by the word of our testimonies, but that doesn't mean that the enemy will not fight back. This is why every believer must have a church, a group of believers to support them. I wanted to find people to support me at this conference.

THE NEXT MORNING, the bus that took us to the conference was so packed I had to stand shoulder to shoulder with some of my fellow attendees. I spent the ride talking to a Methodist woman who stood next to me.

"Tell me about speaking in tongues," she said. "I'm really curious about that."

My heart leaped. "Well, before Jesus ascended into Heaven, He told His disciples, 'John baptized with water, but you will be baptized with the Holy Spirit.'" As I spoke, someone behind me pinched my butt. Because of the crowd, I assumed it was an accident.

"So on the day of Pentecost," *pinch*, "the disciples were filled with the Holy Spirit," *pinch*, "and they began to speak in other tongues." *Pinch*. Waves rippled through every pore on my skin, and my hairs stood on end as I realized that the pinches were not an accident.

I turned around to see Jay. He was another one of the older men attending the conference. I looked down to see his hand mid-pinch at my butt. He looked away, smiling, acting casual, like he was not just about to pinch my butt.

"Can you please stop doing that?" I asked.

Jay blushed, looked at me from the corner of his eyes, and smiled.

I took a deep breath and exhaled to relax. I turned to continue my conversation. "I hear people say that tongues have to be a language that someone around can understand, but Acts 2 is the only specific example of that happening. And the Word also says that when we pray in tongues, we utter mysteries in the Spirit."[2] *Pinch.*

"I'm sorry," I yelled, turning back to Jay. "Can I help you? Is there a problem?"

Jay looked at me and made the same bashful smile. After taking a moment to glare at him, I looked up from Jay and saw another young man from the conference watching the scene. He didn't say anything, but he looked at me with his eyebrows furrowed like he was angry or confused. But he wasn't looking at Jay; he was looking at me. I turned back to the woman. She had the same look on her face. I noticed that the people next to us grew quiet. They didn't know what Jay was doing, but they had all clearly heard me and my tone. No one said anything about it. With one look, I completely shut down.

FOR THE REST of the conference, I could not shake the feeling of Bill and Jay touching my body. Every time I saw them throughout the conference, they taunted me with friendly smiles. At the sight of them, I felt their fingerprints burn into my skin again. When they looked at me, I had to look away.

At one point, all the attendees split up into small discussion groups. In my small group, I was finally distracted from my lingering thoughts of Bill and Jay when a young minister named Jesse asked, "Is it possible to have sex outside of marriage in a godly way?"

Barnabas had already been in a small group with Jesse. He warned me that Jesse was unconcerned with sex outside of marriage, porn, prostitution—everything—which concerned Barnabas and me because Jesse was an ordained pastor in a mainstream, Christian denomination. But I assumed Jesse was in the minority.

"Yes," a man next to me answered. My jaw fell open.

"I'm sure that's fine," a woman sitting across from me replied. To my surprise, five out of the eight people at my small group table agreed that God was okay with casual sex.

Jesse laughed. "Yeah, I'm pretty sure God doesn't care what I do with my penis." Those who agreed with him also laughed. My jaw was on the table.

God doesn't care?

It was the worst trigger. I had just been sexually assaulted *twice* within twenty-four hours, and now, my small group wanted to say that God doesn't care what we do with our bodies.

I wanted this conference to be a safe space. I had hoped that the situation with Bill and Jay was just a few people who may have had a brief moment of poor judgment. I shared my testimony blog with the attendees of this conference because I thought most of them would sympathize with the pain, shame, and trauma of being prostituted. I thought I would be safe without having to worry that they would look at my naked body. But I felt just like I did back in college when the group of guys left me in the car of the man who would eventually rape me. I thought those guys were safe, but they weren't.

My ears buzzed with a high-pitched white noise. My heart slammed against the walls of my ribcage. My entire body shook, and it was my turn to speak.

"I'm sure most of you saw the blog I shared in our Facebook group, but just in case you don't know, I was prostituted in the porn industry. I know what it's like to have sex non-stop and to pretend like it's thrilling and exciting. I have also realized the power of sex. When we have sex, we share a part of ourselves with another person, and they share a part of themselves with us. I know what it's like for sex to be treated like it isn't that big of a deal. I know what it's like to be used and discarded and then feel worthless and lonely and have that empty void deep inside of you that feels deeper and deeper with each person you have sex with.

"I do not believe that's what any of us really want, right? We all long to be loved. We long to be cared for. We long for an intimate relationship. That's why we're here, right? To stand on the side of love, even for LGBT+ Christians."

I looked at Jesse, who was not looking at me as I spoke. His hands sat clasped on the table in front of us, and he watched his thumbs as they slowly circled each other.

I continued, "The Word says to honor marriage because God will judge the sexually immoral.[3] There *is* such thing as sexual immorality, and God *does care* what we do with our bodies. If gay people can be a part of the body of Christ, then we should treat our bodies like they are temples containing His Spirit."

There was a moment where it seemed like we all held our breath. Jesse was silent as he continued to look at his hands on the table. I want to say that what I said moved everyone, and God compelled them to see and understand as the Spirit began to work in their hearts. But that's not what happened.

One man, who was only about a decade older than me, leaned forward. "Aaron, I appreciate where you're coming from, but you're also young and naive. You don't realize that's not how the real world works. I've been married for three years, and my wife and I are about to get a divorce. It doesn't always work out. You sound very *judge-y*."

Judge-y? If I'm judging anyone, I'm judging myself.

The white noise in my ears crescendoed until nothing. I mentally blacked out. I don't remember anything after hearing those words. From the moment Bill held me against his body, the conference felt like I was fighting off one big post-traumatic-stress trip after another, and this man's rebuttal was the last straw. It was the most unsafe I had ever felt in a church environment.

What else were they okay with? Would they care about how Bill touched me?

I know prostitution bears bad fruit. I know porn bears bad fruit. I know casual sex bears bad fruit. When many LGBT+ affirming Christians at this conference said that they believe it doesn't matter what we do in our sex lives, I saw bad fruit. When it came to being gay, the Lord told me that I would recognize where to stand by the fruit. The ex-gay movement seemed to repress romantic love; that was bad fruit. But what I experienced at this conference was worse!

Fruit is born through repentance.[4] Jesse and some other believers were openly unrepentant. They were in the complete opposite direction of the ex-gays, who confessed that they suppress their "sin." But some affirming believers weren't even concerned about sin at all, which made me feel that no one would care about what Bill and Jay had done to me.

When I finally came back from my mental blackout, the discussion group had wrapped up for a break. In the conference room, there was a stage with deep maroon curtains. As others left to go to the bathroom, I snuck behind the curtains to hide. I stood alone in the dark while I did the only thing I knew to do when I didn't know what else to do; I prayed in tongues. As unintelligible words fell from my lips, the Holy Spirit came upon me. Although the backstage was dark, His Presence shined bright within me, and the sense of being trapped subsided. With God, I am truly safe.

The Spirit touched my heart and began to soften an area that I didn't know was still hardened. At that moment, I saw that these people were victims of the same system that had exploited me. During this conference, we examined all of the clobber passages, which are all really about sexual exploitation, but the non-affirming church has insisted that they are about gay people. When we're told that we are something over and over, if we don't know who we truly are in God's eyes, there's a part of us that starts to believe the lies.

Maybe people, like Jesse, Bill, and Jay, had sexually immoral identities thrust upon them by the traditional teaching of the clobber passages. Their sexual orientation had been married to a pornographic spirit, and they complied with it. After all, even our society as a whole had normalized sexual immorality. They were giving in to what the world had told them was normal.

Throughout the conference, the speakers were discussing how affirming Christians could speak to non-affirming Christians about LGBT+ inclusion in the Church. But what was never discussed is that before we can talk to non-affirming Christians, we need to be set free from the sexually immoral system that the mainstream church assumes we are a part of. Otherwise, we've already lost.

As I hid behind the curtains, praying, one of my most favorite Bible stories came to mind: Peter at Cornelius' house in Acts 10. The Holy Spirit compelled Apostle Peter to meet a centurion, a high-ranking Roman soldier, named Cornelius. But Peter and all of Yeshua's first followers were Jewish. They thought Yeshua was sent to deliver His people from their oppressors, which they thought were the Romans. So the Jews believed they should have nothing to do with Gentiles—non-Jews—like Cornelius and his household.

Still, the Word describes Cornelius as "a devout man who feared God, with all his household, gave alms generously to the peoples and prayed continually to God." Cornelius' own servants described him as "an upright and God-fearing man."

When Peter got to Cornelius' house, he said, "You yourselves know how unlawful it is for a Jew to associate with or to visit anyone of another nation, but God has shown me that I should not call any person common or unclean."

It was Cornelius' devotion to God that gave Peter an *aha*-moment. Peter realized that the Lord wanted a relationship with whoever would seek to know Him. By Cornelius' devoted behavior, it was clear that he wanted to know the Lord.

As Peter preached the Gospel at Cornelius' house, God's Spirit fell on Cornelius and his family, and they began speaking in tongues. Peter had just had the revelation that the Church should include Gentiles in God's Kingdom, and the baptism in the Holy Spirit was like the cherry on top of that revelation.[5] Peter had been taught all his life that God was only for the Jewish people, but Cornelius' sanctification, the fact that he was devoted to God, caused Peter to have this paradigm shift.

Standing behind the maroon curtains, thinking about what I had experienced at this conference, I mourned. I knew that if LGBT+ affirming Christians wanted other believers to have a similar paradigm shift, we must be just as devoted and set apart from the world as Cornelius. The Word of God says, "For this is the will of God, your sanctification: that you abstain from sexual immorality; that each one of you know how to control his own body in holiness and honor, not in the passion of lust like the Gentiles who do not know God."[6] It is the will of God that the sex lives of *all* Christians be set apart and look different from the sex lives of people who do not know God. Our sex lives should be more loving than what is normal in the world.

If affirming Christians want to see non-affirming Christians have the same revelation that Peter had at Cornelius' house, then affirming Christians need to be like Cornelius: devout, God-fearing, consecrated, sanctified unto God, giving God *everything* in us and about us, including our sexual orientation. We must be willing to glorify God in our bodies. We must stand against sexual sin. We must be willing to lay down our lives for our spouses just as God laid His life down for His Church. Because that is *love,* and love overcomes sin![7]

I peeked from behind the curtain. People were settling back into their seats as the conference continued. I watched Bill, Jay, and Jesse move about, and I couldn't help but weep.

Do they realize that they are worth dying for?

I tried to hold the tears back, but they streamed down my face. I wiped them away as soon as they came and returned to my seat. A guy from my small group, who had been one of only a few to agree with my stance on sexual ethics, saw that I wasn't okay. As I headed back to our discussion table, he got up and embraced me in a loving hug. He would later tell me that my story gave him hope to continue to wait until marriage. He was a reminder that not every gay Christian is like Bill, Jay, and Jesse.

I was relieved when Barnabas later told me that he overheard a leader of this conference tell Jesse that had he been honest about his beliefs towards sexual ethics, he wouldn't have been a part of this conference. But Jesse still ended up being a conference speaker anyway, and even Jay, the butt pincher, was allowed to teach.

At one point, I wanted to speak to one of the conference leaders about what had happened to me with Bill and Jay. Then I overheard that leader making a crude sexual joke, as crude as a rape joke, and I knew I couldn't open up to him.

He wouldn't understand. This isn't a safe place for me.

AT SOME POINT during the conference, I noticed many people were calling loved ones back home. To ground myself and escape from the PTSD that I was experiencing, I took the opportunity to call Aaron Michael.

"Hey, Aaron," I said when he answered his phone. "Everyone's calling their boyfriends and girlfriends and stuff, so I thought I would call you." As soon as the words came out of my mouth, I realized what I had just said. My eyes widened at the awkwardness of it. Aaron Michael and I had barely just started talking, so it was a bit bold to imply that I liked him like that.

"Aww! That's sweet," Aaron replied. I smiled. It seemed that he liked that I liked him.

"I just wanted to say thanks for being someone who supports me."

Honestly, because of my experience at this conference, if it wasn't for Aaron Michael, I might have become a non-affirming Christian. It was too startling that many people didn't take sexual immorality seriously. To me, it was bad fruit that could only come from bad teaching.

But as I talked with Aaron Michael, I remembered that the bad fruit of sexual immorality isn't inherently rooted in LGBT+ Christians. After all, even some straight Christians are okay with sexual immorality. It's so normal in mainstream society that even doctor's offices and fertility clinics have porn ready as if porn is necessary for procreation. To me, that's a clear indicator that our society is dependent on porn, and it was heartbreaking to realize that what is normal to the world has infiltrated the Church. And how was I, a man who had been prostituted in porn, going to survive in a pornified church?

NINETEEN

THE *PRETTY WOMAN* MINDSET

THE AIR-CONDITIONING was broken at the church where we met for Bible study, but we got together anyway. Sweat poured down everyone's faces, and more of us had pit stains on our shirts than not. But we continued to study the Book of Acts.

One of the guys read the Scripture out loud, "For it has seemed good to the Holy Spirit and to us to lay on you no greater burden than these requirements: that you abstain from what has been sacrificed to idols, and from blood, and from what has been strangled, and from sexual immorality. If you keep yourselves from these, you will do well."[1]

"Stop there for a sec," I interrupted. "I have a thought and a question."

After Peter's experience at Cornelius' house, the Jewish Christians sent a letter to the Gentile Christians explaining that it was important for them to abstain from food associated with idol worship and abstain from sexual immorality.

I explained, "In this verse, the word for 'sexual immorality' is the Greek word '*porneia*.' It's from this root word that we get the

English word 'pornography.' Here in Acts, we're told to abstain from sexual immorality, and in another part of the Word of God, we're told to 'flee from sexual immorality,' to flee from porn."[2]

There it was on the page. Everyone, except for a few new people, knew that I had been exploited in porn. They knew about the pain I suffered. They knew I felt violated when people saw the porn that I was in. Everyone in the room said they loved Jesus and believed the Bible, including the verse we had just read.

"So my question is: do you guys think that my life before I knew the Lord, my life in the porn industry, was it of God or not?"

Everyone's face froze. A derelict, oscillating fan that had been brought in to help with the heat was the only movement around us. It blew the silence from one side of the room to the other.

"I don't think that's a fair question to ask," Barnabas finally said from across the room. His response disappointed me because he and Mike were the only ones, as far as I knew, who believed in waiting until marriage. I had hoped that he would be the person to give what I assumed was the obvious answer. I had hoped that at least Barnabas would take a stand for me.

"Yeah, you're kind of asking us to judge you," a friend sitting next to Barnabas replied.

I thought about it a second. "I'm asking you to judge the fruit that I bore. 'A bad tree can only bear bad fruit.' There's nothing wrong with judging spiritual fruit. I'm asking you to judge everything that I went through. Was that of God? Did it bear good or bad fruit?"

The stillness in the room was interrupted only by the fan turning again toward where I sat. Its breeze frustrated the heat that rose to my face the longer everyone sat silently.

"I think you're asking a very bold question, Aaron," the guy sitting next to me said.

I turned to him, "Is it a bold question? I'm just asking if my life in the porn industry was okay with God?" I looked around at everyone. Many of them were awkwardly adjusting in their seats. They continued to look at me with no response. My face boiled.

"No!" I shouted. "The answer is *no*! My porn, *any porn,* is not of God."

After the Bible study, Barnabas pulled me to the side. "Aaron, I don't think you handled that right. You know that most people there disagree with your sexual ethics, and there were new people there today. The first thing the new people got from you is that they are probably sinning, so you probably scared them off."

I was in shock because none of my friends could tell me that what I went through was wrong, not even Barnabas. It was hard for me to accept that my closest Christian friends couldn't empathize with me. I started to question what I thought I knew.

Do they think God was okay with the times I was raped? Was God okay with the brutal treatment that I received on the porn sets? The degradation? The abuse?

I needed someone, *anyone,* to validate my trauma, to agree that what had happened to me was *not* of God.

At the next Bible study, I publicly apologized. "I'm not saying 'sorry' for my beliefs on sex. I'm not saying 'sorry' for how I feel. But if I used the wrong tone, if I came off as aggressive, I ask for your forgiveness."

I apologized, but I was so tired of apologizing. I was so tired of constantly trying to communicate to Christians that I was exploited in prostitution and that prostitution is *inherently* exploitative. I was so tired of them not getting it or choosing not to get it. I was so tired.

"Aaron, you know, some people *want* to do sex work, right?" one of my friends from the Bible study argued afterward when we went to dinner. "Even *you* enjoyed it at one point."

I understand why many porn users say this. It can be difficult to recognize that your own behavior is unloving and harmful to others. By saying porn is okay because prostituted people enjoy doing it, porn users excuse themselves from any possible harm that happened to create that video. But when people assume that I enjoyed being in porn, they do not realize that they make an assumption my pimp and all of my sex-buyers once made about me.

When I hear stuff like prostituted people "want" to be in porn or prostitution, my mind always flashes back to the same moment. It was right after the porn shoot when the producer asked me what else I wanted my fans to know about me.

I said, "I want people to know that there is more to me than all of this."

The moment those words fell from my mouth, the atmosphere shifted on set. My producer urged me to say something else, but nothing else came to mind.

That shoot happened not long after I heard the Christian man tell me, "Jesus *loves* you." The thought of the Creator of the universe caring about me made me wonder if I was worth more than what I was doing in porn.

After that awkward interview, as I was leaving the studio, the performers for the next scene began to arrive on set. One of them, Brad, stumbled down the hall. After a few steps, he had to lean against the wall to hold himself up. His arms dangled limply at his side. His body reeked of cheap vodka.

"Brad, are you okay?" I asked.

"—'m fine." Brad almost fell over as he mumbled and giggled at himself.

My co-performer, Scott, and I wrapped Brad's arms around our shoulders as we led him to the set where he knocked over almost all of the lights and cameras. We laid Brad on the bed and left him to "perform" the porn scene in that state.

The image haunted me. When I looked at Brad, it was like I was seeing myself for the first time. He was a visible representation of what I already knew about myself but was too afraid to admit. I knew why Brad was drunk. I knew how he felt. I knew exactly what he was doing. I did it too. I was Brad. Like him, I did everything I could to dissociate from the fact that I submitted my body to exploitation.

As I packed up to leave, I couldn't shake Brad's image and the knowledge of where I had left him. By leaving Brad in that state, I became no better than José from college when he took pictures of me while I was blackout drunk and being raped by Brandon. I was no better than the young men who left me in the older man's car before he later raped me.

On my way out, Scott complained to me, "Ugh, I don't want to perform with Brad. He's been a mess lately. He's always drunk or high, and he was crying the other day about how he doesn't want to do porn anymore."

I looked down at my feet. We all had our methods of dissociating from the reality of what we were doing. This time, Brad decided that he needed to get drunk—if that's all he did—to do what he needed to do to make the money that porn offered him.

I looked back up to Scott. "Do any of us want to do this, though?"

Scott was only eighteen, barely legal. His family disowned him because he is gay, so he jumped from friends' couches to hotel rooms. Being young, inexperienced, and with no major job skills, Scott didn't know of any better way to take care of himself other than to be sold for sex. He paid for everything he needed by selling himself.

Scott took a moment before answering, "If I could get a better job, I guess I would."

The reason it was so awkward when I said, "I want people to know that there is more to me than all of this," is because we told the public that we enjoyed being in porn. We *had* to. But my answer to my producer's question was my subconscious pointing out to all of us what I had buried deep within me through dissociation. My subconscious shined a light on the hollow relationship between porn prostitutes and porn watchers. Our fans didn't know us, but they visually had sex with us. They didn't know anything real about us, let alone why we were doing what we were doing. That's why my producer needed me to give another response. In editing, he cut out my actual answer because it was too real for porn.

But in the company of other prostituted people, we could be honest with each other. We all knew that none of us really wanted to do this. It was our crutch "career" that held us up until, hopefully, we could find something better. Unfortunately, many of us never find anything better.

In a pornified culture, sex-buyers like to believe that prostituted people enjoy being prostituted. Sex-buyers often use phrases like, "It was their choice," "They enjoy it," or "Sex work is work," as an excuse for them to buy sex. These phrases are a cover from the reality that sex-buyers treat human beings as sex toys. It gives them an escape from being accountable for renting humans as masturbation tools.

Sex-buyers have, what I like to call, a *Pretty Woman* mindset about prostitution. In the 1990 movie, *Pretty Woman*, a prostituted woman falls in love with her wealthy sex-buyer. Throughout the film, the prostituted woman, played by Julia Roberts, is portrayed as enjoying being prostituted. The film paints her as having so much fun with her sex-buyer that she falls in love with him. Like that movie portrays, many sex-buyers make the romanticized assumption that prostituted people enjoy what sex-buyers do to them.

The *Pretty Woman* mindset is the same mindset that a desperate sex-buyer has in a strip club when he thinks that the naked dancers are actually into him. But they are not into him. They are *never* into him. They are into his money because they *need* his money. The *Pretty Woman* mindset is the same mindset that gay porn fans have when they argue over whether or not the gay-for-pay person secretly enjoys the gay sex he is having. To gay porn fans, it makes the porn more fun and erotic, but the only reason gay-for-pay exists is not that some straight people want to have gay sex. They have gay sex because they *need* the money.

Of course, some prostituted people claim to enjoy what they do. In business, you have to cater to the buyer. If I had answered my producer's question completely honestly with, "I want my fans to know that I only do porn to barely get by and survive," that would have turned our buyers off. If I had told my sex-buyers that I was only having sex with them because I was impoverished and didn't have any other resources to pay for rent, food, and school expenses, a decent human being would probably feel sorry for me, not aroused. I had to betray myself to sell myself.

The *Pretty Woman* mindset protects sex-buyers from recognizing that prostitution is unloving, exploitative, and traumatizing for prostituted people. It accepts the belief that if there is any harm in prostitution, it's not the sex-buyer's fault at all; it's only the prostituted person's fault because they were *asking for it.*

The *Pretty Woman* mindset also argues, "Not everyone likes their job. We all have to make money somehow." In the *Pretty Woman* film, the sex-buyer, played by Richard Gere, even compares his business to the prostituted woman's situation by saying they both "screw people for money," as if implying that prostitution is like any other business. But prostitution is *not* like any other business. Real work is the sale and production of goods and services. Prostitution is the sale and abuse of humans. By its nature, the cheap price paid for humanity in prostitution is inherently unloving and exploitative.

In the Bible, we are reminded that we were "bought with a price" twice: when discussing prostitution and slavery.[3] In both, the idea is the same: if God has already paid the highest price for humanity, then it would cheapen a human's value to treat them like a product to be bought with mere human money. Whether it is for prostituted sex or enslaved labor, humans should not be bought and sold. In God's eyes, we are infinitely more valuable than what money can buy.

Therefore, Christians must choose whether humanity is worth dying for, or humans can buy and rent other humans with dollars. It can't be both. We must choose whether humanity is worth Yeshua's blood shed on the cross or not. God's Word says that humans are not meant for prostitution; humans are meant for the Lord.[4] Either humanity has a God-given worth and value, or we do not. Christians *must* choose.

Affirming Christians *especially* need to make their choice on where they stand with this. With everything I've been through and seen, I know where I stand. My past experiences inform me that all forms of prostitution are unloving. This is the true purpose of the clobber passages. When understood correctly, these verses can bring freedom, not bondage, to LGBT+ people.

It was so discouraging to hear that so many LGBT+ affirming Christians bought into the *Pretty Woman* lie because this mindset undermines the affirming perspective. If prostitution is *not* unloving in every circumstance, then there's an obvious catch-22 for affirming Christians. If prostitution is acceptable, then the interpretation of the clobber passages by non-affirming Christians is correct, and homosexuality is unacceptable.

Two things are going on in the clobber passages: same-sex sex and sexual exploitation such as rape and prostitution. In the traditional view, Sodom's rapists and the male prostitutes throughout the Word of God are "homosexuals." It's as if the problem isn't the circumstances at all; it's the same-sex sex in general. This ignores the degradation inherent to rape and prostitution, like what the *Pretty Woman* mindset does. In 1 Corinthians 6:9, either "male prostitutes" and those who rent them are unrighteous and will not inherit the Kingdom of God because prostitution is inherently unjust, or the verse really condemns "men who practice homosexuality." If there's nothing wrong with prostitution and porn, then the clobber passages really are a condemnation of LGBT+ people. The way I see it, a Christian cannot be truly LGBT+ affirming and support prostitution in any way without throwing out the Bible's authority. Instead, all Christians must tear down the *Pretty Woman* mindset and recognize that prostitution is completely degrading and entirely unacceptable.

When my Christian friends would argue that some people, including me, enjoy being prostituted, I felt trapped in a computer, screaming for help from my friends, but no one listened. Instead, they kept clicking on their screens, masturbating to the abuse. Then to deny that it was unloving in God's eyes, even to dare imply that in *any* circumstance, God would be okay with it, that was too much for me.

I was re-traumatized hearing Christians say that I wanted to be prostituted. These *Pretty-Woman*-mindset Christians turned my past into something they wanted it to be, something sexy and intriguing so that they would not have to confront the fact that what they were doing was harmful and unloving. They denied the reality I experienced so that they could continue to buy fantasies and ignore that they were created through exploitation.

AFTER I WENT HOME from that Bible study, I did what I normally did to remind myself that not all LGBT+ affirming Christians see porn as normal and acceptable. I called Aaron Michael on a video chat.

"They don't get it, Aaron," I cried. "It's like I'm telling them everything I went through, and they either don't believe it, or they aren't listening. They still think porn is okay."

"I'm really sorry they said all that to you," Aaron Michael replied.

"I don't understand their thinking. If I'm their friend, why does it seem like they don't even care?"

Aaron looked down as if looking for the words. "I'm not trying to validate their behavior or anything, but it probably comes from a place of hurt."

"What do you mean?"

"I mean, I watched porn when I felt lonely and vulnerable. We all want to feel connected to other people, and porn kind of makes you feel validated and somehow less alone. Some of them might be struggling with some kind of pain, like rejection or depression, and porn is the way that they've learned to numb that pain. For you to come along and take that away, you might be making them face the pain that they are trying to ignore."

Aaron Michael had a point. Humans need intimacy, and porn, in a way, is like a fake supplement that superficially fulfills that need. So the challenge isn't just pointing out the harms of porn on prostituted people, but also the harms on the viewers. Porn is a fake fulfillment for a deep, natural human need. By using porn, we deprive ourselves of truly fulfilling that need.

I smiled at Aaron. "You're so cute. I wish I could hug you right now."

He smiled back.

Porn can't love us back. Prostituted people will not love us back. Go-go dancers, strippers, and exotic dancers will not love us back. The demand for buying sex comes from a need for love trying to be fulfilled, but it's a counterfeit that only superficially looks like intimacy and love. Everyone is worthy of love. Everyone is worthy of being with someone they want to be with and who wants to be with them. But sex-buyers deprive themselves of love when they seek to fulfill that need through porn or any form of prostitution.

Aaron Michael helped me see that I needed to have compassion for those who were unwilling to repent and still watched porn. I needed to show people who opposed my message the real, authentic love that can only be found in Yeshua. Still, the world even resisted Yeshua, love in the flesh, by crucifying Him. How can you bring real love to people who resist it?

After I got off the video chat with Aaron Michael, I spent some time praying and worshiping. I wanted to share the truth of what happens in porn, but the pushback was hard to deal with. The tree of my faith had broken through the pot of religious tradition. I was burrowing my roots into the earth around me. But as my roots stretched through the ground, they kept colliding into rocky, immovable resistance. My roots could either grow around the stoniness or breakthrough it as I did the pot.

As I prayed, God's Spirit led me to turn my Bible to Revelation 12:11. On the page, I noticed something that I hadn't noticed before. I heard the passage recited at churches repeatedly, but this part seemed to be conveniently left out.

"And they conquered him [the enemy] by the blood of the Lamb and by the word of their testimony, for *they loved not their lives even unto death.*"

It was not just the Lamb's blood or just the believers' testimonies that conquered the enemy. It was because the believers were willing to give up their lives in the midst of the battle against the enemy. God laid His life down for them, and they were willing to lay their lives down for Him. This is our marriage covenant with the Lord. Laying down our lives is a part of love.

If I want to show people real love, I have to be willing to lay my life down to get the truth to them. The world met even early Christians with resistance and opposition. Like Yeshua, the world killed many of them because of their message.

Am I willing to continue to tell my testimony even if people use it to humiliate me? Am I willing to lay my life down to get God's truth to the people even if they resist it? Am I willing to tell my story even if it kills me?

A gust of wind rushed into the room and wrapped me in spiritual comfort. I was reminded that the early Church needed the Holy Spirit's boldness to preach God's message in the midst of resistance and opposition.[5]

Already, I had seen God use my testimony for His glory. My story helped Aaron Michael break free from porn use. I had a Bible study friend confess that he almost slept with someone he had just met, but he couldn't go through with it because my testimony had moved him. Another person messaged me to let me know that they completely quit watching porn after reading my story. I knew God had to be doing something.

"Yes," I said out loud. "Lord, I will continue to tell my testimony no matter what."

If even just one person could be saved, if even just one person would repent, if even one person was set free from this corrupt system, I was willing to continue to share what the Lord had done for me, even if it killed me. Love is worth dying for.

"But Father, please help me find a church where I feel safe and supported so that I can tell this message. I need a sanctuary for when the world gets unbearable."

I sensed in my spirit that God was answering that prayer, but I wasn't sure how.

TWENTY

SEX-POSITIVE GOD

I WENT BACK to Barnabas' affirming church to meet with his pastor. I told the pastor my testimony and asked him how he teaches sexual ethics in his church.

He responded, "While I agree with you that sex is reserved for marriage, I don't really teach much on sex. The LGBTQ community has been hit so hard over the head with the sex topic that I try to stay away from it so that I don't scare anyone away from Jesus."

He sounded a lot like Barnabas, concerned with scaring people, and I understood where he was coming from. I know many people who were raised in the church, but now, they want nothing to do with Jesus because of the traditional teaching on homosexuality. However, there should be a balance. Ignoring the topic of sexual sin altogether leaves people vulnerable to being trapped in a system of sexual exploitation. By refusing to preach about sin, pastors hinder their congregation from being forgiven of much, which hinders people from loving God very much, hindering them from walking in freedom from sin. *"He who is forgiven little, loves little.*" This pastor's response just wasn't enough to make me feel that I would be safe at his church because it meant no one was getting free from sexual sin.

I visited several affirming churches in my area. I questioned the pastors to see where they stood on sexual ethics because I wanted a church where I felt safe. I wanted a church that believed that humanity needed Yeshua to set them free from the world's sexually exploitative culture that we are all victims of. I wanted a church where I wouldn't feel like I was walking around naked.

I expected three things from a church for me to feel safe there.

First, I expected them to teach that sex is godly and loving *only* within a covenantal marriage. God laid His life down for the Church out of love, and laying one's life down for a spouse by waiting until marriage, and then faithfulness in marriage, is the love that He empowers us to walk in. Anything outside of this falls short of God's glory and is sin.

Second, I looked for a church that held this standard for its leaders. By this point, I had seen the negative fruit that churches bear when they refuse to hold leadership to this standard. I wasn't the only one to experience sexual harassment from Christians. Another friend of mine was raped by a leader at a church he visited, and for my friend, that was a reflection of that entire church community. Leaders should be held to higher standards.

The final thing I hoped to see is churches should try to have some kind of supportive culture for those living by this standard. The hardest part about waiting until marriage is the loneliness. Things like singles' Bible studies or connect groups or something that normalizes waiting until marriage in the church's culture would help combat that loneliness and resist the temptation to compromise our worth by having sex outside of marriage.

As I continued to look for sexually moral affirming churches in my area, I visited a church that a friend had been attending. I should have known that this church wasn't right for me because my friend was one of the leaders of this church. When I had told him about my past in porn, his response was, "Cool! What websites are you on?"

It knocked me back. I had to take a moment to determine if he was kidding. He was serious. "No, man! I'm not proud of that."

His pastor was a woman. She was older and stout, and she wore half-moon glasses that magnified her eyes. She responded to my inquiry by asking, "What do you think about polyamorous couples?"

"I'm sorry? What do you mean? What about them?"

"Well, we have several poly couples in this church, so if you're going to ask me about porn, I'm curious about your thoughts on polyamory. Could God bless that?"

"Well, I know that some men in the Old Testament had many wives, but I see it causing major problems as it did with Solomon's wives turning him away from God.[1] And if marriage is to lay your life down for your spouse and forsaking all others—like how we should lay our lives down for God and forsake all other gods—then I would think that monogamy is the most loving option. One God. One Church. One spouse."

How a Christian lives out their sex life is critical to their faith because if marriage is an example of the love between Yeshua and the Church, then a believer's sex life reflects his or her heart towards Yeshua. If a believer cannot be faithful to one spouse, it is unlikely they will be faithful to one God. Solomon worshiped the one God, but he had many wives. And his many wives eventually turned him towards many gods. This revelation was further revealed to me when I found out that this church accepted polyamorous relationships *and* leaned more towards universalism despite maintaining a Christian identity.

Universalism, the idea that all spiritual beliefs are true, is essentially the belief in many gods. The consistent pattern seems to be that those who cannot accept monogamous marriage and/or are unwilling to wait until marriage also cannot completely accept the concept that Yeshua is the *only* Way, the *only* Truth, and the *only* Life.[2] To reject Yeshua is to reject God because He is God. If our hearts are not transformed to love one spouse, our hearts are not geared to remain faithful to one God.

The pastor looked at me from over her glasses like a librarian giving a loud student the "be quiet" look.

I laughed nervously. "One spouse seems like enough to me."

She held her stern gaze on me.

I did not visit *every* church in my area, and I also do not know if I would have this same issue in churches today. But back then, I couldn't find anywhere I felt safe. If it weren't for Aaron Michael, I would have felt completely alone.

AARON MICHAEL had arranged to visit Los Angeles to figure out how he would move here in a couple of months, but he wasn't going to stay with me. A friend offered for Aaron to stay at his place because it was clear that Aaron and I had feelings for each other. To honor each other and God by waiting until marriage, we thought it was best for Aaron to stay with someone else.

Leading up to Aaron Michael visiting, I admitted to him, "I'm kind of nervous about you coming here."

"Why?"

"Well," I stammered, "What if you don't find me as attractive when you see me in person?"

Because Aaron and I had only been speaking through text messages and video chats, he was at a safe enough distance that I could still control what he knew about me and how he saw me. Meeting in person was a whole new step. What if he saw me and was immediately like, "We should just be friends," while I'm over here falling for him?

"What?" he laughed. "I see you right now, and I think you're cute."

"Yeah, but the camera quality isn't like high-def, but in-person you can see *everything* that the camera hides."

He paused for a moment. I wondered if he knew the high demand that I once lived under to remain aesthetically pleasing.

"That makes me sad that you feel that way," he said. "You're fearfully and wonderfully made."[3]

His words, the Word of God, washed over me like warm spring rain. I had never met someone as genuinely sweet as him.

On the day Aaron Michael arrived, I was more nervous than I had ever been. I walked up to the shopping center where Aaron Michael was waiting for me, and I saw him from a distance. He had a skip in his step and a smile on his face. He was so cute!

"God, please let him like me," I prayed under my breath.

When Aaron Michael noticed me, his smile grew wider. He skipped up to me and immediately embraced me in a hug. It was the hug that I needed ever since his reaction to my testimony.

"You are so cute! I can't believe you don't even know it," he said as he released me from his hug.

I sighed with relief. I realized that I could be myself around Aaron Michael. He accepted me as me. He truly believed I was fearfully and wonderfully made. I didn't have to pretend. I didn't have to try to be, or appear to be, someone I'm not. I had the freedom to be me.

Every night that week, I took Aaron Michael to his friend's apartment to stay the night. It was difficult because, if it were possible, I never wanted him to leave my side. But it was also easy to drop him off somewhere else because he was precious to me.

Even though we had just met in person, I felt like I already knew Aaron Michael because of our interactions online. Still, I wanted to know more of him, to know the intricacies of his thoughts, the motives behind every subtle gesture, how deep his love for God went. I wanted to dive into him and truly know him. Know his sweet smile, his sensitivity, the way his hand felt in mine. Being with him was like stepping into a warm shower on a frigid day.

After my first relationship in high school, a relationship where we decided we were "experimenting" and nothing more, I avoided the idea of dating someone. I avoided pain. Guys would ask me out, and even if I were attracted to them, I would turn them down. We could hookup. We could be friends with benefits. But I didn't want a boyfriend. I didn't want that pain again. We could have sex because I thought sex was just a physical act with no strings attached. Sex was like a handshake. But we can't be anything more than friends, even though sex did make us more. I tried to erase the intimacy that was inherent to sex. I wouldn't even talk to guys very much before we slept together. We didn't get to know each other. Then, after we had sex, there was always something that repulsed me about the men I slept with. Today, I know I was repulsed by the intimacy that we shared. I feared that intimacy and the pain that could come with it. Now, after developing a relationship with Yeshua, God was doing something in my heart.

What attracted me the most to Aaron Michael was his innocence. He was waiting until marriage since before I met him, and just the mere fact that he gave someone like me a chance showed me what a pure heart he had. He came from a strict Baptist upbringing, and most people who were raised like him would never, after hearing my past, think it would be a good idea to go on a date with someone like me. But he did. Something about that grace and purity compelled me to want to have some part of it, protect it, honor it, and keep it sacred and uncorrupted.

Aaron and I planned a whole day where it would be just him and me at Disneyland. We held hands almost everywhere we went in the park. There were moments throughout the day that I wanted to tell him what it felt like to be around him, but I wasn't sure how to say it. I didn't have the words, like I was trying to translate some foreign concept that I didn't have the language for.

At the end of our day, we watched one of Disney's nighttime shows. Film projections displayed brilliantly colorful images onto a screen of water that shot up from an artificial lake in the middle of the park as thousands of people looked on in awe and delight.

Aaron Michael put his arm around me as we watched the show. At first, I cringed internally and shrunk back, just as I had always done when someone tried to be that intimate with me. Every other time anyone had ever touched me like that they were doing it to use me, to manipulate me, to get close enough that they could touch my body for their own pleasure. But with Aaron, it was warm, gentle, and pure, like when God first embraced me. Aaron wasn't trying to touch me for a perverted motive. He just put his arm around me, and it was comfortable. It was safe. The show's fantasy around us and Aaron's welcomed touch upon my body rushed from my heart and straight out of my mouth.

"I love you," I whispered into his ear.

He looked at me. We both paused for a moment to take in what I had just said. I hadn't used those words in that way since my "experiment" relationship back in high school. Back then, the true feelings my words expressed were eventually betrayed. Since then, I locked those words away, never to be used again. But now, they broke free from their prison. I said it, and I meant it. This time, unlike the last time, the words were empowered by the Spirit of Love.

"You *love* me?" he asked.

Oh no. He didn't say it back. This is too soon. I probably just made this whole thing awkward and ruined it all.

"Y-yes," I stuttered.

Ugh! What is coming out of my mouth? Why am I saying this now?

He held me tighter and smiled. "I love you too."

The warmth he ignited within me spread to every inch of my being. It was one thing to love, but to be loved in return is better. Our embrace was cozy, comfortable, real, and natural. As the show went on and fireworks exploded in the air, I inched in and allowed my lips to meet his—our first kiss.

AT THE END of our week together, Aaron Michael had to go back home for a couple more months before he officially moved to Los Angeles. As he got into a car to take him back to the train station, it felt like a piece of me was going with him. Like, I was temporarily separating from a part of myself.

For the next few months, we talked every single day. Time with him became a regular part of my routine. I'd come home from work, do some prayer and worship, and spend the rest of the night talking to Aaron before bed. It helped make the distance seem a little less distant.

When Aaron Michael finally moved to Los Angeles, I was ecstatic. He was renting a room in a house less than five miles from where I lived. Just like when he came for that first visit, every night that we hung out, there was always that difficult time where I had to make him leave my place, or I had to leave his.

He used to joke with me as he stood in my doorway, "You love doing this, don't you? You can't wait for me to leave."

The truth is that it was a hard part of waiting until marriage, but it was also easy. It wasn't because of some religious rule or some chastity vow. It was easy because of love. We loved God, and we loved each other. Love made it easy.

"Yes, so go away," I'd play along as I'd shut the door in his face. But then I'd text him.

ME

> Please, don't forget to text me when you've made it home safe.

Then ten minutes later,

AARON MICHAEL

> I'm home. Miss you already. Love you. Goodnight.

ME

> Love you, too. Goodnight.

. . .

AARON MICHAEL joined me in my desperate search for a church. Another gay Christian friend of ours began to attend a new church plant. This friend said that the pastor was very open to discuss homosexuality in the Bible with him and was open to finding ways to reach out to LGBT+ people. Aaron and I thought it was a perfect opportunity for us because it was a mainstream church that took a stand on sexual ethics. It at least had the *possibility* of becoming LGBT+ affirming. Since we couldn't find an affirming church in our area where we felt safe, we thought we could give a not-yet-affirming church-plant a chance.

Despite being openly gay, we were allowed to worship and get as close to the altar as we could get. In fact, at this church, I don't think there was a possibility for them even to suggest that my worship was distracting because everyone worshiped like we were at some Holy Spirit dance party. Actually, everyone else's worship was even more intense than mine, so I had to adapt a little.

The church met in a nightclub, and not just any nightclub; it was a nightclub where I once performed as a go-go dancer.

"We're gonna go hard or go home in this church," the lead pastor shouted. Pastor Doug was a full-on hipster. He wore long shirts and skinny jeans. He had a medium-length beard and long hair that he covered with a rancher hat.

"We came in this morning, and this club still had stripper poles, and in the restrooms, we found used syringes. It was clear that the kingdom of darkness used this club last night, but we know dance and music is a form of worship. The enemy wants to take that and distort it to get us to worship something other than the Lord. But we're gonna take this place back for the Kingdom of God. Amen?!"

The club erupted in praise. "Amen!" We all shouted as the bass dropped, and we began to rave for Jesus.

The worship was very much like a rock concert. The worship band dressed like a rock band—leather jackets, flat-billed caps, skinny jeans, pierced and gauged ears, and tattoos. As we worshiped, a light technician put on a full light show with fog machines and blue and green lasers. They didn't hold back, and they encouraged everyone to give everything in praise.

I did exactly what Pastor Doug suggested. I worshiped the Lord, Who saved me from sexual exploitation, in one of the places where I was once sexually exploited. I was taking back what the enemy had taken from me and giving it back to God. I danced harder for the Lord than I ever danced when I was in prostitution or even at my previous non-affirming church.

Pastor Doug's messages shook me, challenged me, and enlightened me deeper into the Word of God. And I was thankful that he was so candid about sex.

"Sex is supernatural," he preached. "Sex is a *very good* thing. Some people say Christians are sex-negative, but that's weird because we worship a sex-positive God."

It has always been interesting to me that pro-prostitution people tend to accuse people like me of being sex-negative. Oddly, people think an industry built on fake "sex" is somehow pro-sex. On the other hand, the Bible has an entire book dedicated to sex poetry. Through the Song of Solomon, God paints a picture of just how intimate sex is intended to be. Contrary to the pro-prostitution crowd, standing on the side of love and intimacy—the true purpose of *real* sex—is true sex-positivity.

Pastor Doug continued, "Sex is amazing and extraordinary, and I don't just say that because I'm a dude with hormones. I believe that because the Word of God tells me that. And it tells me that sex is designed for one place and one place only: the marriage bed.[4]

"The Word says, 'They shall become one flesh.'[5] So sex is not just for us to make babies. Sex is the supernatural glue that makes a married couple united into one together.

"But you see, what God creates and calls good, the enemy comes along and perverts. God created sex and intimacy; the enemy distorted it into pornography and isolation."

I shifted to the edge of my seat. This was the first time I had ever heard anyone preach about pornography.

"Jesus said that just to look at a woman with lust is to commit adultery with her in your heart.[6] The world believes pornography doesn't hurt anyone, but God says pornography hurts *everyone!*"

At first, I wasn't sure what the appropriate response should be. When I talked like this, I was told I wasn't fair. But this church responded to Pastor Doug with cheers and applause. People around us stood to their feet, clapped their hands, and shouted, "Amen!" I was stunned, but I clapped and cheered as well. I had said some of these same things before, but I never got this type of reaction. People responded to me with rebuke and opposition.

What was different? Pastor Doug's church was a mainstream church with many people who have been in the Church most of their lives. They were familiar with this kind of preaching. They were able to be fully rooted in their church, to grow and soak up all the nourishment that the Church provided them. But many of the people to whom I said these things—LGBT+ people—experienced the Church the way that I experienced my first church. They were told they could only come so close, which left many of them unable to be fully rooted. When we have to hide a part of ourselves from God's Light, that's when the darkness comes in. Without the full stature of membership in churches, many LGBT+ people lack full spiritual nourishment, so they seek what they lack from the world. The world's system becomes normal to them, so when I said things like, "The 'sex' industry is an enemy of God," they resisted it. Because the Church doesn't fully accept them, they cannot recognize the haven the Church offers from this world's corruption, leaving many of them to remain enslaved to sin.

Pastor Doug continued, "Do you know why people sell their bodies?"

I do, I thought to myself.

"Because they don't feel loved," Pastor Doug answered. "They don't believe that they can receive love, especially God's love. And you know what Christians tell them when they use them for sex? They tell them that they *really* are not worthy of love. How can we say that we follow the God Who loves everybody and then go home and do that to people?"

My heart raced. Aaron Michael and I stood up and applauded the message. Pastor Doug took everything that I had ever wanted to say and brought it forth with such boldness and force that the congregation was blown back in their seats.

"Yes!" I screamed. "Yes, that's right! Amen!"

"The Word says, 'Love is patient,'"[7] Pastor Doug continued over our shouts of praise. "Hear me when I say this. Love is willing to wait."

It was the first time I had ever heard anyone get so blunt and so clear from any church, affirming or non-affirming. It's what I had longed to hear preached from the pulpit.

After that service, I went to Pastor Doug. "I like what you said about how people get into prostitution because they don't feel loved. I like that because I was prostituted in porn before I knew Yeshua."

"Wow! And would you say what I said is true?"

"Absolutely, yes. I didn't know that I could be loved by God or by anyone until I found the Lord." As I said it, I looked at a wooden cross the church had set up next to the stage, and then I looked at Aaron Michael. I smiled. "But now, I've found love."

Pastor Doug pulled me into a firm hug. It seemed—I had hoped—that we had found the right church for us.

TWENTY-ONE

THE BODY OF CHRIST

A T WORK, one of the development producers—producers who pitch show ideas to the networks—approached me. "Some networks are wanting to buy a reality show that features Christians. They want something that has a music element, like Christian rock or something like that. Do you have any ideas for people who could fit that description?"

My new church was perfect: youthful, rock-concert-esque worship and edgy preaching that stuck to the Word.

After service that weekend, I pulled Pastor Doug to the side. I asked him if he would be interested in letting me share his contact information with my producer. He was just as excited about the opportunity as I was. The producers contacted him and set up an interview.

The next Sunday, the development producer and our executive producer both showed up at church to shoot some footage of the service. Pastor Doug had seats set up in the very front just for them. My producers both grew up in Catholic families, so their first reaction was, "Wow! This is a church?"

As the band began to praise and worship, the blue and green laser lights began to flash, and the fog machine blasted into the atmosphere. My producers were smiling ear to ear as they recorded the experience. It was great TV material, completely new to both of them, and better than they had expected.

Pastor Doug delivered another one of his fiery messages. "We spread the 'fragrance of the knowledge' of Jesus *everywhere* we go.[1] It's not just about what we do on Sundays at church. It's about Monday through Saturday too. Jesus is a seven-days-a-week, three-hundred-sixty-five-days-a-year God. Everywhere we go, everything we say, and everything we do should be spreading Him throughout all the earth."

He looked at my producers, and then he looked at me. "Aaron!"

Oh, God, why is he calling me out?

"For everyone who doesn't know, Aaron works in television production, and his company just interviewed my wife and me to see if we might do a Christian reality TV show.

"Aaron, you don't know this, but before I had the interview with your producers, they told me, 'Aaron is always so joyful, and he's so friendly to everyone. We know he has hard days, but every time we see him, he always has a smile on his face and seems so happy. We figured it must be this Jesus thing he always talks about.'"

My producers looked back at me and smiled.

"See, Aaron, you're a prime example. You don't just talk the talk; you walk the walk. You represent Jesus everywhere you go, and now, your producers are here. And they want to know Who you know."

It was the most positive thing I had ever heard a straight, not-yet-affirming pastor say about my faith, especially from the pulpit. Pastor Doug knew I was gay and waiting until marriage to have sex. I had seen the footage of the interview, and my producers had asked him what he thought of gay people, what he thought of me. His response was, "It doesn't matter. We love everyone." Since my friend who invited us to this church said that he was having on-going conversations with Pastor Doug about being gay, it seemed that our pastor was on the road to affirming LGBT+ Christians.

Pastor Doug continued preaching. He went on to tell the students in the room that they should represent Jesus at school. He told the married couples that they must represent Jesus to their spouses. And then, he ended his sermon with a prayer for new believers to accept Jesus.

"If you prayed that prayer and you truly accepted the new life that Jesus bought for you, then raise your hand so that we can welcome you into the Kingdom."

I looked up to see that my development producer was in tears as she raised her hand. My pastor looked at her and then looked at me with a grin. I knew that Pastor Doug witnessed the good fruit that could be born in my walk with the Lord, even though I'm gay.

"The Bible says that every time someone says that prayer and comes to the Lord, the angels in heaven throw a huge rager,"[2] Pastor Doug shouted as we all clapped and cheered for the new believers.

AARON MICHAEL and I both started to get a lot more attention at our new church. It was like getting a shout-out during one of Pastor Doug's sermons legitimized our faith in the eyes of the rest of the congregation. This new attention even led our pastor to invite us to join his leadership training classes, which were small-group worship sessions with Pastor Doug's teachings on being a church leader. We both jumped at the opportunity, excited to finally find a church that allowed us to participate fully.

As we went through the courses, Aaron Michael and I grew spiritually. As we grew deeper in our love for God, we also grew deeper in our love for each other.

"When do you think is the right time for a couple to get married?" Aaron Michael asked as we both sat on my bed, studying some of the required leadership books.

I looked up from my reading. "My first pastor suggested about a year and a half to two years because you want to know each other through various seasons. But also, I think it just depends on the couple. I know some people who got married after a couple of months who are still together decades later and seem to be doing well. I also know some people who got married after several years of dating and then divorced shortly after."

Divorce was a somber topic for both of us. Even though Aaron Michael had grown up with his mother and father his entire life, we both watched family members go through divorces. Neither of us ever wanted to go through that.

"Yeah. I think about a year and a half to two years is about right." Aaron Michael turned the page of his book as we both continued reading. "By the way, I want to be the one to propose to you."

I hadn't thought about it much, but I liked the idea of Aaron proposing. It would be the first time I would be allowed to give *real*, pure consent and for the right reasons. I would get to give consent for something that was my true worth: him for me, me for him.

THE BODY OF CHRIST

"Fine, but don't propose before we've been dating for at least a year."

DURING OUR final leadership session with our church, we prepared for an all-day event. We were going to stay in the building to worship, pray, and, most of all, spiritually break off and repent of anything that would hold us back in leadership. After lunch, the pastors handed out a packet that contained examples of various things that we should repent of. The packet was dense. We were asked to find a private place within the room to look through it and pray.

After a moment, Pastor Doug stopped everyone to make an announcement. "Okay, so some of these things are about specific contexts. For example, 'karate' is listed here, but this list comes from our head church in New Zealand. What they mean by 'karate' is probably more of the stuff that's part of other religions that New Zealanders see off Asia's coast. It doesn't mean that if you take Tae Kwon Do, then you'll need to repent of it. If you have any questions, just come talk to me or any of the other pastors."

He wasn't kidding. "Karate" was listed under a section labeled "Idolatry."

As I went through the list, I came to a section labeled "Past hurts," and I noted that I had suffered sexual trauma. And then, there it was. Under "Sexual sin," there was "Homosexuality." I looked over at Aaron Michael, who no doubt saw it as well. I wanted to run over and talk to him about it to see what he was thinking.

I thought, *Maybe this is just an example of something that's about a specific context like Pastor Doug said.*

"Father," I whispered a prayer, "I know You have a plan for this, but what are we going to do if this is our church's stance? What would You have us do?"

I did not select "homosexuality" off my list, and I planned to talk to Pastor Doug to clarify after the event.

After we filled out the packet and prayed individually to break off certain habits, fears, and sins from our lives, the pastors and associate pastors wanted to pray over everyone one-on-one. We formed a line to wait for the next available pastor. Everyone waited silently for their turn. One of the associate pastors beckoned me over as Aaron Michael went to stand in front of Pastor Doug.

I told the associate pastor about my past in prostitution. I told him that I had already severed ties with it, but I needed the grace to communicate my testimony to others. And I needed the wisdom to communicate how inappropriate it is for people to look up those videos. He said a prayer, and then I went to sit at my seat.

I looked over at Aaron Michael with Pastor Doug. Aaron had both of his hands stretched into the air as tears poured from his eyes. It looked like Aaron's legs were noodles, and he would collapse if only Pastor Doug weren't holding him up.

Oh no! What's going on? Did Aaron see "homosexuality" on the list and try to talk to Pastor Doug about it? Is our pastor trying to cast it out of him? Or was Aaron even trying to repent of being gay?

My heart twisted inside of my chest as I looked on. After another minute passed, Pastor Doug began to cry as well. Tears dripped onto his beard. He grabbed Aaron in a firm, loving embrace, in much the same way he had embraced me on the night that I had told him I had been in porn. When Pastor Doug finally released Aaron Michael, they both wiped tears off their faces, and Aaron sat next to me.

"What happened?" I whispered as others continued praying.

Aaron Michael continued to wipe tears off of his face. "I told Pastor Doug about how I was bullied in middle school and high school. How I was called *'faggot'* and stuff like that because they thought I was gay. I told him that I actually am gay, so it made it worse because they somehow knew what I was trying to hide. Pastor Doug prayed with me as I forgave all of those people."

Aaron Michael had told me before that he was severely bullied in school. For Aaron, for me, for most closeted gay kids growing up, it was always the worst thing for someone to notice that you are gay. On the inside, you know, but you hope you can hide it to protect yourself from the pain the world tries to inflict.

"Did Pastor Doug say anything about you being gay?" I asked.

"No." Aaron wiped another tear from his face.

Maybe the packet is just an old-fashioned use of the word "homosexual" after all.

After prayer, Pastor Doug gave one final message to his new class of leaders. He read from the Word, "For the body does not consist of one member but of many. If the foot should say, 'Because I am not a hand, I do not belong to the body,' that would not make it any less a part of the body... But God has so composed the body, giving greater honor to the part that lacked it, that there may be no division in the body, but that the members may have the same care for one another. If one member suffers, all suffer together; if one member is honored, all rejoice together.

"Now you are the Body of Christ and individually members of it..."[3]

243

Pastor Doug closed his Bible as he preached, "Church, we *need* each other. We cannot be a divided body. Look around the room. All of you are different. You are different races, men, women, young, old, and you all have different gifts and callings that are needed to serve as the Body of Christ."

He spoke with a passion and anointing that was not from him but from God's Holy Spirit. Every syllable had a rhythmic diction and a force as if he spoke in tongues, but in English.

"There isn't a single one of you who we do not need for us to be the Kingdom of God on the earth today. It doesn't matter if you're Black or white, native or foreigner, male or female, gay or strai—"

The flow halted abruptly. In a split second, he caught himself and realized what he was saying. The room froze. Our pastor's face contorted as he recognized what he was about to say in front of his church's leadership.

I HAD HEARD the story told at my first church and Pastor Doug's church. Nineteen-hundred years after Apostle Peter's experience at Cornelius' household, the Church looked completely different. The power of God seemed to no longer operate with the same power it once did, and the modern Church was heavily divided into what it called denominations. In the American Church, not only were there denominations, but they were also divided racially.

In 1906, William J. Seymour, a Black minister and son of former slaves, was hired to pastor a church in Los Angeles. During his first sermon, Seymour preached on an experience called the baptism in the Holy Spirit with speaking in tongues. The next Sunday, the elders of the church locked Seymour out. His message was too radical.

However, not everyone rejected Seymour's message. Some congregation members invited him to hold Bible studies and prayer meetings at their house to pray for the baptism in the Holy Spirit. After preaching from the Book of Acts, several people in Seymour's Bible study began to speak in tongues. The experience was so remarkable that those who heard about it visited the meetings out of curiosity only to find that they too began to speak in tongues.

The greatest miracle that happened was that although William Seymour was Black, the signs and wonders of the Holy Spirit drew crowds from all races and backgrounds. Black, white, Latino, Asian, Native American, immigrants, men, women, children, rich, poor, illiterate, educated, all gathered together to worship and experience the power of God. At the height of the Jim Crow era, God's Spirit caused these believers to break through the unholy divides that society had placed upon them, and they stepped out into the holiness of unity.

The prayer meetings grew so much that they had to move out of the house where they met and into an old downtown building on Azusa Street. It was here that Seymour preached messages of salvation, holiness, and power. Miraculous healings, singing and praying in tongues, interpretation of tongues, foreigners hearing the tongues in their own languages, words of knowledge and wisdom, prophecy, and many other manifestations of the Holy Spirit happened regularly at Azusa Street. It came to be known as the Azusa Street Revival.

William Seymour preached in May 1908, "'And when the day of Pentecost was fully come, they were all with one accord in one place.'4 O beloved, there is where the secret is: one accord, one place, one heart, one soul, one mind, one prayer. If God can get a people anywhere in one accord and in one place, of one heart, mind and soul, believing for this great power, it will fall and Pentecostal results will follow. Glory to God!"[5]

Like the religious people in the first century, many religious people looked at the revival with bitter antagonism. Still, God's Spirit continued to move beyond Azusa Street and all over the world. In the coming decades, through continued charismatic movements, the Spirit broke through the denominational and generational boundaries that the religious people had established.[6] The Azusa Street Revival had a lasting legacy. This movement of God has impacted any Christian movement today that has charismatic expressions of worship. The religious people could not stop the wind of the Holy Spirit.

Today, there are still some churches that struggle to break the worldly barriers of race and sex. Even many of those that have conquered those barriers still struggle with the barrier placed between heterosexual, cisgender Christians and their sexual minority brothers and sisters. Even many LGBT+ believers struggle with whether or not they belong to the Body of Christ, and this is evident because many struggle to honor their bodies as if they are a part of *the* Body. But religious people cannot exclude anyone from the power of the Gospel. God will reach even the marginalized and rejected. My story and stories of countless others show that God is already stirring the wells of revival. The revival that started all the way back in the Book of Acts isn't over until the fullness of the Church is brought in and Yeshua returns. The revival can still continue today if the Church—both affirming and non-affirming—is willing to yield to the Spirit of God.

· · ·

THE ANOINTING of the Holy Spirit inspired Pastor Doug's message. He knew that unity was necessary for God's plan to move through the hearts of those on the Earth. Over one hundred years after the Azusa Street Revivals took place in our city, Pastor Doug knew that we needed Black *and* white, native *and* foreign, male *and* female, gay *and* strai— But he stopped the flow.

Aaron and I turned to each other with wide-eyed smiles. Even if Pastor Doug was personally affirming, we knew that he probably would have to keep his affirmation to himself. But at least somewhere within him, we knew Pastor Doug clearly felt some affirmation towards us because the Word says, "Out of the abundance of the heart his mouth speaks."[7] Somewhere within his heart, Pastor Doug knew that the Church needed LGBT+ Christians. The question was, how would the rest of his church handle it?

"Church, you need *everyone* in this room," Pastor Doug cried before moving on to an entirely different topic.

TWENTY-TWO

FATHER, FORGIVE THEM

A BOUT A YEAR after Aaron Michael and I first went to Disneyland together, we went back. The day was perfect. The sky was clear and blue. The park wasn't too busy, and we could go from ride to ride without waiting in too many lines. When we got into Disney's California Adventure theme park, Aaron Michael wanted to head to a ride called *Soarin' over California*. Except, when Aaron took off, he went in the wrong direction.

"Where are you going?" I yelled.

"Come on. *Soarin'* is this way."

"No, that's the wrong way."

"No, it's not. I know a short cut. We can go around. It's quicker."

"There's no shortcut, Aaron," I yelled through the crowd, lagging behind him. "You're going in the complete opposite direction."

Aaron Michael took off to a section of the park designed like a pier. He found a small area where there were no people. I realized it was where we shared our first kiss. The sun's light bounced off the water and reflected into our eyes. The Mickey Mouse Ferris wheel spun in the background, and everyone on the nearby roller coaster screamed for joy. The sky was crystal clear without a single cloud between Heaven and us.

"So when are you going to admit that I'm right, and you're wrong?" I said through a sassy smirk.

Aaron pulled out a ring box and kneeled in front of me.

"Oh!" I exclaimed.

My response threw him off guard. He giggled and started to lose his balance. The sun's rays danced on the white gold ring bouncing around as he righted himself.

"What knee is it that you're supposed to kneel on?" Aaron Michael asked himself as he switched his knees. "I guess I'll just say it," he said, steadying himself as he gave me the biggest smile I'd ever seen on his face. "Aaron Crowley, I love you so much. You are everything I ever wanted. I love how much you love the Lord. I'm ready to spend the rest of my life with you. Will you marry me?"

Getting on his knee was a symbol that Aaron Michael wanted to lay his life down for me. But I didn't want him to be the only one to lay his life down in our relationship. I also got on one knee in front of him.

"Yes!"

He stood up and pulled me in for a kiss.

WE SAT in our church's office, waiting to speak with an associate pastor, Pastor John. His assistant sat across from us, quietly staring. The day after our engagement, Aaron Michael and I received an email that Pastor John wanted to meet with us. We set up a time for the end of the week, and there we were, feeling like a couple of school children called to the principal's office.

Pastor John finally entered the room and sat down across from us. "I wanted to say that we appreciate you guys and what you mean to this church. You two have been to every leadership meeting. You help out everywhere you can, and we notice it. We are so glad that you two are here."

Aaron and I sat motionless in our chairs. He was clearly trying to soften the blow.

"But it has come to my attention on social media, you two went to Disneyland and got engaged to each other?"

It was exactly what we expected. Before going to that meeting, Aaron Michael and I had wondered if this was about our engagement. We noticed that the associate pastor reached out to us, not Pastor Doug, who knew us. This was the first time either of us ever spoke with Pastor John.

His assistant sat through the meeting without speaking, only watching. I wondered if we were some sort of lesson for him, like he was shadowing Pastor John to know how to handle this situation in the future.

"Yes, that's right," Aaron Michael replied.

"Okay," Pastor John continued. "Well, while we know that the world may be changing on this issue, we need you both to know that we do not condone that lifestyle in this church."

That word again! *Lifestyle.* My lifestyle is one of worship. I live to worship God, to give Yeshua my everything. Being gay was just a trait of ours, but it wasn't all there was to us.

Pastor John continued, "Our head church in New Zealand has closed the book on this issue. We do not condone the gay lifestyle here, so if you two want to go through with this engagement, then your growth in leadership stops here."

Aaron Michael and I stared at Pastor John. We had done everything we were asked, everything we were taught, but this one thing—our love for each other—stood in the way of us fully growing in this church.

I finally said the only words I could get out. "Well, Aaron and I will pray about it, and we respect your right to those beliefs."

We ended the meeting there. I tried to set up a time to meet with Pastor Doug, but he had to cancel. And even if we could speak to Pastor Doug about it, if the church had closed the book on the issue, what else was there to say? Even if Pastor Doug really was LGBT+ affirming privately, the church he was a part of was not, and he would have to go against his leadership to keep us on his team. The book was closed. Done.

AFTER FINDING months of safety in the harbor of our Christian rock band church, we were back to swimming through the harsh waves of the world, desperately seeking any shore that would be safe for us to land. I had now been through two mainstream churches. Now, I refused to go to a church that equated my orientation with the sexual exploitation described in the clobber passages. I knew firsthand that what Aaron and I had was vastly different. But we also didn't feel that we would be able to go to most affirming churches in our area because, at least from our experience, we had met too many affirming church leaders who didn't teach sexual morality. We didn't feel safe anywhere.

Even online, there was no escape. Aaron and I had joined a virtual group of LGBT+ Christians who were waiting until marriage. We felt safe in this group because we assumed everyone understood sexual ethics since they were abstinent.

Then a Christian brother from that group named Tom sent me a message asking if we could talk on the phone at some point. As I got ready for a dinner date with Aaron Michael, I gave Tom a call.

"What's going on?" I asked.

Tom took a moment to speak. He was breathing heavily on the other line like he had just finished running. Finally, he said, "I wanted to tell you that I saw some of your porn videos."

Blood rushed to my face. My ears buzzed. My jaw clenched.

He said, "I read your blog and found your porn."

I imagined Tom searching the internet for hours, trying to dig up whatever he could. It had been three years since I had been in porn, so those videos would have been buried under years of pornographic content. He had to have spent a while going through porn video after porn video just so that he could exploit my past for his own pleasure.

"Why would you do that?" I asked through gritted teeth.

I sensed the enemy laughing. This was war. I wielded my testimony as a weapon, and the enemy used the weapon of other Christians' sin to fight back.

"I don't know," Tom said. "You know, maybe you shouldn't have shared your testimony as much as you did."

"Why did you want to tell me this?" I snapped.

"Because, man, I gotta tell you. You ruined porn for me. I see you and Aaron Michael, and you guys look so happy. Then I saw you in your porn videos. You looked so broken, so lost. I couldn't enjoy it. I couldn't enjoy *any* porn after seeing it."

"Good!" I barked. "That's kind of the point. I thought my testimony alone would be enough. You didn't have to participate in exploiting me."

"I know, man," Tom seemed to start crying. "I feel terrible. I guess I just felt like I needed to call you because I need to say that I'm sorry. To you and Aaron Michael, I'm so sorry. Please, forgive me."

He was truly remorseful and repentant. At that moment, it was like something inside me finally shattered from the pressure of it all. The blood diffused from my face. My ears grew quiet. My jaw relaxed.

I was no longer just speaking to Tom. I was now speaking to José and Brandon from college. I was speaking to the older man who raped me. I was speaking to Sean, my pimp. To the sex-buyers and the pornographers. I was speaking to Bill and Jay from the affirming Christian conference. I was speaking to my friends who disagreed with me and to my friends who watched the porn I was in. I was speaking to anyone and everyone who had watched *any* porn. And my heart broke for them.

When Tom called me to apologize for watching the porn videos, my former pimp's face burned in my mind. On the day when Sean started to pimp me out, before he used my body for the first time, he had kept his eyes on me while he took pictures. Then, when he sat in a chair and unzipped his pants, he didn't look at me at all. It was like he was speaking to the floor when he said, "I need to see what you can do. If you want to be in this industry, this is a part of it."

Back then, I couldn't read the hollow expression on his face. I didn't understand why he didn't look at me. But the moment Tom apologized, I realized what Sean was doing back then. Sean was bracing himself in case his confidence was shattered, in case I denied him. He feared my rejection. In the time that I spent with Sean, I got to know a desperately lonely man who longed for intimacy.

There was a time after Sean used me that I asked him, "Is there anyone who is, like, potential boyfriend material for you?" I was desperate for anyone to take Sean's attention off me. I thought that if he had a boyfriend, maybe he wouldn't use me as much.

After I asked the question, Sean made the same face he had made when he first used me. Again, he wouldn't look at me. Instead, he focused on the ground. "Yeah, but it will never happen. He doesn't like me."

I later found out that Sean was talking about one of the other guys he had pimped out. Sean felt guilty for what he had done to this other man, so he didn't believe that he was worthy of true intimacy. Instead, he resorted to manipulating and using me and others to have sex with him. It was the closest thing to intimacy that Sean felt he deserved.

Pimps and sex-buyers are just as broken as I was when I was in prostitution. They are just as enslaved to the corrupt system of this dark, sinful world, a system that tells them that the kind of intimacy they deserve must be bought and sold. They become enslaved to the artificial, aggressive, exploitative, violent "sex" that porn and prostitution offer them.

Sex-buyers buy sex for the same reason that a prostituted person becomes prostituted; they don't know that they are worth more. They don't know that they are worth being loved. They don't know that they are bought with a price, that they are worth dying for. They don't know that they are worth someone laying their life down for them. They buy sex and watch porn because they long for closeness and intimacy, but they do not realize they are worthy of true intimacy. They think that they can only have intimacy if they pay for it, search for it online, and/or force it.

People compromise their worth through all forms of sexual immorality because they don't feel like they are worth waiting for, worth dying for. This compromising of the God-given worth of every human life is why the Word of God says that sexual sin is different from every other sin because sexual sin is sin against one's own body.[1] It is an outward expression of a lack of self-love. It is a form of self-harm. Sex-buyers are enslaved just as much as I was, and like me in prostitution, most of them don't even know they are enslaved.

When Yeshua was hanging on the cross, and the Roman soldiers were beneath Him gambling for His belongings, He didn't look at the people in the world and think about how vilely they had treated Him. He thought about *them*. He recognized that their actions resulted from the broken, sinful world they were a part of. He knew that they were ignorant of their own bondage to the enemy's kingdom. As God in the flesh, Yeshua had every right to curse every single Jewish man who had falsely accused Him and every single Roman soldier who had tortured Him. But He didn't.

Instead, Yeshua cried, "Father, forgive them, for they know not what they do."[2]

Yes, what was happening to Yeshua was corrupt and unjust. But He also knew that shame and condemnation would never solve sin within the human heart. Instead, He knew that His grace would empower humans to break through the bondage of the enemy.

Yes, what Tom did objectified me. What the rapists, sex-buyers, Sean, and even some of my friends did to me was not of God. It was wrong and unloving! But if Yeshua could pour out his grace on humans while they were murdering Him, then by His Spirit within me, I could do the same to those who had exploited me.

I could tell through the phone that Tom was completely repentant. I could hear him on the other line drowning in snot and tears. When we are not walking in the Spirit of God, the most spiritual thing we can do is repent and get back in line with God. When we turn to Yeshua, love is restored within us, and we are empowered by His grace to walk in holiness. It's God's kindness and goodness that lead people to repentance.[3] By holding a grudge against Tom, I would be withholding God's grace within me to empower him to overcome his sin. But if I would allow God's grace to flow out of me to forgive him, then I know that grace could empower Tom to overcome his sin, and that way, he wouldn't hurt anyone else.

The sin Tom committed against me—an imperfect human— was nothing compared to the sin that I once committed against my perfect God. If God could forgive me for my sins, then I could forgive everyone who sinned against me.

"Okay," I finally said, taking slow, cool, deep breaths of air. "I forgive you." There was a sigh of relief on both ends of the line.

The words weren't just for Tom. They were for everyone who had ever exploited me. Sean, the rapists, the sex-buyers, the pornographers, my friends, and for me. As the words came out of my mouth, I was set free from a shackle that I didn't even know had held me down. I thought I was completely set free from my past. However, at that moment, I realized that there was still the remnant of an invisible chain of unforgiveness wrapped around my heart. At the moment that I released forgiveness, I broke that chain, and I was finally, truly free.

I continued, "But Tom, you need to know that I have to tell Aaron Michael about this. I'm used to this, but it's still new to him. He hasn't even seen me naked yet, but people like you have. Imagine how that must feel."

"I understand. Thank you for forgiving me. I hope Aaron Michael can forgive me too."

WHEN I WALKED into the restaurant, Aaron Michael was already there. He looked up from the table with that sweet, innocent smile that lassoed my heart and pulled me in, but every step I took was thick as mud. I could barely move because I knew that when I got to him, I would have to tell him what the guy from our online abstinence group had told me.

Throughout the entire meal, I ran in my head how I was going to tell Aaron Michael. He looked so happy, not knowing, but I had to tell him. We were about to get married, and I didn't want our marriage to be one of secrecy and deceit. We needed to tell one another everything.

I finally said it as we waited for our waiter to bring the check. "I had a call with Tom from the waiting-until-marriage group today. He apologized to us because he watched the porn videos I was in."

Aaron Michael didn't blink as I recounted the story to him, and he didn't seem to breathe. I could see the twinkle in his eyes dim as he listened. As I finished, Aaron looked down, unable or unwilling to look me in the eye.

"Is this what life is going to be like from now on?" he asked a moment after I had finished telling him what had happened. His question was heavy. I didn't want my past to affect my fiancé.

"No," I said. "This is an attack from the enemy that we may have to face now and then, but it's my past. You're my present.

They can't have our present. If they want my past, I guess, let them have it, but they'll never have what we have if they want that."

The Word of God often talks about what we inherit when we become a part of the Kingdom of God. The Apostle Paul said, "For all things are yours, whether Paul or Apollos or Cephas [the leaders of the Church] or the world or life or death or the present or the future—all are yours, and you are Christ's, and Christ is God's."[4]

It sticks out to me that the Word says that the present and the future are ours, but the past is excluded from this list. We own this moment right now, and we own what comes ahead. But the past does not belong to us. It is not ours anymore. It is now Yeshua's. He took our past and nailed it to the cross so that we might be free to walk in His goodness, mercy, and love in the present and the future. All we can do is trust that if we give what the enemy meant for evil back to God, He will take it and use it for good.[5]

But I knew what Aaron Michael meant. He wanted to know if people, especially fellow Christians, our friends, would continue to use my past. He wanted to know if this experience would be a continual part of our lives if I continued to share my testimony. And, most importantly, he wanted to know how all of this would affect our upcoming marriage.

TWENTY-THREE

A COMPLETELY DIFFERENT PERSON

D
URING OUR engagement, Aaron Michael and I did premarital counseling. Since we were without a home church, I called up Mike, the retired pastor I had met while going to my first church's same-sex attraction group. Like everyone else in that group, Mike eventually left. However, he was one of the few who still held onto his relationship with Jesus.

In one of our premarital counseling sessions, I was running late because of work and LA traffic. When I finally arrived at Mike's apartment, he greeted me at his door. Aaron Michael was already there, lying on the couch, holding his stomach as if he were sick. He was pale, and his eyes were red and watery. As I sat down next to him, he sat up and clung to me.

"What's wrong?" I asked.

"I just love you so much," Aaron said, cuddling into me like a lost child finding his mother.

"Why do you look like you've been crying?"

He looked to Mike, who nodded in affirmation. Aaron sat up, took a deep breath, and cried, "I found out that some of our friends watched your porn videos."

My heart sank. I had just told Aaron Michael that this would not be what life with me would be like, but it seemed that our community wanted to prove me wrong.

Aaron explained that someone had casually mentioned that another friend had searched for the porn I was in. What's worse is that he was planning to help us with the wedding, so it stung to think that he would do this to us.

"I hate it," Aaron Michael cried. "All of these people have seen you naked. I'm engaged to you, and I haven't even seen you naked yet. I hate that he did that." Aaron laid his head on my lap. I put one hand on his head, and with the other, I held his hand. "All these people watching those videos, they need Jesus."

"You're right. They do."

Mike had watched our entire exchange. Because of the situation's significance, I'm sure he thought it was best not to speak up until Aaron Michael had finished telling me what happened.

Mike said as he pointed to me, "You know, this Aaron Crowley is not the Aaron Crowley in those videos, right?" Aaron Michael sat up as Mike continued. "The Aaron in those videos is dead and gone." He looked at me, "You consider yourself dead to sin, now, don't you?"[1]

Today, looking back at my time in prostitution seems like a far-off nightmare. Sometimes, I can hardly believe that's who I used to be.

"Yeah. That's not who I am at all anymore."

"Exactly." Mike looked back to Aaron Michael. With his bushy eyebrows wrinkled and his right index finger in the air, he declared the words with authority as if he was speaking on God's behalf. "The Word says, 'If anyone is in Christ, he is a new creation. The old has passed away; behold, the new has come.'[2] The Aaron Crowley you know is a new creation. He is a completely different person than the one in those videos. What people see when they watch those videos is a dead person. He may look like this Aaron, but he is not this Aaron."

"That's right," I said. "Amen!"

"Amen," Aaron Michael replied, wiping his face.

After our session, we confronted the friend who supposedly had seen the porn videos I was in. To our relief, he claimed that he had never even attempted to look them up. The other friend, who had told Aaron about it, admitted to lying. We were upset about being lied to, but also relieved. Yet again, the entire situation was another reminder that we desperately needed the support and fellowship of a church. Still, it wasn't easy to find one that we felt comfortable with, so we did what we could. We prayed.

WHILE ON social media one evening, I saw a post about a new, affirming church starting services just a few hours away from Los Angeles. It was part of a network of churches called the Covenant Network (CN). I had first heard about CN when a pastor from Australia contacted me. He read my testimony and wanted to talk about helping affirming Christians get freedom and deliverance from porn. When I mentioned the Holy Spirit baptism, he said that it was a critical part of his church and CN as a whole.

When I researched the Covenant Network, I found that they are an LGBT+ affirming, Spirit-filled, Christian network with several churches all over the nation and in the world. The head church, New Covenant Church of Atlanta, posted their sermons online. From the videos I watched, I could see that this was a church for people of all races and sexual orientations. The worship team sang powerfully as the rest of the saints clapped their hands, swayed with the music, waved worship flags, and danced. Then I watched the sermon.

Surely, this is where things get watered down, right?

I was wrong. Bishop Randy Morgan got up and preached boldly from the Bible. He was like a white T. D. Jakes. At first glance, he was the stereotypical southern preacher of a mainstream church, but then he mentioned his *darlin'* and tapped the shoulder of a man sitting in the front row, Apostle Johnny Layton.

I grew eager about the Covenant Network. The only problem was that they were mostly on the east coast. That is, until this new church opened up just a few hours from us.

The day that Aaron Michael and I went to check out the new CN church, they had a guest speaker, the network's head prophet. I could sense that Aaron Michael was a little skeptical of the idea of a modern-day prophet. He grew up Baptist, so he was still getting used to the idea of the power of God moving today just like in the Bible. When Aaron and I were first talking, I had mentioned the Holy Spirit baptism, and he said that he had never heard of it. I recommended that he read the Book of Acts. By the time he got to chapter 19, where some believers were filled with the Spirit and began speaking in tongues, Aaron Michael came back to me saying, "Why did I grow up in the church all my life and never hear about this?"

At the CN church, the prophet preached about his testimony. Before he knew the Lord, he was a drug addict. One day, he was on the floor digging through the carpet, trying to find even the tiniest nugget of his drug to quench his addiction. Like the prodigal son, while digging in the carpet, the prophet realized how low his life had gotten. He came to his senses and didn't want to live that life anymore. He knew that God had the power to free him from his addiction, but he was also gay. He grew up believing that being gay and Christian was impossible, so there would be no way for him to find freedom. That is until he walked into New Covenant Church of Atlanta, where he encountered the Presence of the Living God, Who set him free.

After the prophet preached, he looked at Aaron Michael and me and called us up to the front. We crept to the altar with apprehension, unsure of what to expect. I had seen prophetic words given in churches before. I had even gotten words of knowledge, where I suddenly knew something that I could not have known about someone, and told them what I heard the Lord saying about it. But I had never received a prophetic word. And neither had Aaron Michael.

The prophet looked at me, "You're called to ministry, and you know it."

I smiled and nodded, but I thought, *I'm not ready for any mainstream form of ministry. I'm not old enough. I'm not experienced enough. I'm not prepared enough.*

"But the Lord's telling me that you don't feel—"

I have only been saved for three years; I haven't even been saved long enough.

"I keep hearing Him say, 'enough,'" the prophet declared.

My eyes widened, and my mind stopped. My hands shot into the air in surrender to God.

"But the Lord says, 'Son, you are enough. I have prepared you and called you for such a time as this.[3] I am equipping you,' the Lord says. 'I will guide you and lead you into all that I have called you into. Right now is the time for your ministry.'"

The prophet turned to Aaron Michael, who stood next to me watching everything with an innocent wonder in his eyes and a hint of skepticism on his face. "And the Lord says to you, 'You're in your head.' He's showing me that you're one of those people who likes to plan and think everything through and figure it all out. But He's saying to you that He is about to do things with you that you cannot plan, that you cannot think through. And it's going to be good. Don't worry about it. Let Him do what He is planning to do through you."

Aaron covered his face to hide the tears, but it was too late. Tears ran down his cheeks as he sobbed.

"Link arms," the prophet commanded. I wrapped my left arm around Aaron's right. The prophet continued, "The Lord says, 'I have brought you two together for a purpose, to bring My Gospel of freedom to this next generation.'"

After the service, I told the prophet a bit of my testimony. "I hear you that I'm called to ministry. I have this burning passion for sharing what God has done for me, but it's been so hard. Every time I tell my testimony, some people seem to think they are entitled to look up the porn videos I was in." I looked at Aaron Michael. "And now, it affects Aaron too."

The prophet looked from me to Aaron Michael, then said calmly, "Let me pray for you." He put his hands on our shoulders and bowed his head to say a prayer of empowerment over us.

On the car ride home, Aaron admitted to me, "It was like he was reading my mind."

We knew the Holy Spirit was among this LGBT+ affirming network. Back in Acts 2, when the Spirit of God poured out on the disciples in the upper room, people who witnessed it thought they were crazy or drunk. Then Apostle Peter stood up and said that what had happened was fulfilling a prophecy from the Prophet Joel.

> And in the last days it shall be, God declares, that I will pour out My Spirit on *all* flesh, and your sons and your daughters shall prophesy, and your young men shall see visions, and your old men shall dream dreams; even on My male servants and female servants in those days I will pour out My Spirit, and they shall *all* prophesy.[4]

Throughout the Book of Acts, God poured out His Spirit on all kinds of people who were traditionally thought unusable by God. Like the prophecy said, God poured out on young and old, men and women, and then throughout the rest of the Book of Acts, we see God pour out on not just the Jews, but non-Jews, and even sexual minorities, like the eunuch.

When whole groups of people allow God to move through them unhindered like this, it is called a *revival*, a great move of the Living God upon His sons and daughters that transforms the Church and turns the world upside down. God said He would do this in *all* people.

Our first visit to a Covenant Network church gave us undeniable confirmation that the power of God could work through LGBT+ people. We suddenly felt a little less crazy, a little less alone.

The Covenant Network was about to hold its annual conference, the Immersed Conference, in Atlanta. It was going to be held several months after our wedding. We decided that we needed to be there. If the Spirit of God is moving among these LGBT+ affirming Christians, then we wanted to be a part of it.

TWENTY-FOUR

SEXUAL INTIMACY

I N THE MONTHS leading up to our wedding, the production company I had been working for closed down. I was now unemployed. So while preparing for our wedding, Aaron Michael and I struggled financially. We both did little side jobs wherever we could to pick up extra cash, but it still seemed like we weren't going to raise the money we needed for the ceremony we had planned. On top of all that, I kept checking the weather forecast. Rain was expected for the whole week around our wedding, and our ceremony was going to be outdoors.

We had people coming into town from as far as the east coast. If we couldn't afford the wedding, if it rained, if we had to call the whole thing off, what would our friends and family think? Where would they go? What would we do?

As the date grew closer, and as I watched the weather forecast, my breath grew short. My heart raced. I paced the floor. Since growing in faith in Yeshua, I had had less frequent panic attacks, but this wedding was stirring one.

As I attempted to control my breathing, God's Spirit reminded me, *"Do not be anxious about anything, but in everything by prayer and supplication with thanksgiving let your requests be made known to God. And the peace of God, which surpasses all understanding, will guard your hearts and your minds in Christ Jesus."* [1]

I caught my breath. "Father, I want our wedding to glorify You. I want our marriage to glorify You. We have a lot of friends who know my past and still watch porn. We have a lot of friends who don't care about waiting until marriage. We have many friends who think we are crazy for living the lives we live to honor You. Whatever happens, Lord, we want to show everyone that how we have lived, that waiting until marriage, brings You glory.

"So for Your glory's sake, please, help us to afford everything we need for this wedding. Father, You know what the forecast says, but I know that You can control the wind and the waves. If You can bless our marriage, please, remove the rain. Let the sun shine, and let it be the most gorgeous day of the year. Let it be that You are glorified in our marriage. Let it be that Your holiness and righteousness are showcased in us as we glorify You.

"Our friends and family know where Aaron and I come from. They know that we have waited in love for this day, so let them see that it is Your love between us. Let it be the type of day that will inspire everyone to honor You and live for You in the way that we have, if not even more than us. Let our marriage be a marriage that will inspire others to love You and their future spouse the way You love the Church. In Yeshua's name. Amen!"

As I prayed, my heart steadied, and my thoughts slowed. *Peace!*

The Holy Spirit whispered, *"Have faith in God. Truly, I say to you, whoever says to this mountain, 'Be taken up and thrown into the sea,' and does not doubt in his heart, but believes that what he says will come to pass, it will be done for him."* [2]

He spoke it into my heart, and I realized that I needed to speak *to* the mountain. As believers, we aren't supposed to just pray about a situation but speak directly *to* it.

I opened my mouth, "Finances, be made available in Yeshua's name. Rain clouds, in Yeshua's name, be gone from the skies over Los Angeles on March 6, 2015."

A WEEK BEFORE the wedding, despite my lack of regular work, and thanks to some miraculously generous tips that Aaron Michael received at the restaurant where he served, we collected enough money to pay for the ceremony and put together the deposit for our first apartment. We also purchased our first bed together. *Our marriage bed.* The one the Word says to hold in honor and purity.[3] To keep it special, we decided neither of us would sleep in it until our wedding night.

"See, God's providing," Aaron Michael would say each time a big step like this was accomplished, and he was right. God was providing, but the forecast still showed rain.

"Rain clouds, be gone in Yeshua's name," we would declare together.

ON THE MORNING of our wedding, there was the sun! When I arrived at the venue, the bright sky reflected off the grass field that rippled like green ocean waves in the wind. It was a warm mid-seventies with a light, west-coast breeze giving life to the flower arrangements set up around the venue. A friend of ours had spent the previous week preparing the light blue and green floral designs that lined the aisles. Everything was perfect. Even better than what we prayed for.

Aaron Michael and I had asked to be kept separated so that the first time we would see each other would be when we walked down the aisle. I went to a little side room that the venue had for us, and Aaron used the hotel next door that his maid of honor had booked. After I was ready, I prayed with everyone in my dressing room.

"Father, thank You for this beautiful day. All I ask is that we would glorify You in this wedding and this marriage. Show off Your glory! Show off how You can take someone like me, transform them, and redeem their life. You're so powerful, Father. In Yeshua's name, I pray. Amen!"

It was time! Our wedding party consisted of a man and a maid of honor for each of us. They lined up, followed by the ring bearer, my five-year-old nephew, and then me. Aaron Michael waited around a corner where I could not see him.

After Mike announced that the ceremony was about to start, piano music played, and one by one, our men and maids of honor marched down the aisle.

"Go on," I whispered to my nephew, "It's your turn." He stepped forward with his eyes locked on the rings in front of him. Our witnesses awwed as my nephew took his time down the aisle to protect our rings. Finally, it was my cue.

I stepped forward. The flowers, the breeze, the sun, the grass all still there as I had seen them before, and now, the smiling faces of our friends and family filled the rows of seats. My family watched from the front row. My mother wiped tears off of her face. I could tell that these tears were different from the tears she shed on the night when I told her that I was in porn. These were tears of joy.

Behind my family was a mixture of Aaron's and my friends: friends from college, friends from high school, friends from the LGBT+ Christian community. Especially for our LGBT+ friends, our wedding was more than just a celebration of our love. It was a celebration of our legal right to express that love. The U.S. Supreme Court had overturned California's Proposition 8 same-sex marriage ban just two years before, and it was about to overturn the Defense of Marriage Act, which would make our marriage legally recognized across America.

I arrived at the gazebo where our wedding party stood waiting. Then I turned to wait for my husband-to-be. It was his cue. I held my breath.

As he stepped out, my heart leaped into the back of my throat. There he was. He turned the corner with his eyes on the ground, and then he looked up at me. That innocent smile. The sun reflecting from his green-blue eyes. His cheeks pink from the warmth. He was the person I had been waiting for. God called me out of prostitution, and now, He was giving me a husband. When Aaron Michael arrived beside me, we giggled in nervous anticipation, just like we had when he proposed.

The music faded as Mike began his message. He read from the Bible, "Two are better than one, because they have a good reward for their toil. For if they fall, one will lift up his fellow. But woe to him who is alone when he falls and has not another to lift him up! Again, if two lie together, they keep warm, but how can one keep warm alone? And though a man might prevail against one who is alone, two will withstand him—a threefold cord is not quickly broken."[4]

Mike closed his Bible and preached, "As you two come together, you become one. But with you, Jesus Christ is the third strand in your threefold cord. Since God created marriage, it is only right that you build your marriage on the solid Rock of His Son, Jesus Christ. With God, no one can easily break this bond." As we listened, Aaron and I held hands. He massaged my fingers with his thumb.

Mike finished, "The Aarons have written their own personal vows that they would like to share."

I took the mic and looked at Aaron Michael. His eyes were so bright from the sunny day. I said, "Aaron, when I began to follow the Lord, He promised me many blessings, but the blessing I was most eager to find was *you*. Because God made promises to me as a sign of His love, I want to make these promises to you as a sign of my love."

I could see the tears welling up in Aaron Michael's eyes. "Don't cry," I laughed. Aaron bent over laughing, trying to hide his face.

When we composed ourselves, I continued, "I promise to love and cherish you as the blessing you are. I promise to hold you close as a reminder of the Lord's love. I will never leave you, nor forsake you. I will always be by your side, always running towards our Father God with you. I promise to be quick to forgive in our relationship because you are a reminder of God's grace and mercy on me when I was a sinner. I accept you for who you are, and I want nothing more or less than you.

"Today, we fulfill our intimacy. We become one. I will keep this intimacy uniquely yours because you do not need to be burdened or anxious with sharing me. This is my sacred covenant with you. I love you as my own soul."

I passed the mic to Aaron Michael, who wiped his eyes. "Aaron Crowley, you are exactly who I prayed for at thirteen when I thought I might be gay, in the most confusing and scary moments of my life. When I contemplated whether or not these feelings were purposely put inside of me, I prayed, asking God, 'If I were to have a husband, let him love You more than I've ever seen before. Let him be an amazing example of Your glory and grace. And let him have beautiful eyes and not be taller than me.'"

I made a sassy "What?!" face as our witnesses and Aaron laughed. "Thank You, God," he said, clearing his throat. "I love you so much. You are the best blessing I've ever received in my life. You're something I thought for many years I might not get to have: my own family. So to honor God and you for blessing me with all of this, I make these promises.

"I promise always to put Yeshua in the center of our marriage, always to be here to pray and worship with you. I promise always to push you to better yourself and your relationship with God and be open to letting you push me to better myself and my relationship with God. I promise never to leave or walk away no matter what happens in our lives, no matter the trials we go through. I will always stand by your side to be here for you.

"I cannot wait for our life together. I never thought I'd love someone like this, but here we are. I will love you for the rest of my days and into eternity, my *soon-to-be* husband."

After we said our vows, Mike declared, "By the power invested in me by Jesus Christ and by the state of California, I now pronounce you husbands for life."

I gave Aaron Michael the biggest kiss we had shared up to that point.

. . .

THAT NIGHT in our new apartment, I brought out my old sex bag, the one I had sealed three years ago with my STI test results inside. I read what I had written to Aaron Michael.

> Before opening this bag, please consider if you are in love with the person with whom you will commit your entire life and that you have made a promise to love him from this moment on.

I looked at Aaron Michael and smiled. He was who I had written about three years ago. He was who I had envisioned when I decided that I would wait until I found real love to have sex. This was about him.

We ripped open the bag. Although everything inside was expired by that point, I showed Aaron Michael the STI test results. I retold him about the miracles that God had done when He saved me.

Entering into intimacy with Aaron Michael, I assumed that I would be the one to teach him about sex, but it was the opposite. He had no idea what to expect, but the sex I knew before was a perverted form of sex. What I knew before wasn't love. What Aaron and I did was new for both of us. We made *love* to each other.

Sex with someone you love is completely different from sex with someone you just met, especially if that person was paying or was paid to have sex with you. There's a deep level of belonging and security present in making love that was not present in any sexual act that I had experienced before. When love is expressed through sex, when someone loves you so much that they lay their life down in marriage and want to experience mutually pleasurable self-giving with you, it can be a deeply spiritual experience, an immensely healing experience.

I can't believe I used to have meaningless sex. It's so much better when it means something. In all honesty, it always means something, but I had spent years trying to pretend that it didn't. Now, I do not need to pretend. I can enjoy the meaningful intimacy that my husband and I share.

I had gone through the world and experienced sex in the world's way, a way I now hate. Knowing Aaron Michael, knowing his innocence, and experiencing the fullness of a connection with him, made me see just how powerful this intimacy is. And we experienced it together. The deepest and the most beautiful way to *know* someone. It is true intimacy. *It is love.*

TWENTY-FIVE

FINALLY HOME

A FEW WEEKS into our marriage, I was regularly working again. Actually, I was promoted. Before the production company where I worked shut down, I used my spare time to help my editors cut their episodes beyond what I was required to do as an assistant editor. In the process, the executive directors and story producers took notice. Then when those story producers found new gigs, they recommended me on their new shows. I was no longer an AE. I was officially hired and working as an editor.

This was a huge pay increase. Since leaving prostitution, I watched as God took me from making poverty wages that didn't cover my living expenses to making way, abundantly more than what I was making in porn. I give all the credit for this financial stability to my faith in God. I trusted Him with my everything, including my money. I faithfully gave a tithe, ten percent of my income, to any church I attended. I also gave generously to other people above that as the Spirit led me. Just as the Word says, "Whoever sows bountifully will also reap bountifully."[1]

It got to the point that I had a production manager come to me and ask, "Would you like us to increase your rate?"

"Sure," I said. "How much were you thinking?"

He asked, "How much do you want?"

When we step out in faith, it leaves room for God to come through and do His miracles. When I left prostitution for Yeshua, one of my biggest concerns was paying my bills without the income porn provided. But God provided. He provided more than enough so that I could use the income He gave me to bless others.

A few months after I started working as an editor, Aaron Michael texted me while I was at work.

AARON MICHAEL

Can we delete your blog?

ME

What? Why?

AARON MICHAEL

Someone is sharing your porn videos.

I called Aaron, who cried on the phone, "An anonymous account has been sharing videos and gifs of you all over social media. I want you to stop sharing your testimony."

"I can't, Aaron. It is the only way to fight back against the enemy."

"Well, now he's fighting me. I want it to stop."

"No," I said through gritted teeth.

I heard Aaron's heart break through a defeated sigh. "I guess this is just my life now," he cried before hanging up.

As I drove home that evening through LA traffic, I banged my fists on the steering wheel. I planned to tell Aaron Michael off as soon as I got home. I would let him know that he was hindering God from getting the glory that He deserved for what He has done in my life. I was ready to tell Aaron how he was dishonoring God, that he was stealing from me one of the only things that could never be taken away from me: my testimony.

For me, there was no healing from my past without speaking about it. I couldn't just pretend like none of it had ever happened because it did happen. I needed to share my story because it turned my past into something good when someone repented after hearing it. If I couldn't share it, it was like returning my story to the dark crevasses of my heart to be stored away to fester. It was more traumatizing for me to live silently in a world that normalized my abuse than to speak openly about it in the hopes that people would change. I was desperate to tell the world, but my husband was traumatized by me sharing it. I knew I needed to tell my testimony, but I couldn't share it without harming him.

As I drove home, I experienced more road rage than normal. Everyone on the road was in my way. I laid on the horn several times that evening.

"Are you done yet?" The calm of the Lord came upon me as I caught myself.

The Word says, "Be angry and do not sin,"[2] but I was letting my anger control me.

"Father, what am I supposed to do? How are we supposed to handle this? I understand that Aaron is hurt, but what can I do? We shouldn't let other people's sin control what we do, right?"

"Submit to your husband as to the Lord."[3]

Aaron Michael and I had become one. Because of the intimacy that we shared, he started to experience secondary trauma from my former trauma. When sex-buyers exploited my body through porn, he felt exploited too. His heart broke, and I was thinking too much about myself.

The Lord had called me to share my testimony, but Aaron and I had just been married. We were in our honeymoon phase, and that meant there were new dynamics in both of our lives that we needed to figure out. Aaron Michael's heart was hurting, and the only way to heal it—at least, for the time being—was to keep my testimony on the down-low. A loving husband would sacrifice himself and lay his life down for his spouse. Of course, my testimony was a way to honor God, but Aaron had become a part of that testimony when we joined our lives in marriage. The Lord was now calling me to keep his needs in mind when sharing it.

When I got home, I found Aaron curled up in a fetal position on the couch. His eyes were tired from crying.

"I'm sorry," I said, sitting next to him. "If it will help you, I won't renew my blog's web domain. I won't write on it anymore. I won't share it anymore. I'll let it die down so that we can have a moment to figure this out."

Aaron hugged me as he cried tears of relief.

"But," I continued, "I need you to promise me that we will *eventually* be able to share this story. I feel a burden inside of my heart, like a fire shut up in my bones to tell my testimony. I need to know that I can let it out sometime."

He nodded in agreement. "Thank you," he said.

After a few weeks, my blog's domain was past renewal, and the website was removed. I contacted anti-porn groups and other resources that had my story online, and I ensured that they had only the bare minimum of information.

I knew that we would not be able to share this story again until we found a safe church to be a support system and a safe house we could run to when someone misused my past against us. Even with a supportive church, I know we can't stop the world from being the world, but it would be nice to know we have people to stand alongside us when things are hardest. It would be nice to have LGBT+ Christian friends who will comfort us instead of insisting that porn isn't that big of an issue or accusing us of being judgmental and unfair. We still hadn't found any church where we felt safe around us in Los Angeles, but the Covenant Network's Immersed Conference was in just a few months. We looked forward to it with more than hope.

WALKING INTO New Covenant Church of Atlanta for the Immersed Conference, I had the same calm excitement I had when I walked into a church for the first time after experiencing Yeshua's love. The air smelled fresh and pure, like a new book. People greeted each other with warm smiles and hugs. We stepped into the sanctuary and saw exuberant displays of worship all around.

People, all kinds of people—men, women, children, Black, white, Latino, LGBT+, straight, *all* people—got ready to worship and hear the Word of God. I saw Bishop Randy and his husband, Apostle Johnny, in the front row. Aaron Michael and I sat down towards the back because the front rows were already full. Worshipers gathered at the altar, and I anxiously joined them.

As the music began, I allowed it to sweep over me. I lifted my hands to the Lord, danced, clapped, and swayed with joy. People in the back waved worship flags of various colors, and, on the other side of the room, an artist painted her devotion to the Lord. Her brush strokes flowed with the music.

During the first session, Aaron Michael and I were shocked by the speakers' passion. They declared the Word of God with such power and authority. One brother took a tambourine and preached, "We should be waiting on God to fulfill His promises like this." He ran around, banging the tambourine and shouting, "Hallelujah!"

After a lunch break, we returned that evening for the night service. When worship began, there was a moment where no one sang. The keyboard played, and everyone just soaked in the Presence of God. I closed my eyes and lifted my hands as I continued to worship.

Then, a deep, soft, yet powerful voice roared, *"Aaron!"* I knew this voice.

I opened my eyes and looked at the stage, thinking that someone had said my name, but no one spoke. Everyone seemed to have their eyes closed, standing silently, soaking in the tangible Presence that flooded the room. Then I realized that the voice was His voice, the voice Who called me in the beginning, the voice Who told me, *"I love you."*

"Speak, Lord," I whispered. "I'm listening."

Time snapped to a halt. The moment suspended in that millisecond.

"When you are given the microphone, tell them what I am showing you now. This is to confirm that what you sense in your heart is from Me."

Time snapped back into movement. The worship team began to lead us in a song where we declared that we would see God's promises. People continued to worship, some on their knees, some prayed discreetly in English, and others prayed in tongues. Many had their hands raised high in the air. They all felt familiar; they all felt close. They felt like home.

But I barely knew anyone here, except for the few people from the new CN church we visited and the prophet we met before. I had not been invited to speak beforehand. We were new to this body of believers. It would be completely inappropriate to expect, or even think, that I would be given the mic at this conference.

Then the prophet came to the front to give a message. After preaching from the Word, he had everyone under the age of thirty-five stand. He had a prophetic word for our generation. Then he went through and prophesied over individuals.

After prophesying over a youth group from one of the CN churches, his eyes met mine, and he paused for a moment. "Aaron and Aaron, I have to follow the Holy Spirit. Will you two please come down here for a minute?"

Aaron and I crept out of our row towards the front altar. As I looked around, I realized that we were just a few of several hundred people. When we got to the front, the prophet leaned in and whispered in my ear, "Do you have something from the Lord that you'd like to share?"

"Yes," I whispered.

The prophet leaned back and faced the congregation. "I have some head knowledge about these guys, but that doesn't mean my calling them out is of my head knowledge. I believe I have a word from the Lord for them."

As the prophet spoke, I whispered to Aaron Michael, "Do you mind if I tell them?"

"Tell them what?" he asked.

"Our testimony."

The prophet leaned in to ask my husband, "Are you okay with this?"

"Yeah," he said, but I sensed he was hesitant. The prophet handed me the mic.

"Are you sure? Can I tell them about both of us?" I whispered.

"Do what the Lord tells you."

The prophet looked at the congregation and said, "For those of you who aren't married yet, this is called submitting to your spouse." We all laughed. It was a needed break from the silence that the church was now sitting in.

"Are you *absolutely* sure?" I asked Aaron again.

"Follow the Lord."

Although I could tell that he was nervous, it seemed that even Aaron Michael sensed a safety with the people in the Covenant Network. I finally turned to the congregation, took a deep breath, and spoke what was going on in my heart.

"While we were worshiping, I heard my name called, and I thought it came from the stage. But when I looked up, I realized no one was speaking. It was God's voice. When the worship team started singing about seeing God's promises, I knew it was confirmation.

"I've received a lot of promises from God, and the one that came to my heart the most while we sang that song is," I gave a little chuckle at what I was about to say. It was bold. I looked to Aaron Michael and declared, "We will see the porn industry shutting down." At those words, a dozen people began to clap their hands. Everyone else seemed mostly clueless.

"Come on! Yes!" I heard an excited voice shout from somewhere in front of me.

I knew it was an extremely bold statement. Porn is a multibillion-dollar industry. How was it going to shut down? By taking away its demand. By telling the truth about what happens on porn sets. By making it clear what porn really is. By leading people to encounter the freeing power of the love found only in the Living God, Who revealed Himself to humanity through His Messiah, Yeshua. I'm not seeking to impact legislation, but if the demand for porn were to end, the entire institution of prostitution would begin to shut down. Laws can only go so far as to cause behavior modification; I want to see a world changed by heart transformation. I don't want to see a world where people stop watching porn because of shame or fear of legal repercussions. I want to see a world where people see all forms of prostitution as the unloving institution that it is. I want to see people empowered by love, God's love, to where they cannot find pleasure and enjoyment in the sexual exploitation of others.

I continued talking while looking at Aaron Michael to make sure he was okay with the words coming out of my mouth in front of the congregation. "Aaron Michael and I come from similar but different pasts. I was prostituted in porn, and Aaron used to struggle with porn addiction. Now, God has joined us together to go out and reach people who are where we were."

It started with just one person on the front row, but within a couple of seconds, the congregation erupted. People stood on their feet, clapped, and cheered, praising God. A knot developed in my throat. I could hardly believe the reaction. Not only was this an LGBT+ affirming network of churches from around the world, not only were these affirming churches who believed in the baptism in the Holy Spirit and God's power for today, but this was also an affirming church that did not mock, did not shudder, did not attempt to exploit us when I uttered the words, "I was prostituted in porn."

As they continued to clap, the prophet leaned over and whispered into my ear, "You don't know this, but you've been prayed into this moment. We have interceded for someone just like you two to come into this network."

I looked up at him as I envisioned that it was the prayers of these saints that led me to drunkenly stumble upon the Christian outreach group to hear the guy tell me, "Jesus *loves* you." I envisioned that they had prayed for me to grow uncomfortable with selling myself. I envisioned that they had prayed for me to be protected and healed from the STIs that I experienced in prostitution. That they had prayed for me to receive the baptism in the Holy Spirit and the empowerment to walk free from my pornified sexuality. That their prayers had led me to meet Aaron Michael after seeking the Kingdom of God *first*. I envisioned that their prayers had led me to this very moment, right here, right now, showing them that the Lord had heard and answered their prayers.

As the applause died down, I finally said, "Thank you. That's very encouraging because it's very difficult to stand here and say that. Usually, when I say things like that, a lot of people don't like us."

In front of me, Bishop Randy shouted, "We *love* you!"

I laughed as I handed the mic over to the prophet, who spoke the word that he received from the Lord.

"The Lord says, 'I'm giving you ease. I'm opening doors and relationships that will allow you to minister as you've never done before. Some people once turned and snubbed you and criticized you. They will call you to apologize, and you will have an open door to minister to them.' And the Lord says that He will change a stronghold that has bound the LGBT community for so long. The next generation that's rising will break the chains that once bound our people."

The prophet laid his free hand upon my head. "In the name of Jesus, I declare that you are protected." He moved his hand to Aaron Michael's head. "You are protected."

Protected. Aaron Michael and I needed spiritual protection. Every time we wielded our testimonies as weapons, the enemy was prepared to strike back. But God, in His infinite wisdom, has provided a means for spiritual protection.

When a sheep strays away from the flock, that sheep becomes vulnerable. When a hungry wolf comes along, he isn't going after the many sheep who remain close to the Shepherd. The hungry wolf will go after the sheep who has wandered off and is alone. That lone sheep is easy prey. That's how the enemy operates.[4]

There's strength in numbers, which is why we need the Church. The Church's role is to equip every believer for their ministry and provide the protection they will need. The Church enables us to go out into the world with the right spiritual equipment necessary to fight off the enemy and spread the Gospel to *all* people.[5]

As the prophet declared protection over us, we recognized that we had just found the people who would equip and protect us. By this point, I had been saved from porn for three and a half years. During that time, I had sought where I belonged in the Church, only to feel like I was wandering alone through the wilderness. Now, we were finally home.

My faith was once no more than a small seed that was planted the night a stranger told me, "Jesus *loves* you." Even in the rocky, infertile environment of my life in porn, that seed found soil and sprouted into a new life. I had gone from rocky wilderness to a restrictive planting pot, and then empty forest. My faith had grown and grown, and my roots stretched out deeper and wider until they found themselves intertwined in the roots of others. Now, I finally found myself in an orchard of righteous oaks nourished directly from the river of Living Water.[6]

After the prophet was done speaking what he heard from the Lord over Aaron Michael and me, he turned to the congregation. "Church, this is the next generation!"

BEFORE WE headed to the airport to fly back to Los Angeles, Aaron Michael and I asked if we could have a moment to meet with Bishop Randy and Apostle Johnny. One of his assistants led us to Bishop's office, where we waited for them. There were windows with open blinds that let the sunlight fill the room. Our eyes were open to the spectacle of walls filled from floor to ceiling with all kinds of Christian books. It was like a small, sunlit library.

When Bishop Randy and his husband came in, they smiled at us as they sat down. Bishop Randy sat directly in front of me, and Apostle Johnny sat directly in front of Aaron Michael. I couldn't help but think we were looking at a mirror of our future.

I said, "I wanted to know, what exactly does it mean to be a part of the Covenant Network?"

"Well, to be a part of the network means that y'all align with our vision for the Spirit of God to be poured out on *all* people," Bishop replied.

"I was thinking we might need a Covenant Network church in Los Angeles."

"That would be awesome," he said with a huge smile.

I adjusted in my seat as I said, "The only thing is—I've had problems with churches in the past, so forgive me—I need to ask this upfront. Do you guys teach sexual ethics? Do you teach that Yeshua's love is resembled in our sex lives *only* by waiting until marriage?"

Bishop Randy smiled as he looked at Apostle Johnny. "Absolutely, yes!"

I smiled. It was like breathing fresh air for the first time.

Apostle Johnny said, "After hearing y'all's testimony, I can understand why that would be so important to y'all."

Then Bishop Randy squared his shoulders and looked me dead in the eyes with narrowed brows that let me know that he was a man of authority. "And if you want the Covenant Network in Los Angeles, I have a couple of questions for you." He leaned forward. "Do y'all believe that the Bible is the Word of God?"

I smiled. Aaron and I said it together, "We do."

"Do y'all believe that Jesus is the *only* Way to salvation?"

I looked at Aaron. He was also smiling because we had both encountered people who identified as Christians but leaned more towards universalism. It was nice to know the Bishop of CN was not a universalist.

"We do," we responded.

"Do y'all believe in Hell?"

Oh, he was asking the tough ones, the most controversial of all questions in Christianity. But it meant to me that Bishop Randy accepted even Yeshua's hardest teachings.

Yeshua said that there would come a day when He will say to some people, "Depart from Me… for I was… naked and you did not clothe Me… As you did not do it to one of the least of these, you did not do it to Me."[7]

God says that He has justice in store for those who have taken advantage of people's nakedness in prostitution. I used to take comfort in the thought that those who abused me would get what they deserved, but I've learned that isn't even God's will that He should have to tell those people to depart from Him. He longs for them to repent, to be born again, and to spend eternity with Him.[8] Now, it is my prayer that everyone would repent and be saved.

We worship a God who won't force Himself on people. He wants everyone to spend an eternity in intimacy with Him, but not everyone wants Him. The only way a person can be isolated from God is to isolate themselves, but if they are willing to come to Yeshua, He greets them with wide-open arms. If they don't want a relationship with Him, He won't force Himself on them like a rapist would, so there is a place where spirits go when they want to remain separated from God.[9] But if God is the fullness of joy and the fullness of peace, then an existence separated from Him would be the most joyless and peace-less existence. It would be *Hell.*

Aaron and I answered, "We do."

"Okay, finally," Bishop Randy continued, leaning back in his seat. "Do y'all believe in the baptism in the Holy Spirit with speaking in other tongues?"

"We do," I laughed. "And you know what, Bishop," I said as I leaned back in my seat, finding comfort in the company we shared. "Once affirming churches get all that, that Yeshua is the only one Who saves and delivers from sin, including sexual sin, that the power of His Spirit sets us free, it's going to change the Church and the world. There will be a worldwide, sweeping revival."

EPILOGUE

END THE DEMAND

A s I STARTED writing this book, I saw a social media post from an old friend who was still in the porn industry. He shared the pictures of several prostituted young men. These men had died. This post was in memoriam. The causes of death ranged from drug overdose to suicide.

I recognized some of their faces from my time in porn, and as I looked at their pictures, my eyes flooded with tears. I wished that I could turn back time, find each of them, and tell them about God's love. I wished I could reach into my computer, pull each of them out, and tell them that freedom is available through Yeshua. But even though it was not God's will that these men passed away at such young ages,[1] it was too late.

The strangest part about seeing that image was knowing that I was almost one of them. I had attempted suicide so often while in prostitution. I sometimes purposefully drank myself so drunk that I hoped it would kill me. But God pulled me out before that could happen. It was God's will to transform my life. It is God's will to transform *every* life. That is why I had to tell my testimony and write this book.

I am now an ordained pastor in the Covenant Network. I have the honor of preaching and ministering the Word of God throughout America, and every time, I'm in awe of the Lord's work. We see Him move among our people, break the chains that once held them in bondage, and empower them to walk in His love.

There are still those who use my testimony as an excuse to exploit and harass us. But because we now feel connected to a supportive, Spirit-filled body of believers, Aaron Michael and I now feel more comfortable sharing our story. Because of the Covenant Network, its leaders, and especially our Bishop, I felt safe enough to write this book. It has been the final nail in the coffin of my past.

As Aaron and I have shared our story, we have seen prostituted people, sex-buyers, and sex-sellers come to know the Lord. Every time, it is a reminder of Yeshua's love, grace, and mercy on us, on all of humanity. It is a reminder that one night, at the lowest point in my life, Yeshua came into my room—the room of a young, prostituted, gay man—and told me, "*I love you.*"

We have seen so much fruit from sharing our testimony, but we need your help! This story is not over. This is the part where you come in. You get to decide what happens next. I told you what happened to me because of porn, now what are you going to do about it?

The most important step that you can take to help us stand against prostitution is to repent. If you've been struggling with porn or any sexual sin, then turn to God, right here, right now. Ask Him to pour out His grace to strengthen you to overcome your weakness to sin. If you need help, seek pastoral counseling at your church or even speak with a therapist. As you walk in freedom, you've already helped to end the demand for sexual exploitation. If there are no sex-buyers, then there won't be any sex-sellers to prostitute human bodies.

Next, share your testimony. If you were once prostituted, the world needs to know what your life was *really* like in prostitution. I encourage you to share how the Lord saved you. If you were a sex-buyer or sex-seller, tell the world how the Lord has delivered you and caused you to see the true worth of humanity. If you once lived promiscuously, tell your experience of God empowering you to now wait until marriage. If you're married, tell how God empowered you to love your spouse like Yeshua loves His Church. If someone tries to show you pornography, don't act like it's normal. Say, "Man, that's not cool," and tell them your testimony. If they try to say that porn and prostitution are okay because "some people want to be in the sex industry," share my testimony. Please give them a copy of this book. These testimonies will expose the world to the truth, and when we know the truth, we—even LGBT+ people—are made free from sin.[2]

Finally, pray! When I saw the images of the prostituted men who had died in the porn industry, I got on my knees, and I prayed. My friend's post was a painful reminder that many people still live the life I used to live. It was a painful reminder that there are still sex-buyers who demand the explicit material those young men made to survive. We need to pray to end the demand. There are many people in the world today who are not living God's will for their lives. Like the young men I saw in that post, they are heading towards death without ever knowing the goodness and love of God. That is *not* God's will, and the only way to receive God's will on the earth is to pray.[3] Pray and ask the Lord to lead people into repentance and freedom from this bondage.

Churches, especially LGBT+ affirming churches, must see the truth that prostitution in all its forms is inherently harmful, traumatic, and exploitative. It is time to rise and take a stand to love people out of this system.

It starts with *you*.

LORD, let the reader of this book encounter Your love with the same force and same power that I did, if not more, so that their lives will never be the same again. Holy Spirit, flood them to overflow so that their lives are filled with Your power. Empower them to walk in Your love and holiness. Father, whether they are straight, gay, trans, intersex, Black, white, Latino, Asian, Jewish, whatever, show them who they are in You. Open their eyes to see that they are worth dying for, that all of humanity is worth dying for. Give them the revelation that they have been bought with the absolute highest price of Your blood so that they will live their life to glorify You in all that they do.

In the mighty name of Yeshua HaMashiach, Jesus the Messiah, I pray. Amen!

ENDNOTES

PROLOGUE: FROM THE AUTHOR'S HUSBAND

1 Ephesians 6:12
2 Romans 8:28
3 Psalm 139:14

TWO: PIMPED OUT

1 Fight the New Drug, a non-profit organization that helps people struggling with porn, states, "Although it's fallen in the ranks the last few years, since 2012—but remained in the top 10—a wildly popular search term on a porn site that got 33.5 billion visits in 2018 is TEEN." Fight the New Drug, "'Teen': Why Has This Porn Category Topped the Charts for 6+ Years?," August 28, 2019, https://fightthenewdrug.org/this-years-most-popular-genre-of-porn-is-pretty-messed-up/.

THREE: ASKING FOR IT

1 A study of over 300 of the most popular pornographic scenes found that "88.2% contained physical aggression, principally spanking, gagging, and slapping, while 48.7% of scenes contained verbal aggression, primarily name-calling." Bridges, Ana J., Robert Wosnitzer, Erica Scharrer, Chyng Sun, and Rachael Liberman. "Aggression and Sexual Behavior in Best-Selling Pornography Videos: A Content Analysis Update." *Violence Against Women*,

16, no. 10 (October 26, 2010): 1065-1085. https://doi.org/10.1177/1077801210382866.

2   A research study states, "Males shown imagery of a woman aroused by sexual violence and then shown pornography that involved rape were more likely than those who hadn't, to say that the rape victim suffered less and that she enjoyed it, and that women in general enjoy rape." Layden, M. A. "Pornography and Violence: A New look at the Research," in J. Stoner and D. Hughes (Eds.) *The Social Costs of Pornography: A Collection of Papers,* (Princeton: Witherspoon Institute, 2010), http://socialcostsofpornography.com/Layden_Pornography_and_Violence.pdf.

3   According to a study on social pressure and masculinity, 60% of men in the US, 51% of men in the UK, and 42% of men in Mexico believe that society as a whole tells them that a "'real man' should have as many sexual partners as he can." 63% of men in the US, 55% of men in the UK, and 53% of men in Mexico believe that society as a whole tells them that a "'real man' would never say no to sex." Heilman, B., Barker, G., and Harrison, A. *The Man Box: A Study on Being a Young Man in the US, UK, and Mexico.* (Washington, DC and London: Promundo-US and Unilever, 2017), 23-25.

FOUR: UNWANTED

1   Psychologists say, "When trauma has included sexual abuse or rape, the numbing and intrusion symptoms typically involve body sensations and somatic complaints, as well as sexual desire, arousal or orgasm... Traumatized individuals may develop a sexual desire disorder with hypo-, hyper-, or asexuality." Schwartz, Sc.D., Mark F., Lori D. Galperin, L.C.S.W., Williams H. Masters, M.D.,

"Post-traumatic Stress, Sexual Trauma and Dissociative Disorder: Issues Related to Intimacy and Sexuality," Masters and Johnson Institute, March 17, 1995, https://www.ncjrs.gov/pdffiles1/Photocopy/153416NCJRS.pdf.

SIX: THE OPPOSITE OF LOVE

1   A survey of prostituted people states, "We interviewed 854 people currently or recently in prostitution in 9 countries (Canada, Colombia, Germany, Mexico, South Africa, Thailand, Turkey, United States, and Zambia)... 89% of these respondents wanted to escape prostitution, but did not have other options for survival. A total of 75% had been homeless at some point in their lives..." Farley PhD., Melissa, et al. "Prostitution and Trafficking in Nine Countries: An Update on Violence and Posttraumatic Stress Disorder," *Journal of Trauma Practice,* The Haworth Maltreatment & Trauma Press, an imprint of The Haworth Press, Inc. Vol. 2, No. 3/4, 2003, http://www.prostitutionresearch.com/pdf/Prostitutionin9Countries.pdf.

2   The Harvard Civil Rights-Civil Liberties Law Review states, "Urgent financial need is the most frequent reason mentioned by people in prostitution for being in the sex trade... Disproportionately, people in prostitution are members of socially disadvantaged racial groups or lower castes." MacKinnon, Catherine A., "Trafficking, prostitution, and inequality." *Harvard Civil Rights-Civil Liberties Law Review* Vol. 46 (February 23, 2011): 276-277, https://prostitutionresearch.com/trafficking-prostitution-and-inequality/?highlight=inequality.

3   The National Transgender Discrimination Survey (NTDS)
    states, "An overwhelming majority (69.3%) of sex workers
    reported experiencing an adverse job outcome in the
    traditional workforce, such as being denied a job or
    promotion or being fired because of their gender identity
    or expression (vs. 44.7% of non-sex workers). Those who
    lost a job due to antitransgender bias were almost three
    times as likely to engage in the sex trade (19.9% vs. 7.7%)."
    It also states, "Transfeminine NTDS respondents were
    twice as likely to participate in the sex trade compared to
    transmasculine respondents (13.1% vs. 7.1%)." Fitzgerald,
    Erin. "Meaningful Work: Transgender Experiences in the Sex
    Trade." *National Center for Transgender Equality.* December 9,
    2015, https://transequality.org/issues/resources/meaningful-
    work-transgender-experiences-in-the-sex-trade.

4   The National Sexual Violence Resource Center states, "46% of
    LGBTQ youth run away because of family rejection of sexual
    orientation or gender identity... 1 in 3 teens on the street will be
    lured into prostitution within 48 hours of leaving home. More
    than 1 in 3 homeless youth engage in survival sex. Of them:
    LGBTQ youth are 3x [three times] more likely to have engaged in
    survival sex..." "Homeless Youth & Sexual Violence," *National
    Sexual Violence Resource Center,* 2014, https://nsvrc.org/sites/
    default/files/nsvrc_publications-infographic-homeless-youth-
    sexual-violence-infographic_0.pdf.

5   The previously cited survey done on prostituted people also
    states, "Prolonged and repeated trauma usually precedes entry
    into prostitution. From 55% to 90% of prostitutes report a
    childhood [before age 18] sexual abuse history." Farley PhD.,
    Melissa, *Journal of Trauma Practice,* 35.

6   The same survey done on prostituted people also states, "68% [of prostituted people] met criteria for PTSD. Severity of PTSD symptoms was strongly associated with the number of different types of lifetime sexual and physical violence... the person with PTSD experiences fear and powerlessness, oscillating between emotional numbing and emotional/physiologic hyperarousal. PTSD is likely to be especially severe or long lasting when the stressor is planned and implemented by humans (as in war, rape, incest, battering, torture, or prostitution) rather than being a natural catastrophe." Farley PhD., Melissa, *Journal of Trauma Practice,* 34, 36.

SEVEN: WORTH DYING FOR

1   McDowell, Dr. J.D., and Jones, Dr. C., "*The Bibliographical Test,*" Christian Research Journal, August 13, 2014, https://www.josh. org/wp-content/uploads/Bibliographical-Test-Update-08.13.14. pdf, 1-7.

2   Zukeran, Dr. P., "The Dead Sea Scrolls Shed Light on the Accuracy of our Bible," Probe for Answers, April 17, 2006, https://probe. org/the-dead-sea-scrolls/.

3   1 Corinthians 6:9 (NRSV)

4   1 Peter 1:18-19

5   Luke 10:7

EIGHT: BORN AGAIN

1   John 3:3

2   Ephesians 2:1

3   Isaiah 59:2

4   Romans 3:23

5   Romans 8:38-39

6   Matthew 5:21-22

7   Matthew 5:27-28

8   Matthew 15:19

9   Layden, M. A. "Pornography and Violence: A New look at the Research."

10   Karen Countryman-Roswurm, LMSW, Ph.D., reported, "Working with those who had been sex trafficked, we already knew that pornography was a part of the experience while they were being sex trafficked. What is most interesting though, is to see that pornography is a common thread... pornography was used as a means to normalize, to desensitize them to the sexual acts that they would experience. As well as pornography was used as some sort of advertising for their sexual abuse. So through different modes of pornography, they would be filmed, and they would be used, and they would be advertised for the various acts that could be done to them... And it was rape on camera." Fight the New Drug, "Karen Countryman-Roswurm, LMSW, Ph.D., Interview Truth About Porn," YouTube video, 1:08-1:58, posted by "Fight the New Drug," January 18, 2019, https://www.youtube.com/watch?v=uDo4xy2d9CM.

11   A study with data from 150 countries states, "Countries with legalized prostitution have a statistically significantly larger reported incidence of human trafficking inflows." Cho, Seo-Young, et al. "Does Legalized Prostitution Increase Human Trafficking?" World Development, (2013), 68. See also Jakobsson, Niklas & Kotsadam, Andreas, "The Law and Economics of International Sex Slavery: Prostitution Laws and Trafficking for Sexual Exploitation," European Journal of Law and Economics, (2013), 87. and Di

Nicola, Andrea et al. *Study on National Legislation on Prostitution and the Trafficking in Women and Children.* Commissioned by the European Parliament, (2005), 132.

12 Trafficking Victims Protection Act (TVPA) of 2000, Pub. L. No. 106–386, Section 102(a), 114 Stat. 1464.

13 "Hotline Statistics." *National Human Trafficking Hotline,* December 31, 2019, https://humantraffickinghotline.org/states.

14 "Sean Paul Lockhart, Biography." Accessed May 20, 2020, IMDb, https://www.imdb.com/name/nm1851320/bio.

15 Mohan, Megha, "'I was raped at 14, and the video ended up on a porn site,'" BBC News, (February 10, 2020), https://www.bbc.com/news/stories-51391981.

16 1 John 4:8

17 Romans 6:23

18 Ezekiel 18:4, 20

19 Malachi 3:1, John 1:1-5, 14, Colossians 2:9

20 Romans 5:8, 1 John 3:16

NINE: SEEK, AND YOU WILL FIND

1 Ephesians 4:11-13

2 1 Peter 3:7

3 1 Corinthians 14:34-35

4 Judges 4:4

5 Matthew 28:10

6 Acts 18:26

7 Acts 21:9

8 Biblical scholars state, "Some modern translations, not willing to acknowledge the possibility of a woman apostle, change this name to a man's name, *Junius,* but the earliest writers all identify Junia

as a woman. For example, Chrysostom (4th century) comments on Romans 16:7, 'How great the wisdom of this woman must have been that she was even deemed worthy of the title apostle!'" Pierce, Chuck D., and Robert Heidler, *The Apostolic Church Arising* (Denton: Glory of Zion International Ministries, Inc., 2015), 190.

9 1 Corinthians 11:5

10 1 Thessalonians 5:22

11 "Policy and Position Statements on Conversion Therapy," Human Rights Campaign, accessed May 25, 2020, https://www.hrc.org/resources/policy-and-position-statements-on-conversion-therapy.

12 Luke 14:33

13 Matthew 7:7

14 Matthew 7:20

TEN: THIRSTY

1 Matthew 7:16-18

2 Matthew 3:8

3 Galatians 5:22-23

4 Fight the New Drug, a non-profit organization that provides information on porn addiction and recovery, states, "Neurochemicals act as ingredients in a sort of neuro-cocktail that, during a healthy sexual experience, trigger feelings of pleasure and bonding, followed by relaxation and ongoing longing for one's partner. The problem is, porn can short-circuit this otherwise healthy system… For a lot of people, often starting around age 11, porn hijacks this process, and the associated natural urges and curiosities. Many became dependent on a stimulus that offers a cheap counterfeit for what they naturally yearn for." Fight the New Drug, "Quitting Porn? Learning

the Brain Science Behind Compulsivity Can Be a Game-Changer," June 4, 2019, https://fightthenewdrug.org/brain-science-behind-compulsivity-game-changer/. See also, Hilton Jr., Donald L., and Clark Watts, "Pornography addiction: A neuroscience perspective," National Institutes of Health, February 21, 2011, https://www.ncbi.nlm.nih.gov/pmc/articles/PMC3050060/.; Love, Todd, Christian Laier, Matthias Brand, Linda Hatch, and Raju Hajela, "Neuroscience of Internet Pornography Addiction: A Review and Update," National Institutes of Health, September 18, 2015, https://www.ncbi.nlm.nih.gov/pmc/articles/PMC4600144/.; and Wilson, Gary, "Start here: Evolution has not prepared your brain for today's porn," Your Brain on Porn, https://www.yourbrainonporn.com/miscellaneous-resources/start-here-evolution-has-not-prepared-your-brain-for-todays-porn/.

5   "Consider This," The Novus Project, accessed May 22, 2020, http://thenovusproject.org/resource-hub/parents.

6   "The Detrimental Effects of Pornography on Small Children," Net Nanny, December 19, 2017, https://www.netnanny.com/blog/the-detrimental-effects-of-pornography-on-small-children/.

7   A study on pornography's effects on young men reported, "ED [erectile dysfunction] accompanied by a low desire for partnered sex is now a common observation in clinical practice among men seeking help for their excessive sexual behavior, who frequently 'use pornography and masturbate.'" Park, B. Y., et Al., "Is Internet Pornography Causing Sexual Dysfunctions? A Review With Clinical Reports," *Behavioral Sciences* 6, no. 3, (Sep 2016): 17, https://www.ncbi.nlm.nih.gov/pmc/articles/PMC5039517/.

8   Research states, "Individuals who never viewed sexually-explicit material reported higher relationship quality on all indices compared with those who viewed sexually-explicit material

alone. Those who viewed sexually-explicit material only with their partners reported more dedication and higher sexual satisfaction than those who viewed sexually-explicit material alone. The only difference between those who never viewed sexually-explicit material and those who viewed it only with their partners was that those who never viewed it had lower rates of infidelity." Maddox, Amanda, Galena K. Rhoads, and Howard J. Markman, "Viewing Sexually-Explicit Materials Alone or Together: Associations with Relationship Quality," Archives of Sexual Behavior, U.S. National Library of Medicine, December 29, 2009, https://www.ncbi.nlm.nih.gov/pmc/articles/PMC2891580/.

9   1 Corinthians 6:16
10 Exodus 22:16
11 John 7:38-39
12 James 5:16

ELEVEN: HEART TRANSFORMATION

1   Psalm 141:2
2   Acts 1:4-5, 8
3   Ezekiel 36:27
4   Ephesians 1:13
5   Acts 8:14-17, 19:1-6
6   Acts 2:4, 10:45-46, 19:6
7   1 Corinthians 14:1-4, 14
8   Deuteronomy 31:6, John 14:16
9   John 8:11
10 2 Corinthians 12:9
11 John 8:1-11

ENDNOTES

12　2 Corinthians 12:7-10

13　Titus 2:11-12

14　Luke 7:36-50

15　John 14:15

16　Matthew 22:37-40

TWELVE: THE FRUIT

1　2 Corinthians 3:18

2　Psalm 37:4-6

3　Galatians 5:17-18

4　Matthew 7:20

5　1 Corinthians 7:9

6　Galatians 5:22-23

7　Matthew 11:28-30

8　Romans 8:12-13, 12:1

9　"Major Group Devoted to 'Curing' Gay People to Shut Down," Southern Poverty Law Center, November 20, 2013, https://www. splcenter.org/fighting-hate/intelligence-report/2013/major-group-devoted-%E2%80%98curing%E2%80%99-gay-people-shut-down.

10　"Policy and Position Statements on Conversion Therapy," Human Rights Campaign.

11　"LGBT Equality," National Association of Social Workers: New York State Chapter, accessed May 25, 2020, https://naswnys.org/ legislation-and-advocacy/nys-issues/lgbt-equality/.

12　American Psychological Association, "Report of the American Psychological Association Task Force on Appropriate Therapeutic Responses to Sexual Orientation," August 2009, https://www. apa.org/pi/lgbt/resources/therapeutic-response.pdf.

THIRTEEN: THE SPIRIT OF PORN

1   "Sodomy," Merriam-Webster, accessed May 26, 2020, https://
www.merriam-webster.com/dictionary/sodomy#h1.

2   2 Timothy 3:16

3   Encyclopedia Britannica states, "Although Israelite prophets and
reformers repeatedly denounced sacred prostitution, the early
Israelites seem to have adopted the local Canaanite rites, which
they apparently practiced publicly until the reform of King Josiah
about 621 BC." The Editors of Encyclopedia Britannica, "Qedesha
Temple Prostitute," Encyclopedia Britannica, accessed May 26,
2020, https://www.britannica.com/topic/qedesha.

4   The Stanford Encyclopedia of Philosophy states, "…
homosexuality, as a specific sexual construction, is best
understood as a solely modern, Western concept and role. Prior
to the development of this construction, persons were not really
'homosexual'… The differences between, say, ancient Greece,
with its emphasis on pederasty [sex between an adult man and
a prepubescent boy], role in the sex act, and social status, and
the contemporary Western role of 'gay' or 'homosexual' are
simply too great to collapse into one category." Pickett, Brent,
"Homosexuality," *The Stanford Encyclopedia of Philosophy* (Summer
2020 Edition), Edward N. Zalta (ed.), first published August 6,
2002; substantive revision April 28, 2020, https://plato.stanford.
edu/entries/homosexuality/.

5   The previously cited online encyclopedia states, "Given
that only free men had full status, women and male slaves
were not problematic sexual partners. Sex between freemen,
however, was problematic for status. The central distinction
in ancient Greek sexual relations was between taking an

active or insertive role, versus a passive or penetrated one. The passive role was acceptable only for inferiors, such as women, slaves, or male youths who were not yet citizens... Ancient Rome had many parallels to ancient Greece in its understanding of same-sex attraction..." Pickett, Brent, "Homosexuality."

6 Romans 1:23

7 Pickett, Brent, "Homosexuality."

8 The previously cited online encyclopedia states, "...less is known about [ancient] Greek attitudes towards women [in same-sex sexual activity]." Pickett, Brent, "Homosexuality."

9 Levine, Amy-Jill (ed.), Brettler, Marc Zvi (ed.), Lander, Shira (contributor), *The Jewish Annotated New Testament: New Revised Standard Version, 1 Corinthians* (New York: Oxford University Press), 295.

10 "Strong's Greek: 4205. pornos," Bible Hub, accessed May 26, 2020, https://biblehub.com/greek/4205.htm.

11 "Strong's Greek: 405. andrapodistés," Bible Hub, accessed May 26, 2020, https://biblehub.com/greek/405.htm.

12 Proverbs 18:21

FOURTEEN: EUNUCHS

1 "FAQ: What is intersex?" InterACT, May 18, 2020, https://interactadvocates.org/faq/#definition.

2 Matthew 19:3-12 (paraphrased)

3 Years after my conversation with Pastor Andrew, the evangelical Council on Biblical Manhood and Womanhood drafted the Nashville Statement to oppose same-sex marriage and transgender identity. In that statement, they admit that people born with "a

physical disorder of sex development" are acknowledged in the Bible when Jesus mentions "eunuchs who were born that way from their mother's womb." However, they also state that people with "a physical disorder of sex development" should "embrace their biological sex insofar as it may be known," as if completely unaware of the complications that standard could bring to intersex people. "Nashville Statement," Article VI, The Council for Biblical Manhood and Womanhood, August 29, 2017, https://cbmw.org/nashville-statement/. See also Simon, Lianne, "An Intersex Christian responds to the Nashville Statement," Intersex and Faith, September 4, 2017, https://www.intersexandfaith.org/news/2017/9/4/an-intersex-christian-responds-to-the-nashville-statement.

4   John 2:24-25
5   Leviticus 21:20, Deuteronomy 23:1
6   1 Corinthians 6:20
7   1 Corinthians 7:9
8   Ostrer, MD, Harry, et. al.,   "Swyer syndrome," National Organization for Rare Disorders, 2019, https://rarediseases.org/rare-diseases/swyer-syndrome/#:~:text=Swyer%20syndrome%20is%20a%20rare,anatomic%20sex%20development%20is%20abnormal.

FIFTEEN: UNLESS SOMEONE GUIDES ME

1   Frankowski, Barbara L., and Committee on Adolescence, "Sexual Orientation and Adolescents," *Pediatrics, Official Journal of the American Academy of Pediatrics*, June 1, 2004, https://pediatrics.aappublications.org/content/113/6/1827.long.
2   Hebrews 13:17
3   Isaiah 56:3

SIXTEEN: LONELY

1 Genesis 2:18
2 Matthew 6:33
3 Psalm 37:4
4 Psalm 16:11
5 Philippians 4:7
6 Psalm 34:8
7 Revelation 12:11

SEVENTEEN: DIGNITY

1 Potter, Karen, "The Church's Role in Addressing the Porn Problem." Presentation at the Coalition to End Sexual Exploitation Summit 2020, Covenant Eyes, July 20, 2020.
2 2 Corinthians 5:17 (paraphrased)
3 Ephesians 5:25-28
4 Galatians 5:23

EIGHTEEN: GLORIFY GOD IN YOUR BODY

1 Ephesians 5:18
2 1 Corinthians 14:2
3 Hebrews 13:4
4 Luke 3:8
5 Acts 10:1-2, 22, 28, 34-48
6 1 Thessalonians 4:3-5
7 1 Peter 4:8

NINETEEN: THE *PRETTY WOMAN* MINDSET

1   Acts 15:28-29
2   1 Corinthians 6:18
3   1 Corinthians 6:20, 7:23
4   1 Corinthians 6:13
5   Acts 4:31

TWENTY: SEX-POSITIVE GOD

1   1 Kings 11:1-8
2   John 14:6
3   Psalm 139:14
4   Hebrews 13:4
5   Genesis 2:24, Matthew 19:5, 1 Corinthians 6:16
6   Matthew 5:28
7   1 Corinthians 13:4

TWENTY-ONE: THE BODY OF CHRIST

1   2 Corinthians 2:14
2   Luke 15:10
3   1 Corinthians 12:14-15, 24-27
4   Acts 2:1 (KJV)
5   Martin, Dr. Larry (ed.), *Azusa Street Sermons by William J. Seymour,* (Joplin, MO: Christian Life Books), 1999, 107.
6   Sherrill, John, *They Speak with Other Tongues,* Grand Rapids, MI: Chosen Books, 1964, 43-87.
7   Luke 6:45

ENDNOTES

TWENTY-TWO: FATHER, FORGIVE THEM

1   1 Corinthians 6:18
2   Luke 23:34
3   Romans 2:4
4   1 Corinthians 3:21-23
5   Genesis 50:20, Romans 8:28

TWENTY-THREE: A COMPLETELY DIFFERENT PERSON

1   Romans 6:11
2   2 Corinthians 5:17
3   Esther 4:14
4   Acts 2:17-18, Joel 2:28-29

TWENTY-FOUR: SEXUAL INTIMACY

1   Philippians 4:6-7
2   Mark 11:22-23
3   Hebrews 13:4
4   Ecclesiastes 4:9-12

TWENTY-FIVE: FINALLY HOME

1   2 Corinthians 9:6
2   Ephesians 4:26
3   Ephesians 5:22 (paraphrased)
4   John 10:11-16
5   Ephesians 4:11-12

6   Isaiah 61:3
7   Matthew 25:41-46
8   2 Peter 3:9
9   2 Thessalonians 1:9

EPILOGUE: END THE DEMAND

1   2 Peter 3:9
2   John 8:32
3   Matthew 6:9-10

ACKNOWLEDGMENTS

ONE OF THE BIGGEST moments I realized that I was going to marry my husband was in one of the biggest moments where he most displayed his support for me. A few months before he proposed and almost a year before our wedding, the Lord called me to go to a conference called the Coalition to End Sexual Exploitation Summit hosted by the National Center on Sexual Exploitation (NCOSE) in Washington, D.C. After reaching out to Dawn Hawkins at NCOSE, she gave me a scholarship to waive the conference fees, and she provided a dorm. Thank you, Dawn and everyone at NCOSE, for your help and all that you do to end sexual exploitation.

The only thing that was lacking for me to attend the conference was the cost of my flight. Even though finances were tight for both of us, Aaron Michael said he believed the Lord was asking him to provide me my flight. Thanks to my then-boyfriend, I was able to attend this conference, which provided me with much of the information and resources that would later aid me in writing this memoir. Aaron Michael, you have been my longest and strongest supporter since the moment I first shared my testimony with you. I know this book was not easy for you, but I couldn't have done it without your help and support. Thank you! I love you!

While writing this book, it was difficult to go through and relive many of the memories, but the support I received from my editors and beta readers made it much easier. Thank you to my developmental editor, Katie Bernath, for your spot-on edits and your support when I almost wanted to throw the entire book out. Thank you for believing in this project and for your support for all survivors of sexual trauma. Thank you, Wendy Danbury, for reminding me of the power behind telling a story. Thank you, Hank Musolf, for verifying and fact-checking all the research. And thank you, Ariel Allen, for your keen eye with proofreading.

Thanks to my beta readers, this book is much more readable than its earliest forms. Thank you to Aaron Michael Crowley-Guest, Bishop Randy Morgan, Apostle Johnny Layton, Prophet Mary Thompson, Apostle Mike Whited, Apostle Mark LeGear, Pastor Jasmine Jones, Pastor Tanzanika Ruffin, Pastor Jonathan Cardenas, Paul Creekmore, Lauren Wright, Michael Piechoinski, and Aaron Simnowitz. All of your thoughts encouraged and challenged me in ways that brought this book to a higher level and strengthened its impact. Thank you so much!

Publishing a book is not cheap. I couldn't have done it without the financial support of everyone who preordered an advanced copy to help raise the funds. To everyone who gave, thank you for letting the Lord provide through you. I pray that He returns your generosity 100 times over. As a thank you to those who gave $250 or more, I want to specifically thank Apostle Shelly Planellas and Pastor Tanzanika Ruffin from New Covenant Church of New Orleans, Pastor Jasmine Jones from The River—New Covenant Riverside, Pastor Doug Sewell from All Saints Community Church, Pastors Jonathan and Leonard Cardenas from New Covenant Church of San Antonio, Apostle Mike Whited and Dan Hall of New Covenant Ministries of Charlotte, and David Lemke.

Finally, I want to thank Bishop Randy Morgan and Apostle Johnny Layton for your leadership and accountability. The word "author" comes from the root word for "authority." I know that I have no true authority unless I'm able to submit to authority. Like the centurion in Matthew 8:5-13, who submitted his faith to the authority of Yeshua and received a miracle, I can say, "I too am a man under authority." Therefore, I'm expectant for the Lord to do miracles through this book. Thank you, Bishop Randy, Apostle Johnny, and everyone who has believed in me and this message.